New Security Challenges Series

General Editor   :ity in the
Department of   of Warwick,
UK, and Directo
                                                                      their causes
The last decade   )onses from
and manifestati      nity. In the
the social scien

past, the avoidance of war was the primary objective, but with the end of the
Cold War the retention of military defence as the centrepiece of international
security agenda became untenable. There has been, therefore, a significant shift
in emphasis away from traditional approaches to security to a new agenda that
talks of the softer side of security, in terms of human security, economic security
and environmental security. The topical *New Security Challenges series* reflects this
pressing polit   and research agenda.

Titles in ude:

Angela Pennisi   'oristella
THE ASEAN RE   NAL SECURITY PARTNERSHIP
Strengths and L   ts of a Cooperative System

Natasha Underh
COUNTERING C   3AL TERRORISM AND INSURGENCY
Calculating the R   of State-Failure in Afghanistan, Pakistan and Iraq

Robin Cameron
SUBJECTS OF SECU !Y
Domestic Effects of F eign Policy in the War on Terror

Sharyl Cross, Savo Ken era, R. Craig Nation and Radovan Vukadinovic (*editors*)
SHAPING SOUTH EAS: EUROPE'S SECURITY COMMUNITY FOR THE
TWENTY-FIRST CENTURY
Trust, Partnership, Integration

Tom Dyson and Theodore Konstadinides
EUROPEAN DEFENCE COOPERATION IN EU LAW AND IR THEORY

Håkan Edström, Janne Haaland Matlary and Magnus Petersson (*editors*)
NATO: THE POWER OF PARTNERSHIPS

Håkan Edström and Dennis Gyllensporre
POLITICAL ASPIRATIONS AND PERILS OF SECURITY
Unpacking the Military Strategy of the United Nations

Hakan Edström and Dennis Gyllensporre (*editors*)
PURSUING STRATEGY
NATO Operations from the Gulf War to Gaddafi

Hamed El-Said
NEW APPROACHES TO COUNTERING TERRORISM
Designing and Evaluating Counter Radicalization and De-Radicalization
Programs

Philip Everts and Pierangelo Isernia
PUBLIC OPINION, TRANSATLANTIC RELATIONS AND THE USE OF FORCE

Adrian Gallagher
GENOCIDE AND ITS THREAT TO CONTEMPORARY INTERNATIONAL ORDER

Kevin Gillan, Jenny Pickerill and Frank Webster
ANTI-WAR ACTIVISM
New Media and Protest in the Information Age

Ellen Hallams, Luca Ratti and Ben Zyla (*editors*)
NATO BEYOND 9/11
The Transformation of the Atlantic Alliance

Christopher Hobbs, Matthew Moran and Daniel Salisbury (*editors*)
OPEN SOURCE INTELLIGENCE IN THE TWENTY-FIRST CENTURY
New Approaches and Opportunities

Janne Haaland Matlary
EUROPEAN UNION SECURITY DYNAMICS
In the New National Interest

Sebastian Mayer (*editor*)
NATO's POST-COLD WAR POLITICS
The Changing Provision of Security

Michael Pugh, Neil Cooper and Mandy Turner (*editors*)
WHOSE PEACE? CRITICAL PERSPECTIVES ON THE POLITICAL ECONOMY OF
PEACEBUILDING

Aglaya Snetkov and Stephen Aris
THE REGIONAL DIMENSIONS TO SECURITY
Other Sides of Afghanistan

Aiden Warren and Ingvild Bode
GOVERNING THE USE-OF-FORCE IN INTERNATIONAL RELATIONS
The Post 9/11 Challenge on International Law

New Security Challenges Series
Series Standing Order ISBN 978–0–230–00216–6 (hardback)
and ISBN 978–0–230–00217–3 (paperback)
(*outside North America only*)

You can receive future titles in this series as they are published by placing a standing order. Please contact your bookseller or, in case of difficulty, write to us at the address below with your name and address, the title of the series and the ISBNs quoted above.

Customer Services Department, Macmillan Distribution Ltd, Houndmills, Basingstoke, Hampshire RG21 6XS, England

---

Extremists in Our Midst

Confronting Terror

Abdul Haqq Baker

Founder and Director of Strategy To Reach Empower & Educate Teenagers (STREET UK)

First published 2011
First published in paperback 2015 by
PALGRAVE MACMILLAN

Palgrave Macmillan in the UK is an imprint of Macmillan Publishers Limited,
registered in England, company number 785998, of Houndmills, Basingstoke,
Hampshire RG21 6XS.

Palgrave Macmillan in the US is a division of St Martin's Press LLC,
175 Fifth Avenue, New York, NY 10010.

Palgrave Macmillan is the global academic imprint of the above companies
and has companies and representatives throughout the world.

Palgrave® and Macmillan® are registered trademarks in the United States,
the United Kingdom, Europe and other countries.

ISBN 978–0–230–29654–1 hardback
ISBN 978–1–137–56976–9 paperback

This book is printed on paper suitable for recycling and made from fully
managed and sustained forest sources. Logging, pulping and manufacturing
processes are expected to conform to the environmental regulations of the
country of origin.

A catalogue record for this book is available from the British Library.

A catalog record for this book is available from the Library of Congress.

This edition is dedicated to my beloved wife, Amatullah and my sister, Aqilah who continue to be unwavering in their love and support for me.
It is also dedicated to the memory of Sulaiman (Henry) Amankwah; one of the shining stars that emerged from our community.

Contents

List of Figures

List of Tables

List of Charts

Foreword

The 9/11 and 7/7 terrorist attacks unleashed a combination of fear, outrage, and concern from citizens and policymakers alike. Many asked, 'Why do they hate us?', 'Can Muslims be loyal citizens?', 'Is multiculturalism a failed policy', 'How do we fight a war against global terrorism?'. The US and UK among others were quick to introduce anti-terrorism legislation; organisations such as government tended to focus on fighting terrorists abroad and the threat from home-grown terrorism.

After 9/11, I received a call from a congressional staffer on the Hill. A group of members of Congress wanted to meet with Muslim leaders but were concerned that they be 'moderate Muslims'. I was asked if I could come up with a list of such leaders and then meet with the staffer to discuss (vet) my candidates. Obviously, this request raised many questions for me. I wondered, 'Why is the term "moderate" rather than "mainstream" Muslim used?' and 'When they speak of Jewish and Christian leaders, do they ask for moderate Jews or Christians?'. I thought to myself, 'Treating Jews or Christians in this way would create a public outcry!'. Most important, I wondered what asking about 'moderate Muslims' says about our governments' failure over the years to get to know and work with the mainstream in Muslim communities, its leaders and institutions as fellow citizen partners rather than suspects. Former Prime Minister Tony Blair commented at a conference he hosted in London shortly before he stepped down that, in its zeal, his government focused so much on extremism that it did not sufficiently seek out and work with the Muslim community itself.

The legacy of the 9/11 and post 9/11 terrorist attacks has been exploited by media commentators, hard-line Christian Zionists and far-right political candidates whose fear-mongering targets Islam and Muslims. Islamophobia is fast becoming for Muslims what anti-Semitism is for Jews. Rooted in hostility and intolerance towards religious and cultural beliefs and a religious or racial group, it threatens the democratic fabric of American and European societies. Like anti-Semites and racists, Islamophobes are the first to protest that their stereotyping and scapegoating of these 'others' as a threat, incapable of integration or loyalty, are not Islamophobic. Yet, examples illustrate that the social cancer of Islamophobia is spreading across Europe and the United States, threatening and infringing upon the constitutional rights of their Muslim citizens and resulting in an increase in discrimination, hate speech and hate crimes.

Ironically, failure to distinguish between a very small but dangerous and deadly minority of extremists and the vast majority of Muslims contradicts hard data from major polls by Gallup, PEW and many others that demonstrate the extent to which the majorities of European and American Muslims, who span the spectrum from conservative and fundamentalist to secular reformers, are in fact part of the mainstream mosaic in their societies, concerned about and contributing to the peace and security of their societies as witnessed by grassroots community-led initiatives that have addressed and are still addressing violent extremism.

Abdul Haqq Baker's *Extremists in Our Midst: Confronting Terror* tells an extraordinary story of one such community and effectively responds to those who continue to ask: 'Why aren't Muslims in our country addressing and combating religious extremism and terrorism?'. This first-class study by an insider practitioner of a British Muslim convert community in countering extremism offers an extraordinarily important counter-intuitive response that challenges conventional wisdom in addressing the question of whether British Muslim converts are more susceptible to violent extremism, or whether they are the most effective members of the Muslim community in countering it. To rephrase the question slightly, are British Muslim converts best placed by virtue of their identity/ies to act as effective conduits between the majority (host) society and immigrant, second/third generation Muslim communities in understanding and effectively leading the fight against violent extremism in the UK today?

Equally importantly, this book challenges a popular stereotype of Salafi Islam, prevalent among many experts and many Muslims and non-Muslims alike, who fail to distinguish between mainstream and violent Salafism, equating all Salafis with violent Jihadists.

Too often popular discourse speaks of so-called 'moderate' Muslims over and against Salafi Muslims, simply equating Salafism with religious extremism and terrorism. Thus, for many Western secularists, moderate Muslims are those who advocate secular liberalism. Conservative or traditionalist Muslims are regarded as fundamentalists: theologically closed-minded, suspicious, or extreme. Liberal or self-styled progressive Muslims often fall into a similar trap, appropriating the term 'moderate' solely for themselves and using the term Salafi and 'fundamentalist' to dismiss or ridicule those espousing more conservative and theological positions.

In a world that continues to be threatened by foreign and domestic acts of terrorism, and in which Western governments and societies are challenged to counter the growth of extremism and 'home-grown' terrorists, *Extremists in Our Midst: Confronting Terror* is a 'must read.'

JOHN L. ESPOSITO
University Professor and Founding Director
Prince Alwaleed Bin Talal Center for Muslim–Christian Understanding
Georgetown University
USA

Preface to the Paperback Edition

Since the first publication of this study in 2011, religiously motivated terrorist attacks have adopted new, more simplified but visually shocking trajectories of violence. The murder of drummer Lee Rigby in London on 22nd May 2013 provides a stark example of the extent to which violent radicalisation has taken root among a small minority of British Muslims. The fact that the two convicted for Rigby's murder were converts again raises questions surrounding their susceptibility and propensity for violent extremism.

The original scope of this study examined the challenges faced by a British Muslim convert community in the face of extremist propaganda and the violent radicalisation of former members such as Zacarius Moussaoui (the 20th 9/11 attacker) and Richard Reid (the Shoe Bomber). Theoretical frameworks, which are applied from an insider's participant-observer perspective, enable unique narratives and insights to unfold and illustrate some of the processes of radicalisation within an urban societal setting. Empirical evidence highlights key precursors that can either catalyse or divert an individual's path toward or away from violent extremism.

This study also examines continuing discourses that allege Salafism to be an ideological precursor toward violent radicalisation and an intrinsic part of the extremist mosaic belonging to terrorist entities, like the self-proclaimed Islamic State (IS) or ISIS as they commonly referred to. Discussion of Salafism within the context of other community ideological delineations ensues, examining whether existing academic and media portrayals of the movement are accurate.

These discussions are significant insofar as they relate to the present government's definition (or lack of it) of what constitutes non-violent extremism – terminology that has gained increasing currency and been largely attributed to Salafism – following David Cameron's Munich speech on radicalisation and Islamic extremism in 2011.

The Paris attacks in January 2015 and western governments' increasing concerns at the prospect of 'returning jihadis' from Syria and Iraq have witnessed a raft of new and contentious legislation aimed at preventing further terrorist attacks and protecting civil liberties. However, alarmingly for many British Muslims, these new laws continue to ignore and fail to adequately address root causes of radicalisation, resulting in more socially conservative communities being targeted as suspect and opposed to core societal values.

This study remains particularly relevant today in view of its first-hand, insider account of the radicalisation of individuals who became intent on wreaking havoc in societies among which they were raised due to a distorted ideology. It provides a foundation upon which to further examine and compare current trends of extremism affecting angry disaffected young Muslims today.

Preface to the First Edition

This empirical study is aimed at examining and evaluating a convert community's approach in countering the effects of extremist and terrorist propaganda in the UK. Failure to avert terrorist attacks in London on 7 July 2005, and the subsequent attempt a fortnight later, have led to the government and its agencies seeking alternative strategies to combat what has now been established as a legitimate home-grown threat of terrorism among British Muslim citizens. Legislation subsequently introduced after 11 September 2001 failed to acknowledge or, indeed, recognise the threat of terrorism from British Muslims and instead targeted, primarily, Muslim asylum seekers/immigrants. This approach, together with the government's foreign policy on Iraq and support for the US-led 'War on Terror' confirmed emphasis on a restrictive 'top down' approach to tackling extremism, failing to recognise significant and timely contributions that could be made from marginal grassroots communities.

Not until the events of 7 July has the British Muslim convert community within the UK been under so much scrutiny, as being especially susceptible to extremist teachings which allegedly lead to terrorist activities. As focus increasingly centres on community-led initiatives, due to the above mentioned factors, it has become necessary to research and analyse the effectiveness of the British Muslim convert community in countering extremism against the prevalent backdrop of violent extremist propaganda. The Salafist ideology is examined and discussed in light of existing academic and journalistic debates which posit it among the contributory causes of violent extremism. Adherents of Salafism, Salafis consider their practices mainstream, away from the extreme spectrums of both liberalism and terrorism. They have been, up until recently, marginalised among both Muslim and non-Muslim communities, resulting in various inaccuracies being attributed to the movement, ideologically, historically and politically; leading to conclusions that extremist 'violent Jihadis' (takfeeris) are of identical schools of thought, but at the other end of the same spectrum, so to speak. The study seeks to determine, first hand, factors which influence and affect the Islamic education and development of British Muslim converts within the UK including the cultural and social motivators, as well as existing tensions that may exist between them and established Muslim communities. Additional factors which serve as catalysts in propelling a small number of them towards extremism will also be examined.

Acknowledgements

I must begin by thanking members of the Brixton Mosque convert community for the trust they afforded me to conduct research relating to their religious beliefs and practices. The challenges faced by British converts coming from a predominantly grasssroots background led me to embark on studying a small but increasingly significant section of Muslims whose profile continues to attract attention since the events of 7/7. Their position among wider British society and the more culturally embedded Muslim communities is unique when considering the UK's present socio-political climate in light of its foreign policy and support for the US-led 'war on terror'. In fact, this work would not have been possible without the contribution and support of these converts which includes family and friends. I am therefore indebted to a number of these individuals and feel it prudent to refer specifically to some of them. My family deserve special mention for their academic contribution, support and patience during the time it has taken to complete this book.

Abu Murad and Abu Kais (Tamim) are acknowledged for their support of the Brixton community during its formative years and for recognising its need to become more established. The community's ambition to have its own place of worship became a reality through the charitable donations of the Megrisi family which enabled the purchase of the mosque premises in 1998. I must thank all of the above mentioned for their commitment and contributions towards the community's development at that time.

I thank Muhammad al-Malkee, Taalib Alexander, Abdul Malik Edwards, Rasheed Amer, Abdul Haq Addae, Shaun (Musa) Danquah, Abu Hajirah and Sameer Koomson for their support and encouragement to complete this study. The 'light bulb moments' I experienced in my discussions with Sameer were truly inspirational and helped me to structure specific areas of my research. I cannot forget to mention Aslam and the entire Daniel family who have been on this journey with me since childhood. They continue to be my extended family that symbolise Strength within Strength. My colleagues and friends at STREET UK and ELS Jeddah are to be commended for continuing their excellent work while, on occasions, I have been preoccupied with completing this study.

Professor Stuart Croft, Doctors Basia Spalek, Jonathan Githens-Mazer and Robert Lambert are also acknowledged for their unfailing support and encouragement to complete this book. I have endeavoured, throughout this book, to highlight some of the challenges facing us today and the possible solutions which can contribute towards addressing them more effectively.

Permission to use figure 4 from *Making Terrorism History* by Scilla Elworthy and Gabrielle Rifkind, published by Rider, has been granted by Random House.

1
Introduction

Overview

The rationale behind this book is to provide a practitioner's insider perspective on a convert community's approach to tackling violent extremism during the early 1990s and up until 2009. The significance of conducting this research can best be illustrated by reference to practitioner authors in another field of study, namely, education, and their attempts to gain credibility by articulating theoretical frameworks that inform successful and established practices. Whitehead and McNiff observe:

> while practitioner research is generally held in high regard for its contributions to quality practice, it is not held in equal regard for its potential contributions to quality theory. Part of the reason is that its methods for assessing quality have not yet been fully worked out, and in some cases not even addressed.
>
> (Whitehead and McNiff 2009: 1)

They further observe:

> The new openness to practitioner research is therefore offset by caution that perhaps practitioners are still not capable of doing quality research or generating theory because they are not fully conversant with the appropriate methods for judging the quality of their work, and, given that the topic is seldom raised in the practitioner research literature, it would seem of low priority. So, if practitioners themselves do not take care in addressing these core issues, the wider

educational research community could be forgiven also for not taking them seriously.

(Whitehead and McNiff, 2009)

The challenges faced by practitioners in the educational circles described here could easily be transferred to those facing practitioners in the counter terrorist field today. In fact, despite acknowledgement by governmental and other statutory bodies regarding the success of grassroots community-led initiatives in addressing violent extremism, a preference for academic research, mainly from outsider perspectives, still proliferates in the counter-terrorist arena, it being the preferred and safer option for government. Added to this somewhat inhibitory approach is the more recent statutory alignment to self-confessed alleged former extremists who have apparently renounced violent extremism and embraced a more liberal and secular variation of Islam.[1] Such affiliations ignore practitioner entities that have never espoused violent extremism and have been at the forefront of countering violent extremist propaganda and its protagonists since the early 1990s. The consistency of their counter extremist efforts has often been overlooked by the authorities who prefer alternative voices considered to provide a more palatable brand of Islam. In any event, Whitehead and McNiff's observations remain relevant to the ambit of this book. Academic research in this field, particularly from a *western Muslim convert*'s perspective, is minimal and there is a need to introduce this dimension to existing discourses on the subject. The authors further acknowledge that:

> Practitioners themselves need to define and articulate the standards of judgement they use to evaluate their own work, and make these standards of judgement available to the wider... research community.
>
> (Whitehead and McNiff, 2009: 1)

This book examines British convert Muslims who faced violent extremist propaganda at a grassroots level during the early 1990s. It also discusses the effects of these Muslims being labelled as extremists because of their adherence to the orthodox Salafi (Salafist) branch of Islam. The book focuses on the following research question:

> Are British Muslim converts more susceptible to violent extremism or, are they the most effective members of the Muslim community in countering it?

Or, to rephrase the question slightly:

Are British Muslim converts best placed by virtue of their identity/ies, to act as effective conduits between the majority (host) society and immigrant, second/third generation Muslim communities in understanding and effectively leading the fight against violent extremism in the UK today?

In order to place the research question within an appropriate context, it is necessary to discuss the socio-political and socio-religious climates that have developed in the UK. These climates have arguably contributed to the marginalisation and criminalisation of certain sections of the Muslim population within the UK today. Such sections include adherents to the Salafi doctrine of Islam. The author wishes to demonstrate what a participant observer's insider perspective can contribute to academic literature in this field. A unique academic insight can be gained on a convert-led Muslim community in view of the author's position as community leader and chairman of the Brixton Mosque and Islamic Cultural Centre between 1994 and 2009. This position provides an alternative perspective to existing research in this field, given the duality of roles as both author and practitioner. The inability of many authors to obtain sufficient primary empirical data from this particular, very insular section of the Muslim community leaves a significant knowledge gap which has failed to record the experience of British Salafi Muslims in addressing violent extremism. Academic research therefore needs to be conducted among the Salafi community itself and compared to existing research in similar, related fields. Presently, there exist few insider perspectives whereas an increasing plethora of outsider perspectives on Salafism and its adherents abound.[2] Relatively few of these perspectives provide accurate, primary research findings. In any event, these sources will be cited as a means of correlation or contrast, whatever the case may be in each instance (Wiktorowicz, 2006a: 207–39 and Olivetti, 2001). In the absence of a genuine insider perspective, external analyses, based largely on secondary data, are inevitably flawed. Despite the input of western Muslim academics on the subject, the author will suggest that they continue to provide an outsider perspective. The ideological differences and unswerving adherence to different schools of jurisprudence arguably influence non-Salafi academic findings. An example of this can be witnessed in the increasing contributions of Muslim academics from the Sufi tradition who have entered the arena to expound upon Salafism, often providing inconclusive data based on secondary sources of research without substantiation from primary evidence.[3] This book endeavours to bridge the above mentioned knowledge gap by providing and examining primary data, and correlating it with existing secondary sources.

The book is likely to be of general interest in view of the current climate of concern surrounding Muslim communities in general and British Muslim youth specifically. Counter Intelligence agencies and other statutory bodies' assessment that extremist cells and sympathy for violent extremism have increased since the 7 July 2005 bombings, only serve to perpetuate public concern.[4] Societal concerns and sensitivities regarding the possibility of further 'home grown' terrorist attacks from British Muslims have been further exacerbated by continuing anti-Muslim sentiment and negative media portrayals of Islam and Muslims. This has, in turn, raised the issue of identity and what 'Britishness' entails within multi-cultural Britain today. The book aims to provide, on one hand, insight into a community of British Muslim converts who possessed intrinsic values of Britishness prior to conversion to Islam. On the other hand, it intends to explain the orthodoxy of Muslim converts' practice within the context of more mainstream practices in Islam. The objective in this instance is to provide an alternative insightful narrative from which a more comprehensive debate can develop regarding the extent of the societal contribution of British Muslim converts in countering the violent extremist phenomenon in Britain.

From a practitioner's perspective the research aims to provide a similar insight to that already mentioned above; however, additional empirical evidence will hopefully provide a wider platform upon which existing theoretical frameworks can be further examined and tested. Counter terrorist agencies and related bodies, such as the Metropolitan Police are expected to be interested in the approach adopted in this research primarily due to the fact that no research of this nature, i.e. a participatory observer perspective among an altogether insular Salafi community, has been conducted to date in the UK. The apparent inability in the past of such agencies to examine or even penetrate communities of this nature means that possibly, for the first time, they will have an academic insight, from a community practitioner (this being the author having a duality of roles) to inform their practitioner perspective. It has proved necessary to address some of the more predominant and prevalent discourses on radicalisation and Salafism in order to place the latter movement within a specific, discernable context. Therefore, it is not unusual for ensuing discussions to proceed along tangential avenues around radicalisation, usage of terminology, etc. before refocusing on the key research question. The distinctive themes of discourse are interwoven and, in some instances, interchangeable throughout this book in an attempt to illustrate the complexities that surround research into violent extremism and Muslim communities in Britain today. They are by no means conclusive, however, and serve only to complement existing as well as emerging research on contemporary Salafism in the UK.

The initial part of this study (Chapter 2) will provide a historical prologue to the research question, illustrating the establishment and progress of, arguably, the first Salafi convert-led mosque in the UK and how issues of identity, both British and Muslim, contributed to the continuing evolution of a distinct convert identity. It provides a contextual backdrop against which the analyses/research chapters can be examined. The chapter also provides a distinctive narrative which highlights the issues that affected the community's struggle to thwart the increasing attempts of violent extremist propaganda that was threatening to effectively take control of the mosque.

Chapters 3 and 4 will encapsulate the literature review, highlighting academic, scientific and religious discourses surrounding identity and religious conversion. Chapter 3 focuses particularly on the issue of identity formation in the UK and how it is defined from multi-cultural or pluralistic perspectives. Chapter 4 examines theoretical aspects of religious conversion in order to identify potential circumstances and environments against which Muslim conversions have occurred in the UK during the past two decades (Kose, 1996 and Zebiri, 2008).

Chapter 5 introduces the methodological approaches applied in this study, discussing the research methods employed.

Chapter 6 focuses on three case studies of extremists who resided in the UK; Richard Reid, Zacarias Moussaoui and Abdullah el Faisal, all of whom were convicted of terrorist related offences and imprisoned. The fourth case study will examine Sean O'Reilly (a pseudonym); a convert initially invited to and attracted towards violent extremism but, upon encounter and engagement with Salafis, moved away from his former position and embraced Salafism. This particular case study will examine the reasons behind his gravitation from violent extremist narratives.

Chapter 7 introduces interviews conducted on the target group of British Salafi converts. Dissemination of the data extrapolated from these interviews will then take place so as to provide distinctive time lines/periods over which conversions took place. This will enable the opportunity to determine whether socio-political/religious events during specific periods (between the 1990s and 2008) affected the target group and their choice of Islamic practice. It will also provide an illustrative narrative against which the previous case study chapter can be compared to establish whether similar drivers existed between the two research groups (i.e. interviewees and case studies) and whether their respective responses in dealing with these led to similar religious conclusions.

Chapter 8 (the conclusion) will address the research findings and place them within the context of the primary research question, querying whether the findings are conclusive and the extent to which additional research is required. These will also be compared and contrasted with the Brixton Mosque's account of community approaches towards tackling violent extremism during the 1990s, with particular focus on more recently established counter extremist intervention strategies and programmes. The chapter will, thereafter, discuss: i) implications for the government's Preventing Violent Extremism agenda, ii) the implications for the counter terrorist policing policy and iii) the implications for Muslim communities throughout the UK.

Statement of the problem

Since the early 1990s, significant international events affecting the Muslim world have continued to politicise Muslim youth in Britain.[5] Various Islamic movements and groups, such as Hizbut Tahrir, Supporters of Sharia (SOS) and The Committee for Defense of Legitimate Rights (CDLR) emerged during this period to highlight and, in some cases, exploit the tensions prevalent in the Arab and Muslim world (Wiktorowicz, 2005: 9).[6] Such tensions were to be played out on British soil and proliferate throughout university Islamic societies across the country.[7] The most notable of groups was Hizbut Tahrir in view of their well organised media campaigns, intellectual appeal to undergraduate Muslims, and their spiritual guide and leader, Omar Bakri (Wiktorowicz, 2005: 3) however, it did not take the masses long to realise that this group was, by and large, centred largely around rhetoric. More serious and extreme ideologies were being expounded by individuals who appealed to a wider audience that included non-academic, street-wise youth, converts (some of whom came from a background of crime), and disillusioned second/third generation British Muslims. Abu Hamza al Misri, Abdullah el Faisal and Abu Qatadah were able to engage a captive audience with their extreme understanding of Islam, experience and studies abroad in the Muslim world.[8] The latter was to bear the brunt of their extremist rhetoric in the early to mid-1990s.[9] Islamic scholars were subsequently belittled and discredited by extremists' highlighting of, and reference to, contentious legal rulings (Fatawa) that contributed to the dissension that ensued.[10]

The Salafi position

Salafi communities in the UK arguably became the sole voice to effectively counter the developing extremist rhetoric and propaganda, recognising the popularity and indeed, threat of an emerging *'takfeeri'* (excommunicating) ideology in Britain. Their effectiveness stemmed from recognition and familiarity of violent extremist roots, and the sources of Islamic legislature and texts that are often distorted in extremists' attempts to justify terrorism. The increased popularity and attention to the extremist narrative was fuelled primarily by the aforementioned conflicts involving Muslim countries and communities. The perceived double standards of the West in addressing these conflicts further exacerbated the progression of Muslim youth towards extreme radicalisation which would consequently make them vulnerable to violent extremism. Salafism came under immediate attack from the proponents of extremism and British Salafis were derided alongside religious clerics in the Muslim world.[11] The effectiveness of Salafis countering the arguments of takfeeri propaganda led to the extremists' uniting in their attacks against Salafism.[12] Hizbut Tahrir's opposition to Salafism, for example, was continually emphasised in universities throughout the UK (Husain, 2007).

Surprisingly, despite the availability of extremist material that points, unequivocally to its opposition and rejection of Salafism, academic, government and media perceptions hold the movement's ideology to be a contributory proponent or precursor to violent extremism. Difficulty has arisen, however, in the application of relatively new terminology to define what comprises various strands of Salafism. In using such terminologies it has increasingly been suggested that ideologies/movements that have historically been considered disparate in the Muslim world, are now being defined as one and the same in the contemporary era. For example, Takfeeri (violent extremist), Ikhwani (Muslim Brotherhood/Islamist) and Salafi ideologies and groups are now being considered as one and the same movement, but with differing political aspirations (Wiktorowicz, 2006b: 207–39). Little, if no, consideration appears to have been given to the possibility of marginalising and indeed criminalising the Salafi community. Failure to make informed and properly researched distinctions between the above mentioned ideologies has already contributed towards the movement's marginalisation.

Although similar in many respects, the three movements still differ in rudimentary aspects of their respective beliefs and practice. Another example of newly introduced terminologies which emanate largely from western academia and journalistic discourse can be seen in Stemmann's distinction between *'academic Salafism'* (*Salafiyyah al-ilmiyyah*) and *'jihadi'* or, *'Fighting'* Salafism or *Salafiyyah al-Jihadiyyah*, (Stemmann, 2006: 3). Pargeter observes:

> rather than being an organization, Salafiyah Jihadia is more akin to a current of thought ... It is also a term used primarily by Moroccan and other security agencies to label their Islamists.
>
> (Pargeter, 2008: 118–19)

She cites, as evidence to illustrate the coining of this new and somewhat alien terminology a prominent 'Salafist preacher', Ahmed Al-Rafiki, who explains Salafia Jihadia to be:

> a media and security term because I don't know anybody who claims to represent that current. There is no organization or group that carries that name.
>
> (Pargeter, 2008: 119)

Others have, unsurprisingly, rejected this new terminology, and few rebuttals of what is seen as disingenuous neo-classification of Muslims are as emphatic:

> As for what is called salafiyah jihadia, this is part of the imagination of the atheist media ... we, Ahl Sunna wal Jama'a, are not salafiyah jihadia. We pray, so why don't they call us salafiyah praying, we go to pilgrimage and they don't call us salafiyah pilgrimage?
>
> (Pargeter, 2008: 119)

The introduction and subsequent use of new terminology to describe groups or phenomena as methods of denigration, etc. gathered momentum among the Muslim world during the mid- to late twentieth century. In acknowledgement of this existing method, McCants et al., recommended the following strategy as a means of reducing the popularity of Jihadis among Salafis:

> Label the entire Jihadi Movement 'Qutbism' in recognition that the Jihadis cite Sayyid Qutb more than any modern author. Muslim opponents of the Jihadis (including mainstream Wahhabis) use this

term to describe them, a designation Jihadis hate since it implies that they follow a human and are members of a deviant sect. Adherents of the movement consider 'Qutbi' to be a negative label and would much rather be called Jihadi or Salafi.

(McCants et al., 2006: 10)

Figure 1.1 below presents an interesting depiction of where Salafis may be located among the wider Muslim community. It is more accurate, however, in its illustration of precisely where Jihadis (or more accurately, takfeeris/violent extremists) are likely to be positioned. The author suggests that the continuing usage of inaccurate terminologies and typologies to define and categorise Salafis and takfeeris as one and the same entity, serve only to isolate and stigmatise the former movement who have, thus far, proved among the more effective in countering the violent extremist ideology. Continuing negative portrayal of Salafis may in fact result in a return to their previous insularity/isolation from wider society which, in turn, may further marginalise them and lead to proliferating the threat of 'Jihadis' embedding themselves even further among the former's communities. It is important to note that the illustrations in Figure 1.1 are, to a greater extent, mutually exclusive in that each constituency does not necessarily encapsulate the positions and ideologies, etc. of the other. In other words, it should not be incorrectly understood from the diagram that all 'Jihadis', for example, are Salafis but not all Salafis are 'Jihadis', etc.

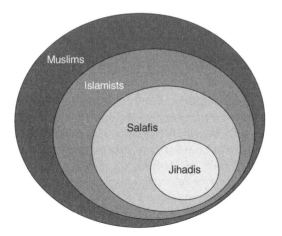

Figure 1.1 Jihadi constituencies
Source: McCants et al., 2006: 10)

Stemmann's research further emphasises the author's above-mentioned concern when discussing the impetus and process of extremist recruitment. Unfortunately, his classification of extremism, as it relates to Salafism, is that the ideology and movement are in fact precursors to violent extremism and, most notably, terrorism. Irrespective of this assumption, some of the transitional drivers towards extremism described by him correlate with takfeeri, violent extremist descriptors. He suggests the:

> radicalization process begins with the emergence of anti-integration tendencies and the desire to disengage from the host society.
>
> (Stemmann, 2006: 11–12)

This, he claims:

> continues with hostility towards the host society, rejection of the principles and institutions of liberal democracy, and the growing acquisition of violent attitudes.
>
> (Stemmann, 2006: 12)

Figure 1.1's depiction of the 'Islamist' *locality* among the wider Muslim community is, to a greater extent, accurate. However, the author suggests that it requires amendment if it is used to illustrate *'gravitation'* towards violent extremist ideology and thought. In other words, so far as politicisation and extremist philosophy are concerned, 'Islamists' would be positioned in the adjoining circle to the 'Jihadis' position with 'Salafis' occupying the penultimate 'outer circle' beside the 'Muslims' constituency. In effect, therefore, the Islamist and Salafi constituencies would be swapped. Further discussion on ideological positioning and the binary usage of Figure 1.1 takes place later in the book. However, in order to more accurately portray the UK context of both the ideological and gravitational positioning of some Muslim communities in Britain the author proposes additional theoretical frameworks (Figures 1.7 and 1.8 below). Behavioural traits which contribute to the extremist mosaic will be referred to briefly. In the meantime, perhaps the most telling aspect of Stemmann's conclusion is that the above mentioned descriptors he refers to make susceptible individuals potential targets for extremist recruitment. He discusses the transitional stages from Salafism to terrorist militancy as being an easy process 'given the radicalization that accompanies integration in the Salafi community' (2006: 11).

When considering Figure 1.1, and the positioning of 'Jihadi' constituencies, it is important to note that a more conclusive assessment would be that Stemmann's process becomes particularly poignant if Salafi communities resort, once again, to the insularity witnessed prior to 9/11 as a knee-jerk reaction to continuing inaccurate and often negative portrayals of their practice. To reiterate the earlier warning, 'Jihadis' could then embed themselves among Salafi communities to the extent that they recruit unsuspecting young Muslims who are unable to discern the finer aspects of ideology, methodology and practice, as was witnessed in the case of Richard Reid, aka the 'Shoe Bomber' during the late 1990s.

The author is well placed as a member of a Salafi community and is aware of the effects of extremist propaganda upon susceptible youth coming from backgrounds similar to that of Richard Reid. While in the process of learning the foundational aspects of Islam, Reid was violently radicalised towards extremism owing to his relative naivety and misplaced enthusiasm for his new found religion. After all, 'Recruits tend to have little knowledge of the Koran, and thus it is easy for the recruiter to mask the religious content of their core message; namely, that Islam is under threat from enemy action (2006: 12). This research will endeavour to establish the validity of such claims that Salafism contributes towards extremism and, therefore ultimately, terrorism.

Part of the remit of this ethnographic study is to examine the effect(s) of religious terminology used to define aspects of Islam, i.e. Jihad, and religious groups deemed to be part of the violent extremist phenomena. In this regard, the author's participative observant role will enable comparisons between an insider and outsider perspective of a British Salafi community and, in doing so, bring to the fore the research question concerning their susceptibility to, or effectiveness against, violent extremism. Acknowledgement is, however, given to the possibility of the subjective bias that can occur in studies of this nature and to mitigate such bias Chapter 5 addresses the methodological approaches applied in this instance. Subsidiary questions invariably emanate from the research question around the susceptibility of convert Muslims to violent extremism. Although raised in media circles, there appears to be little, if any, academic discourse on this topic (Pipes, 2005). Further questions are also raised addressing British and Muslim identities of converts and how both tackle areas of perceived conflict of the two constructs. The author suggests that the majority of converts in this study do not necessarily undergo or face the conflict experienced by second/third generation British Muslims so far as dual or multiple identity issues are concerned. However, some converts from the older, African-Caribbean target group may have experienced racism from the host society during child/adulthood.[13] This resulted in them developing resilience to racism or subsequent stereotypical profiling. The younger target group are arguably more integrated and part of the fabric of multi-cultural Britain. It is, therefore, unlikely that they experienced the same degree of racism, if any, as their more senior peers.

Framework of study

Figure 1.2 provides the framework around which this study will examine stages of the sample group's pre- and post-conversion progression/regression in order to determine any pre-existing or post-related drivers that may have contributed to any identified susceptibility to violent extremism. In contrast, observations will also highlight the drivers that have prevented such susceptibility, possibly enabling individuals to be effective conduits against violent extremism.

This model has been adapted from Hudson's work in a completely separate field from that which this study is addressing; namely, management. However, it is proposed by the author that it can be adapted as an effective process of charting stages of religious conversion (Hudson, 1995: 45).

Founding (conversion) phase

This stage of conversion shall examine the influences/drivers that caused individuals to convert to Islam and compare these to other existing theoretical frameworks and models that cover the same phenomena (Roald, 2004). Discussion will then ensue around whether pre-conversion influences and perceptions continue to affect individual's lives thereby impeding their assimilation to Islam or, on the other

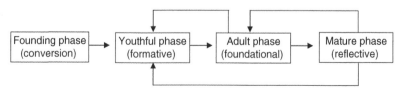

A convert's contextualisation and understanding of Islam moves forwards and backwards

| Founding phase (conversion) | → | Youthful phase (formative) | → | Adult phase (foundational) | → | Mature phase (reflective) |

Figure 1.2 Proposed model for the life cycle of a convert's post-conversion process

hand, they have been able to fully embrace new ideological, cultural and religious practices once considered alien to them.

Youthful (formative/overzealous and idealistic) phase

Particular focus will be put on this stage of conversion which is, arguably, the phase in which converts are most susceptible to extremist propaganda and teachings. Overzealousness is a common feature of many conversions as, in many instances, a new convert possesses a heightened sense of self-righteousness with a desire to directly address/tackle perceived ills of society (Roald, 2004: 160). Social affiliations, if not effected at the founding phase of conversion, can possibly still occur at this particular stage. This phase will highlight observations surrounding the possible correlation between pre-conversion practices that may continue or even proliferate during the youthful phase (i.e. gun, knife and gang criminality) and violent extremism. Reference will be made to existing de-radicalisation programmes that address such issues at grassroots level to determine the validity of, and possible reasons for, such correlation.

Adult (foundational) phase

This phase looks at longer-term Muslim converts who have practised the religion long enough to have perhaps progressed from earlier understandings and practices of the first two phases. Reasons behind such progressions will be examined and discussed to determine whether an *'actualisation'* of the religion is in fact the significant factor that enabled such progress. *Actualisation* of the religion, as opposed to practising it in *abstract*, means that the adult phase convert has better understood and experienced the religion as a way of life, i.e. lived or travelled abroad to Muslim countries and engaged/participated in those societies, thereby enhancing his/her understanding and practice of Islam. This is contrary to their previous understanding and practice which, as mentioned above, was previously applied in an abstract form, i.e. learned from books, cassettes and videos in a predominantly non-Muslim environment. Research results are intended to show whether converts have come to terms with their new found, and often dual, identities or whether conflicts still arise during this phase.

Mature (reflective) phase

Converts' perceptions may further develop or, indeed, change if they have not already at earlier stages of post-conversion, owing to a multiplicity of socio-economic and/or religious factors. For example, marriage, birth of a new child or even the death of relatives or friends (irrespective of their religion) may be contributory factors towards an individual reflecting on his/her religious understanding, practice and development. These potential drivers shall be examined and discussed shortly; however, at this juncture, it is necessary to briefly examine Roald's three-stage conversion process which, to some extent, lends support to the four-stage model proposed above. When suggesting that new Muslims undergo a process of '*culturalisation*' into their spouses' or friends' cultural contexts, she identifies a preliminary stage of ' "falling in love with Islam", where one wants to practise every Islamic precept' (2004: 288).

The second stage is described as a period of discovery where the convert realises the difficulty or, indeed, impracticality of implementing Islamic practices in their entirety. S/he therefore realises the 'discrepancy' between Islamic ideals and Muslims' actual practice. In other words, the new convert recognises the difference between: 'the Ideal Islam', as it is illustrated in Islamic books and that of Muslim understanding/practice in various parts of the world. Roald's observations at this stage accord to the author's earlier explanations regarding 'abstract' and 'actualised' understandings of the religion. Finally, she mentions the third stage of conversion being the convert's ultimate realisation that Muslims are not too dissimilar to their non-Muslim counterparts and that 'it is possible to understand Islam in a Scandinavian framework' (Roald, 2004: 288).

The proposed model introduced below (Figure 1.3) illustrates the process of cognition and development so far as ritualistic aspects of conversion are concerned. Rambo suggests:

> Ritual actions consolidate the community through singing, recitation, and gestures in unison, which instill a deeper sense of belonging. Ritual is also a way to tell the story of the new faith to outsiders... ritual provides experiential validation of the religious belief system being advocated. (1993: 115)

As already intimated above, Rambo's model is applicable insofar as it relates to the initial phase, i.e. 'founding phase' of Hudson's amended framework (Figure 1.2) because it illustrates process of change prior to conversion ('Separation'), during cognitive openings and changes ('Transition'), leading to actual conversion ('Consolidation').

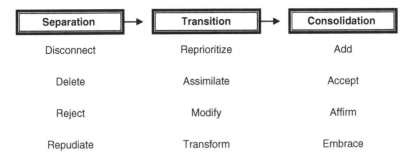

Figure 1.3 Ritual processes
Source: Rambo, 1993: 115

A bipolar perspective of extremism

It is necessary to introduce another perspective to the debate on extremism as focus has been specifically on violent extremism and its drivers. 'Liberal extremism' is arguably considered by significant sections of the Muslim community to be another form of extremism and a contributory factor towards young Muslims, including converts, *swinging* from a more moderate or, indeed, liberal perspective towards violent extremism. However, unfortunately, statutory authorities are perceived to show a clear preference in inviting and accommodating Muslim support from this end of the spectrum. After all, 'participating in ... demonstrations is relatively non-confrontational ... and ... is rendered friendly and safe' (Greaves, 2005: 76).

This spectrum could possibly act as a general indicator of where groups, movements and, indeed, ideologies are situated among the Muslim communities in Britain today. Subsequent to the models shown in Table 1.1, the introduction of two additional gauges that determine possible drivers of violent extremism among British Muslims is also necessary. In response to a booklet entitled 'Making Terrorism History', the author proposed a measure by which catalytic drivers of violent extremism could be made (Elsworthy and Rifkind, 2006).

The simple continuum shown in Figure 1.4 served to reflect the extent of Muslim sentiment in light of perceived injustices implemented by the government and statutory agencies against the religion of Islam, Muslim countries or the Muslims themselves. The author submits that this continuum can be used when considering the case studies to determine each subject's perception of external, socio-political or socio-religious factors

16

Table 1.1 Bipolar spectrum of religious extremism among the Muslim community in Britain

Liberal Extreme	Moderate Perspective	Fanatical/Violent Extreme
Secular	Addressing Muslim concerns within context of Islamic law (Sharia) and common law	Imbuing emotional responses from its followers
Failure to adequately address Muslim concerns		Propelling them to react/respond physically
Lack of religiously knowledge based decisions		
Reliance more upon intellect than Islamic edicts and rulings	Action relative to what is required	Urgency of reaction/ response
More concerned with public perception and position with higher authorities etc.	Contact with bona fide, experienced & knowledgeable scholars	Instilling uncontrollable hatred/resentment towards own society
Self appointed and often not representative of Muslim masses/involvement in politics	Engaging with wider society acting as effective conduits between Muslim community and wider host society	& those who do not subscribe to their view
Failure/refusal to acknowledge shared Muslim sentiment regarding government policies and subsequent actions that adversely affect Muslim communities/societies	Involvement in politics	Misinterpretation/ distortion of religious texts to justify extreme beliefs
Belief only in Jihad un-Nafs (personal, inward struggle) and condemnation of all physical Muslim action/reaction	**Belief in and advocacy of Jihad in its correct context, whether it be offensive or defensive**	Justifications for criminality in societies considered Darul Harb (a place of war)
Passivism/Inaction	**Measured/balanced response**	**Violent extremism/ Terrorism & empathy/support for it under the banner of Jihad**
		Misplaced Activism/ Reaction

Source: Baker, 2006: 8

Sense of Injustice------Actual but Conceivable Injustice------Ultimate Injustice
(Perceived injustice)   (Atrocity)

Figure 1.4 Perceptions of injustice continuum

that propelled them towards violent extremism. A more comprehensive framework that can further illustrate these particular elements can also be used. The definition of 'atrocities' in this instance is restricted to general Muslim perceptions of injustice by some western governments against Muslim countries and/or communities. Examination of at least two of the case studies in this research will reveal the extent of politicisation among adherents to violent extremism. Violent terrorist acts or attempted acts are, according to some experts in the field of counter terrorism 'a considered political act triggered by a set of [these] circumstances' (Briggs et al., 2006: 41).

The author suggests that by placing 'atrocities' at the starting point of 'the cycle of violence' a tacit acknowledgement is given which indicates that such atrocities cannot be prevented and must, therefore, be considered a normal or acceptable initiator of events as illustrated in Figure 1.5. This can be perceived as a precarious initiator to the above mentioned cycle. Precursors to atrocities – which invariably exist – must be equally considered and highlighted, due to the fact that violent reactions can also stem from these areas. Muhammad Sadiq Khan and his colleagues arguably witnessed what they perceived to be the failure of the country's democratic process of the masses rallying to dissuade its government from going to war with Iraq. They (Muhammad Sadiq Khan and his colleagues) shared the anger, frustration and humiliation of many Muslims around the world at the lack of diplomacy afforded over

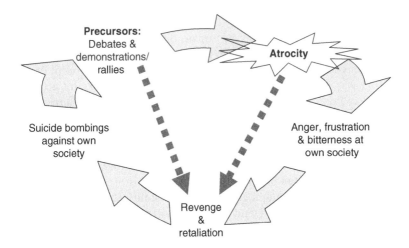

Figure 1.5   Cycle of violence (modified)[14]

the March 2003 invasion of Iraq. Arguably, these individuals had already developed extremist ideologies and beliefs before the commencement of the war. This possibly explains their resultant capitulation across the 'cycle of violence' spiral to the anger/retaliatory and eventual terrorism stage. The model refers to 'international atrocity' and highlights alternative routes to the 'cycle of violence' model; one emanating from an almost knee-jerk reaction of those already imbued with extremist ideologies and beliefs, and the other – those who realise what they conclude to be the ineffectiveness of democratic processes, i.e. rallies, etc., recognising violence as the only effective tool against imminent (and often additional) ultimate injustices. Perceived international atrocities can be, on occasions, easier to envisage than national or local ones. A clear example of this was witnessed during the build-up to the war on Iraq in 2003; the world witnessed mass protests by societies unconvinced of the arguments expounded by the US and its allies, perceiving that a great (ultimate) injustice was about to be committed against the Iraqi people. National/local 'atrocities', on the other hand, can sometimes be more difficult to detect until the act has actually been effected (successfully or unsuccessfully, depending on from which perspective it has been considered.) The June 2006 Forest Gate incident can be cited in support of this assertion. An incident/atrocity committed within a national framework can effectively propel recipients of that particular injustice, or those sympathetic to them, into the international arena of violence and terrorism. This book aims to examine the validity of such assertions when considering the case studies in Chapter 6.

Finally, the author proposes that the following 'Funnel' theoretical frameworks (Figures 1.6 and 1.7) incorporate the existing models discussed below, and illustrate the significance of the primary research question within the context of this entire research. The concept of the funnel was developed and first proposed by the author and a fellow trustee of Brixton Mosque in 2006 to the extent that it was referred to as a theoretical model during the Wilton Park Conference Summary Report on counter terrorism in March 2006.[15]

The three dimensional illustration (Figure 1.6) shows the positioning of the Salafi community at the neck of the funnel where the 'gravitational pull, translated in this context, as extremist propaganda, intensifies. This positioning highlights the Salafis' ability to address extremist propaganda at the 'hard end' of the bipolar spectrum illustrated in Table 1.1, particularly at a stage when Muslim youth are considered most susceptible to violent extremism. It also portrays the stark context of the primary research question so far as Salafis' susceptibility to extremism,

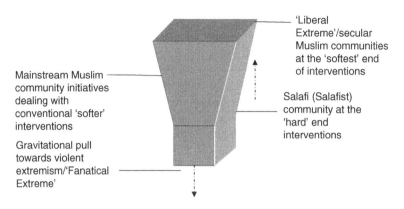

Mainstream Muslim community initiatives dealing with conventional 'softer' interventions

Gravitational pull towards violent extremism/'Fanatical Extreme'

'Liberal Extreme'/secular Muslim communities at the 'softest' end of interventions

Salafi (Salafist) community at the 'hard' end interventions

Figure 1.6 The funnel model

or effectiveness in countering it, is concerned. Other more conventional Muslim communities are located higher up the funnel, with the most liberal at the very summit, thus depicting the 'softer' degrees of work with their respective communities. Young Muslims who are actively *engaged* with these communities are not considered at risk to violent extremist propaganda, although it must be acknowledged that they will inevitably empathise with the anger and frustration of Muslim communities towards perceived injustices against the Muslim world. Depending on the degree of liberalism that underpins these types of communities, such feelings, when running high, could result in a 'pendulum swing effect' from the liberal extreme to the violent, fanatical extreme (see Table 1.1).

The cross section overview of the funnel (Figure 1.7) illustrates the societal parameters surrounding disenfranchised young Muslims and

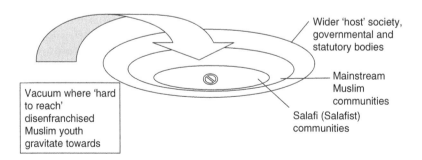

Wider 'host' society, governmental and statutory bodies

Mainstream Muslim communities

Salafi (Salafist) communities

Vacuum where 'hard to reach' disenfranchised Muslim youth gravitate towards

Figure 1.7 Cross section of funnel model

also provides a context to the second part of the research question regarding converts' positions as potential conduits between Muslim communities and wider 'host' society. The wider circle depicts the non-Muslim 'host' society and governmental/statutory bodies, with the Muslim community being located more centrally among the inner circles. The author suggests that, in the event of both wider society and Muslim communities failing to address various socio-economic, political and religious factors facing such youth, there is a risk of them gravitating towards a central, more covert, societal 'vacuum' which exists within an even smaller inner circle.[16] This is where extremist rhetoric is most potent. The risk of being effectively 'sucked' into extremism is then substantially increased; however, such risk remains undetected. This observation accords with the earlier positioning of 'Jihadis' illustrated in Figure 1.1. Unfortunately, some journalistic investigations discovered that, instead of addressing this area of concern, the previous Labour government's apparent intention appeared to be one of attempting to 'police' extremist *thought* among Muslim communities. This particular approach was apparently in response to accusations that too much focus had been on countering violent extremist *action* but not *thought*:

> Ed Husain, of the Quilliam Foundation think-tank, said the root causes of terrorism were extremist views, even if those advocating the views did not call for violence.[17]

A repositioning of significant sections of the Muslim community would prove inevitable when considering the funnel concepts (Figures 1.6 and 1.7) in this instance. Particular concern would surround Figure 1.7's illustration of Muslim communities and the risk of them being marginalised to a greater degree than at present. This in turn poses the potential of these communities being targeted as the 'alien other' by the surrounding, non-Muslim 'host'/majority society. Such a regression at this stage of academic and public debate regarding the threat of homegrown terrorism would be reminiscent of the stigmatisation received by the Jewish community in parts of pre-war Europe during the early to mid-twentieth century. That said, acknowledgement is given to the fact that not all government agencies subscribe to the approach advocated by Ed Husain and are aware that a government strategy that targets individual or collective views and beliefs could prove 'incendiary' to existing relations with Muslim communities in Britain.[18]

Chapter conclusions

Earlier presumptions regarding the roles of Muslim converts within the multi-layered spheres of wider, non-Muslim/host societies and the more insular Muslim communities, need to be re-examined in light of recent events which witnessed home-grown terrorist attacks in the UK. Increasingly, it has become necessary to complement existing research on Muslim converts in Europe and the UK in particular as a result of these events. The second aspect of the research question will be addressed in light of this observation. The theoretical frameworks proposed in this chapter will be referred to throughout the research with the objective of highlighting their complementary and, possibly, interconnecting components. At the same time, however, the ensuing chapters will also serve to challenge the validity of these frameworks in order to test their rigour and applicability to this subject.

2
Brixton Mosque's Early Encounters with Extremism

The events that immediately followed the 9/11 terrorist attacks led to an increased focus on communities like those who attended the Brixton Mosque in south London.[1] Although much has been written by media sources and academics providing external, observatory analysis and conclusions about the Mosque and its community, there still remains the need to provide a more empirical, historical account from an insider's perspective. The author of this account is appropriately placed, as an established member of the community, to provide a first-hand account of the mosque's evolution since 1990 and how the community dealt with, and continues to tackle, factors which shape its development today. Participant Observation, therefore, forms the basis of the research methodology applied throughout this particular chapter.The Brixton Mosque and Islamic Cultural Centre (aka Masjid Ibnu Taymeeyah) is centre for a diverse multicultural community that largely comprises converts from African Caribbean backgrounds.[2] The initial founders of the community (the 'elders') first began congregating in each others' homes in the mid-1970s, culminating in their establishing a small meeting venue and place of prayer in Bellfields Road, a short walk from the mosque's present locality. The community continued to expand until, in 1990, the move was made to 1 Gresham Road, the current site. With the rapid social development of the community and increasing numbers attending the mosque the elders realised the need for a cohesive development strategy to accommodate the requirements of the attendees who came from refugee backgrounds, not to mention new Muslim converts. However, up until 1994, when the present leadership was elected, the centre was managed by a series of administrations that failed to implement effective policies for social and educational development. Additionally, their inability to access available resources from local government for community requirements further strengthened perceptions among the congregation that the leadership at that time was unqualified or uninterested in the community's needs.[3] Tensions reached a climax in March 1993 when the majority of community members called for an open meeting with the leadership, failing which they would be ousted by a majority vote with a new management team assuming responsibility.

There are several factors to note which led to tensions developing in those formative years and these played pivotal roles in the present leadership's election on 11 January 1994:

1. The Mosque was considered a novelty by other established cultural centres around South London owing to the fact that no such institution had, up until then, been managed and administered by convert Muslims. Furthermore, unlike the other established communities which had established cultural ties to their countries of origin, e.g. Pakistan, Bangladesh, Morocco, etc., the convert community of Brixton had few options other than to be self-reliant.
2. Unlike the majority of mosques in the UK, Brixton Mosque's congregation did not adhere to a single ideology at the time. Many British mosques adhere to Islam's four established schools of jurisprudence, the Hanafi School being predominant among the South Asian community. Further sub-branches are found within this school, such as Deobandis, Tablighis and Barelvis to name but a few; however, the source of jurisprudence is largely the same.[4] In contrast to a generally singular adherence to an ideology or methodology, Brixton Mosque's leadership accommodated a variety of practices, irrespective of ideology, so long as it subscribed in some way to Islam. This resulted in Sunnis, Shia, Sufis (the Murabitun Sect) and even Nation of Islam members attending and worshipping there.
3. Instability and obscurity in such a fundamental area as ideology invariably attracted the attention of individuals and groups seeking a platform to exploit this vulnerability and propagate their beliefs. Abu Hamza, Muhammad al Misri, Omar Bakri and Abdullah el Faisal were a few who attended the Mosque either by way of invitation from the previous unsuspecting management or simply to worship there and assess the prevailing climate. Abu Qatadah even attended on one occasion, shortly after arriving in the UK.
4. Study circles were established after prayer by various individuals, many of them being of Arab/North African descent, under the pretext of teaching converts Arabic. In an effort to counter this growing

influence the mosque leadership was keen to promote any African-Caribbean convert who had graduated from one of the Islamic universities in Saudi Arabia or elsewhere in the Muslim world as a viable alternative.

At the same time as welcoming the unfortunate attention of such individuals and groups, the unsuspecting leadership began increasingly to ostracise the Salafi members because of the latter's quiet opposition to the melting pot of ideologies which was a primary cause of tension in the community. Conflicts and divisions were increasingly witnessed in areas such as congregational prayers and the manner in which they were performed according to religious delineation. It is important to note that the Salafi youth had become an integral part of the community at that stage. Street wise and in touch with much of the youth in and around south London, the Salafis were deemed a threat by the elders, although they had formerly welcomed them. In an effort to address the rising tensions and reach some form of compromise, the leadership acceded to the request of the Salafis, after engaging in dialogue with them, to ban Shia and Nation of Islam adherents because of the variance of their fringe beliefs, considered unacceptable to mainstream Sunni ideology. Part of the agreement was that classes be conducted by the little known Abdullah El Faisal, a recent graduate from Riyadh's Muhammad Ibn Saud University, Saudi Arabia, who professed his belief to be in accordance with Salafism. Relative stability was subsequently established in 1992 and the community continued to develop; the leadership appeared to have a coherent strategy which witnessed the establishment of one of the first Muslim Housing Associations in London.[5] Community members were being housed in improved accommodation for the first time; however, the strategy behind such developments was soon to be made clear.

The leadership had been successful in bringing together members from all sections of the community. A weekend workshop had been arranged for a new management committee in Lampeter, Wales. The workshop was well organised and effective in brainstorming mission objectives and strategies, etc. However, unbeknown to a few of the participants, it had been part of a covert plan to develop and strengthen the leadership's Murabitun/Sufi manifesto before announcing it as policy to the community upon returning to London. This resulted in mass resignations from the new management committee and the outright rejection of the manifesto by the entire community. The Salafis, despite avoiding the political manoeuvrings and strategies of other groups within the community, were deemed a threat once more by the administration, and Abdullah el Faisal (who was initially introduced by the leadership), was prohibited from teaching in the mosque because of his apparent Salafist inclination. El Faisal's study circles were transferred to one of the elder Salafi's homes and it was shortly after this occurrence that he (el Faisal) began espousing his extremist views – much to the consternation and surprise of those in attendance. Despite el Faisal's prohibition from having lessons in the mosque and being censured by the leadership, Salafi attendees were opposed to any violent action against the mosque.[6] This was contrary to the increasingly polemical position adopted by el Faisal who threatened to ignite a violent revolt in an attempt to oust the Murabitun leadership from the mosque. Suffice it to say that el Faisal's study circles ceased immediately upon his attendees' realisation of his extremist interpretation of the religion. He had successfully managed to suppress such beliefs up until this time. Subsequently, he proceeded to establish study circles elsewhere in the local vicinity, hiring public venues to continue propagating his increasingly extreme beliefs.

March 1993: 'Black Sunday' – the first crisis

The increasing tensions culminated in members across London calling for a public meeting to discuss how best to resolve conflicts surrounding the leadership. Expectations in the wider community were that the subsequent meeting would produce a new leadership to replace the existing Murabitun management. Coincidentally, the leadership had already conceded that they had lost popular support. Their observation was compounded by revelations that they had transformed the mosque's charitable status into a limited company (Masjidullah Ltd). The outcome of the subsequent public meeting was unanimous and the Murabitun lost their position in the mosque and among the community. The next stage was to decide on the most appropriate mechanism for electing a new management. The procedure most widely accepted was loosely modelled on the Islamic election of the first leader and Caliph after the death of Prophet Muhammad in Madina in 622 CE (Christian Era):[7]

1. Nominations for leaders were received from the congregation attending the meeting.
2. The nominees would then sit privately among themselves to decide who was the most suitable and/or qualified to become leader.

3. Once they had reached a unanimous or majority decision, this would be conveyed to the community who would accept it.
4. The new leader would be responsible for choosing his management and administrative committees which would be reflective of community requirements.

One surprising outcome from these nominations was that four of the five nominees were Salafi, confirming the popularity of their doctrine among the community. Consequently, the process of selecting a new chairman was relatively easy. The new leader was announced, heralding the introduction of Salafi leadership, arguably for the first time in a British mosque. However, difficulties were set to continue because of some community members' suspicions about the motives of the Salafis who had been accused of trying to 'Saudize/Arabize' the attendees. The newly elected leader's failure to engage with and embrace community sensitivities only served to exacerbate these suspicions.

Within nine months, tensions resulting from the election needed to be addressed, with requests being made for another general meeting where the previous decisions surrounding the leadership would again be reviewed. Aside from the leadership's alienation of the community other significant developments were noticed:

- El Faisal's study circles in the local vicinity gained prominence, attracting a much larger audience as a result of disgruntlement with the new Salafi leadership in the mosque.
- Many of the North African attendees, also disillusioned and upset by the non-representative composition of the new leadership, started to hold their own functions, also within the local vicinity.
- Some members from the West African community members migrated to less controversial waters and established a more liberal cultural centre further along Brixton High Road – the North Brixton Mosque.

The obvious level of disaffection among the local Brixton Muslim community had reached unparalleled proportions and serious concern arose about a potential bloody conflict in an attempt by other groups to remove the leadership. These waters were tested in October/November that same year (1993) when el Faisal announced in one of his study circles in south-east London that, despite his explusion from Brixton Mosque, he would nevertheless attend and conduct a study session there the following week. The news of a potential confrontation spread rapidly throughout south London and heightened existing tensions. While the leadership was more than prepared to deal with the potential conflict, it was conscious of the need to avoid exacerbating the already fragile climate. El Faisal attended the mosque as planned and entered it with approximately 30–40 supporters. He proceeded to the main prayer area, sat and began his lecture, despite the presence of the mosque leader. Security around him was immediately approached, as was el Faisal, and reproached. The subsequent measures taken by the leadership served to thwart his agenda to continue; the PA system was switched off, as was the electricity, effectively rendering el Faisal mute. He attempted to proceed with his programme in another area of the mosque; however, the impetus had been lost by the continuous presence of the leadership and community members, and their ability to stifle his attempts. Both he and his supporters eventually left the premises with promises of reprisals. Fearing the worst, appeals were made by many of the community groups in Lambeth to find a solution to the impending crisis. The mosque leadership and self-appointed 'Committee of Elders' agreed to select a group of independent arbiters to convene over the issue as to who should lead the community. The existing leadership's removal was almost a foregone conclusion and came as no surprise to all parties involved. However, the surprise was the unanimous request of the non-Salafi representation that another Salafi be appointed leader of the mosque and community again. Their reasoning was that a unified, authentic ideology had, for the first time, been introduced to the mosque. However, the way it had been disseminated to the community by the chairman was divisive and alienating. They believed the Salafi methodology would be expressed more wisely by a leader coming from a similar background to the community members.[8] The outgoing leader, while known to the community, was not *from among* them especially considering his east London roots. The present leadership was elected and given parameters within which to develop its own administration and committees.

On 11 January 1994, the arbiters' conclusions and final decision were announced in a general meeting. Among the immediate undertakings of the new leader (the author of this account) was to amend the charitable status of the mosque, providing a more secure process of election. This was also done to avoid the recurrence of incidents that preceded the new administration (such as el Faisal's confrontational attendance). The mosque changed its charitable status and become a charitable trust in 1997.[9] The new status would ensure protection of mosque assets such as the existing premises acquired on 27 March 1998. It also afforded more security than the previous status in that only the six trustees possessed legislative powers over community affairs.[10]

The period of new leadership ushered in an era of growth and a strong sense of communal identity started to develop. A number of strategic initiatives, described below, were devised and implemented to facilitate progress.[11]

Community engagement

Friday Khutbas (sermons) were used as an avenue for the leadership to familiarise the community with its objectives and vision of progress, as well as to commence a structured process of learning fundamental tenets of Islam and how to contextualise these within British society. It provided a platform of religious instruction for the community. As mentioned earlier, up until the new leadership was elected the community had never received a coherent, structured Islamic education, causing conflict with both their Muslim and British identities. Sermons were also delivered in English, another essential factor contributing to the mosque's success in attracting attendees from all over London. Admittedly, the use of English as the sole medium of communication unfortunately marginalised the North African and Arabic speaking attendees of the mosque. This was remedied, albeit to a minimal degree, by providing one sermon each month in Arabic. This was subsequently translated into English for the non-Arab speaking attendees. Additional reasons for the success of the mosque's sermons were their topical nature, which always addressed contemporary issues such as the 9/11 attacks on the US (Baker, 2001).

There was a need to establish more communal activities where new and existing members of the community could socialise and invite non-Muslim family and friends into their new environment. Community Dinners, therefore, enabled engagement on an informal level. Short lectures were delivered amid discussions relating to various issues affecting the community and society as a whole. The leadership seized upon these events to familiarise itself with members and enlist voluntary support in relative fields of expertise required in the mosque.[12]

Meetings took place between local government representatives between May and July 2001 to discuss programmes enabling the empowerment of women among the Muslim community. This included participation in seconded youth work in order to facilitate women-only sporting activities which the mosque had recently initiated.[13]

Such liaisons were considered by local authorities as a progressive step towards the inclusion of Muslims into the wider community. In fact, the local council had recently conceded that its previous failure to work with the mosque had in fact been to its disadvantage.[14] Irrespective of their initial oversight of Brixton Mosque's contribution among the wider non-Muslim community, an effort to forge stronger links between the two entities was made:

> The Brixton Islamic Community Centre now seeks to establish a positive and healthy working relationship with Lambeth Council. We believe that both parties could be inspired by the example set in the neighbouring Local Authority, where Wandsworth Council and the local Muslim Community have developed a positive working relationship which has enabled that community to go from strength to strength, socially, educationally, culturally and even recreationally.[15]

Despite the Mosque leadership's readiness to engage with the wider community, a degree of conflict still ensued.

Confrontation with the local non-Muslim community: Its context and implications

Some members of local Muslim groups continued to remain insular, refusing to engage entirely with the wider non-Muslim community. In many instances, they also avoided engaging with other culturally-led Muslim communities owing to negative experiences they had previously experienced post conversion (Reddie, 2009: 190–2). One major reason for not engaging with the wider non-Muslim community, of which they were formerly an intrinsic part before conversion, was suspicion and mistrust. Alienation from family and/or friends, coming out of prison and having to adjust to a new but different life, etc. were some of the reasons for negativity. These factors created vulnerability among some members and Brixton Mosque was the ideal environment to accommodate them.[16] Roald confirms the feelings of 'strangeness' and frustration from Muslim converts in her study of Scandinavian converts (Roald, 2004). Initially, such negativity was not addressed directly by the leadership for fear of provoking more suspicion and causing further alienation of community members. Instead, the mistrust and pessimism of the wider society was in fact used to focus on an initial sense of religious belonging, providing a context within which they could define their identity and reasons for converting to Islam. This initial approach, although precarious, proved successful as it fostered an atmosphere of trust for the leadership who empathised with its members. As a result, the foundation was then established for a process of change in perspectives; namely, how members should contextualise the correct Islamic understanding of residing within Western society, and the most effective means of integrating this with their newly established Muslim identity.

Undoubtedly, on many occasions this process of change would result in social and psychological conflict for some members, and this would require mosque involvement at various levels. Such occasions initially included increasing confrontations with the local police in view of the developing sense of an '*us and them*' mentality, and the perceived ineptitude of the police to handle domestic complaints from Muslims sensitively and in the same way they would deal with other minority- or faith-led communities.

The Stockwell Park Estate incident

Incidents of this nature culminated in a confrontation between mosque members and the police when a non-Muslim robbed and attempted to assault a female Muslim community member during the summer of 1997. This was met with a robust response from the mosque with members visiting the Stockwell Park estate and entering the premises of the assailant who was well known in the area. This action resulted in the wider non-Muslim community threatening reprisals against the Muslim community and a direct threat against Muslim residents living on the estate. The mosque leadership held an emergency meeting with some community members and it was interesting to note that two opinions emerged on how to deal with the prevailing circumstances which threatened to escalate. Never before had the Brixton Muslim community taken such a public stance, highlighting unequivocally its identity, and emphasising the significance of its presence as a distinctive but integral part of the wider non-Muslim populace. However, one opinion emanating from the elders was to calm things down and apologise for entering the assailant's home. The other contrary opinion was that a firm stance should be maintained to reflect the seriousness of the situation at hand. The leadership decided to incorporate both positions and devised an appropriate strategy. The ensuing confrontation with armed police resulted in a directive that the group of Muslims present disband immediately or face arrest. This request was rejected on the premise that the police refused to provide security for the Muslim family which lived on the estate where the initial robbery and attempted assault had taken place. Undeterred by threats of action, community members remained. The confrontation passed without further incident with a police withdrawal from the estate. This incident established the Muslim community's presence as part of the wider community. It also imbued members with a self-dignity and confidence that had previously been lacking post conversion. Nevertheless, negative perceptions of the Muslim community persisted, resulting in similar incidents between community members and local police. In the event, serious confrontations like the storming of Brixton Police Station's reception following the unannounced entry by the police into the mosque in order to apprehend a community member (September 2000), led the leadership to embark on a series of meetings with local police in an effort to avoid further similar incidents. The meetings proved successful, reducing pre-existing tensions between community members and the police, as well as fostering a mutual understanding of parameters within which both entities could operate. The mosque leadership took this opportunity to promote positive citizenship among its members, reinforcing its strategy to foster improved relations with the local non-Muslim community. Unfortunately, the reputation emanating from incidents like those mentioned above attracted extremist elements to Brixton seeking young converts unafraid of confrontation *and*, unwittingly, criminal activity (Cole and Cole, 2009: 96). A few members of the mosque began attending the study circles that opened in the local vicinity. Zacarias Moussaoui and Abdur Rahim (Richard Reid) were included among those who gravitated towards such events.[17] The mosque leadership, when approached by the police or other local statutory bodies, confirmed that these events were unrelated to its own activities.

Extremist propaganda subsequently increased in Brixton with the frequent circulation of leaflets outside the mosque after congregational and Jumuah (Friday prayers). This ignited frequent confrontations between mosque members and extremist sympathisers. In an attempt to counter the latter's propaganda weekly sermons focused on highlighting the differences between mainstream and extremist ideologies. However, these achieved limited success. Scholars conversant with, and experienced in, countering extremist propaganda were required to tackle the issues at hand.

Islamic conferences and lectures

'Return to Ilm' (knowledge) conferences were then instituted as a result of the above, inviting recognised scholars and students of knowledge from the Muslim world. Wiktorowicz acknowledges the significance of some scholars' impact upon such conferences, attesting to their prominence:

> Among the elite students (of Shaykh Muhammad Nasirudeen al-Albani [d.1999]) were Ali Hasan al-Halabi and Salim al-Hilali... who... went on to become prominent non-violent scholars in their own right with substantial international influence.
>
> (Wiktorowicz, 2006a: 213)

These scholars' superior knowledge of religious texts meant they were able to defeat the extremists' arguments and effectively render them impotent. The only remaining recourse for the latter was their attempt to discredit the scholars. This succeeded so far as takfeeri adherents and sympathisers were concerned owing to widespread negativity towards the Muslim and Arab world, considered to be led by despotic, infidel governments. This tactic, coupled with distortions of religious texts and edicts, served as extremist protagnonists' only effective counter measure to the conferences. The most vocal of the extremists during this period were Abdullah el Faisal and Abu Hamza al Misri respectively. They were challenged to substantiate their extremist beliefs during some conferences.[18] Heated discussions between mosque attendees and adherents to extremist propaganda intensified resulting in occasional physical confrontations. Concern regarding escalating tensions resulted in the mosque management expelling attendees who had been adversely influenced by extremist propaganda and were contributing to the conflict within the community. Previously, as a communal property, the mosque was unaccustomed to preventing entry to any Muslim; however, in view of the increasing concerns surrounding security, decisive action had to be effected immediately. One particular obstacle to implementing such preventative action was the fact that the premises, being council property, did not belong to any private entity at the time.[19] An additional measure to stem the tide of extremist propaganda was introduced: all leafleting was prohibited outside the mosque premises. However, it proved difficult to extend this policy beyond the immediate vicinity of the mosque and extremist propaganda continued to be distributed across the road from the mosque, adjacent to Brixton Police station. Nevertheless, as a result of its emerging position, Brixton Mosque rapidly became recognised among the wider Muslim community for its socially conservative adherence to Salafism and its unwavering stance against extremism. Warnings emanated from some areas of London, particularly Finsbury Park Mosque, where Abu Hamza and his followers had gained control, that Brixton Mosque was a government organisation sponsored by 'apostate and puppet regimes' from the Middle East, and that its sole objective was to pacify the Muslim community.[20] Among young Muslims a clear distinction had now been emphatically drawn between extremist propaganda and Salafism, second / third generation and converts being polarised between the two ideologies.

9/11 attacks and their effect on the community

Immediately after the attacks of 11 September 2001 the mosque leadership convened a meeting in which the following measures were decided:

1. to close the Community School, Iqra, in the interim owing to its vulnerability as a primary school with predominantly female staff,
2. to contact the leader of Lambeth council to show solidarity with the wider community and confirm the local Muslim community's abhorrence with the attacks,
3. to obtain scholarly advice on how to proceed in the prevailing climate,
4. to contact concerned community members, especially the most vulnerable, such as single parent families, to ensure their safety, and
5. to speak to the local police, highlighting concerns about reprisals, etc.

In the ensuing atmosphere, suspicion arose as to the identity of the culprits of these attacks. Muslims were the first to be accused, even as the World Trade Center towers were collapsing, placing international focus on the Muslim world. Reprisals against Muslims were reported across Europe and America; the most severe incidents culminating in fatalities.[21] The momentum with which evidence was gathered heightened suspicions among Muslim communities of an underlying agenda to provoke conflict between the West and the Muslim world in an attempt to make western hegemony more dominant in those resource filled regions.

Unwelcome attention – 'the twentieth bomber' (Case study 1)

It was amid this atmosphere of mistrust that the Brixton Muslim community braced itself for another crisis, this time on an international scale. Zacarias Moussaoui came to the attention of the world as the alleged twentieth suicide bomber. His efforts to participate in the

9/11 attacks had been prematurely thwarted because of his arrest prior to these events for unrelated visa violations. Moussaoui's connection with Brixton Mosque in the early to mid-1990s, led to the almost inevitable attention and investigation of its members from Scotland Yard's Anti-Terrorist branch. Media coverage was, as expected, intense and coverage of Brixton and its multicultural, multi-faith community was a constant source of attention. Moussaoui had lived and worked among the Brixton community, renting accommodation from local community members (Shaykh Abu Bakr and his then wife, Christine Abdullah). Ms Abdullah's name and address were found among Moussaoui's possessions as was the address of his previous employers, Black Crescent, whose owners were also a part of the local Muslim community. When locating Ms Abdullah's address, officers from the Anti-Terrorist Branch actually met the author. The constant attention and visits by Scotland Yard yielded very little as far as they were concerned. They visited the now ex-husband of Ms Abdullah, travelling to the Gambia as soon as they had ascertained his whereabouts. Other than superficial information concerning Moussaoui's residence and temporary employment, the authorities were unable to obtain any substantive information. The Brixton Muslim community therefore remained suspect, despite its efforts to be transparent and cooperative.

Three months after the 9/11 attacks, Brixton Mosque was thrust into the unprecedented position of defending its socially conservative adherence and practice of Islam while distinguishing itself from violent extremism. However, suspicions in the Anti-Terrorist Branch regarding the mosque as an extremist conduit were substantiated, as far as they were concerned, by ensuing events which highlighted Richard Reid, aka the 'Shoe Bomber', as a British Muslim convert who had, like Moussaoui, also attended Brixton Mosque.

Unwelcome attention 2 – 'the Shoe Bomber' (Case study 2)

Revelations in media reports that an unknown individual had attempted to explode a device on a transatlantic flight in December 2001 caused tremors across the western world as it sent an emphatic reminder that extremists were intent on implementing their agenda on or across western soil. Unbeknown to many at the time, Reid had previously been a member of the Brixton Muslim community prior to his violent radicalisation to extremism. Abdur Rahim, as he was known among the community, had joined the mosque after leaving prison in the mid- to late 1990s. Upon realising his identity, the mosque management met to discuss how to tackle this new and impending dilemma. It was agreed to contact Scotland Yard in an effort to avert further suspicion from the mosque and its community, especially in view of the recent Moussaoui affair. Also, in view of conversations with Reid's mother during the previous summer, it was apparent that he was no longer in contact with family or friends. Indications were that she would also contact the authorities to confirm Reid's identity and that he was a Muslim convert from Brixton. By establishing this initial contact the mosque management would, at this sensitive stage, avert further suspicion from the authorities who could be justified in believing the Muslim community actually knew more than previously disclosed. Such was the urgency of contact at this particular stage that the first unsuspecting patrol officer passing along on the high street was approached, and confirmation as to Reid's identity and nationality provided impromptu with a request that this be conveyed to Scotland Yard and that they make contact with the mosque management immediately. Subsequently, a telephone call was received from the Anti-Terrorist Branch with a request that the chairman visit Scotland Yard without delay. Offers to drive there were firmly declined by senior officers who stipulated that no personal transport approach anywhere near the vicinity of the Yard as it would invariably be stopped, searched (and possibly destroyed). Instead, a representative from the Anti-Terrorist Squad would travel to Brixton to collect the chairman for questioning. Their sudden change in approach was confirmation that the community was now under suspicion.

The Media

On 25 December 2001, media reporters contacted the mosque. In an attempt to avert negative media from sensationalist journalists, the author of this book, in his capacity as chairman, agreed to conduct an interview with *The Times* newspaper. Few members were notified or consulted at the time as, indeed, it was never expected (albeit naively) that the story would warrant the attention it subsequently received. This lack of consultation caused severe consternation and chastisement from many members of the community who, after the story became public, feared for the future of the mosque and its associated institutions. Concern was also expressed, once the story broke, about the frankness with which the leadership spoke and publicly exposed the protagonists of extremism. On the other hand, some members appreciated the need to clarify and distinguish the community from extremists. These numbers increased once members witnessed the favourable media coverage and empathy of wider non-Muslim communities. That said, the anger displayed among sections of other Muslim communities was severe. The intensity of media coverage continued for at least six to eight weeks; however, the position and focus on Brixton Mosque and its community had, from that moment in time, been irreversibly altered. It, alongside Finsbury Park Mosque, became one of the most well-known Muslim centres in the western world, initially for the wrong reasons – association with terrorism. Characters like Moussaoui, Reid and Abdullah el Faisal who had, at some stage, frequented Brixton Mosque, meant it would forever be associated with extremism. Fortunately, this negative association has, to some degree, been dispelled by way of an active campaign to distinguish the mosque's beliefs and practices as one of *opposition* to violent extremism. The Mosque management had, to some extent, successfully steered the community away from potentially damaging assertions that it was a 'hotbed of extremism', highlighting the fact that it had always been one of the few centres over the past 20 years to effectively combat extremism at grassroots.[22]

Conclusions

The failure of previous mosque administrations to provide strategic direction or a clearly defined ideological delineation could arguably be considered a contributory factor that led to the community's initial exposure to violent radicalism and extremist propaganda. The succeeding Salafi managements only served to highlight this failure and the dangers it could invariably manifest. As expected, the Salafi assumption of leadership to a strategically significant institution resulted in an important avenue of extremist propaganda being stifled. Unfortunately, such propaganda was able to proliferate via alternative venues within the local vicinity. The relative success of extremist protagonists in tapping into the emotional psyche of young, disillusioned individuals such as Richard Reid and Zacarias Moussaoui highlights the effectiveness of their propaganda, especially in the absence of experienced and qualified opponents who could effectively tackle them at a grassroots level. This chapter has highlighted how, historically, there was little or no involvement or indeed attention paid by other Muslim communities and authorities to extremist propaganda which rapidly attracted the attention of younger second and third generation Muslims, not to mention new British Muslim converts. Despite universities effecting measures to prevent extremist organisations such as Hizb ut-Tahrir among others from propagating their destructive ideologies, the authorities failed to heed warnings regarding the catalytic nature of the violent extremist narrative. This chapter suggests that, historically, Brixton Mosque was itself considered an extremist entity by authorities, resulting in a deliberate oversight of what was considered at the time as local religious rivalries and factionalism. Few centres can provide a historical perspective charting the path of their encounters with extremism. Fewer still can accurately reference strategies employed to deter susceptible youth from extremist propaganda, being aware of its eventuality, namely, terrorism. Brixton Mosque may arguably be considered as having been unsuccessful in its attempts to deter Richard Reid and Zacarias Moussaoui from extremism. However, see Chapter 8 for a discussion regarding successful intervention/counter radicalisation initiatives and engagement with young British Muslims, many of whom are considered hard to reach by statutory bodies today. The current chapter has also provided vital background to the analysis of the empirical data that will be introduced in Chapters 6 and 7. It is important to understand the debates taking place among the Brixton Mosque community even though the perspective given is from that of the author. In the event, this perspective will assist future authors in identifying any unconscious bias.

Considering the conflict of identities faced by new Muslim converts alongside the foundational phases of learning a new religion, their potential susceptibility to extremist propaganda is unsurprising. The theoretical framework presented in Figure 1.2 reflects the ideological vulnerabilities that exist during early stages of conversion; however, it fails to incorporate the challenges converts face with their new identity constructs of being both British *and* Muslim. Chapter 3 explores these issues, highlighting the fact that such conflicts of identity are not restricted to new Muslim converts alone.

3
British Muslims and Identity

This chapter discusses issues surrounding identity and its implications for the Muslim communities in Britain today. Academic and Muslim perspectives are discussed within the context of examining whether a distinctive British Muslim identity exists, or can be developed, and whether such identity conflicts with the majority society's common perceptions of 'Britishness'. It also seeks to determine the validity of such examination in view of (r)evolving discussions around what actually constitutes 'Britishness' and meaningful (as opposed to legitimate) citizenship. Legitimate citizenship, for the context of this research, is considered the more tangible aspect of belonging to society, i.e. possessing a British passport, National Insurance number, etc., whereas *meaningful citizenship* is considered to involve the more intangible 'sense of belonging'.

The chapter also examines existing data and typologies that distinguish the heterogeneous nature of Muslim communities, and discusses whether these remain accurate post 7/7 or whether more specific research into the composition of Muslim communities is now required. By placing emphasis on the above areas of discussion, the focus of this research is clarified; namely, British convert Muslims and the factors that encapsulate the duality of their identity as being British *and* Muslim; particularly Salafi (Salafist) Muslims.

The primary research question – whether British Muslim converts are more susceptible to violent extremism, or whether they are the most effective of the Muslim communities in countering it – is then placed within the context of existing academic and journalistic debate, as is the second part of the question: whether they (British convert Muslims) by virtue of their identity/ies, act as effective conduits between the majority (host) society and Muslim communities in understanding and effectively tackling the threat of home-grown violent extremism facing British society today.

Identity

Rennani argues that the issue of identity initially developed from the social science of psychology and gradually evolved into a sociological concept. The psychological perspective places emphasis on 'an expressed sense of personal distinctiveness, personal continuity and personal autonomy' (Renani, 2001: 15). That said, he acknowledges the wider sociological concepts of identity as being the more encompassing so far as the individual and society are concerned. This accords with Evans's observation of identity formation as a result of dialectics between the two entities (Evans and Potter, 1970). This position is also shared by Berger and Luckmann who see identity as a 'phenomenon' that emerges from the dialectic between the individual and society (Berger and Luckmann, 1967). Erikson's understanding of identity, while similar to the above concepts, does not highlight the symbiotic nature of the relationship between the individual and society. Instead, he refers to the: 'sharing of some kind of [the individual's] essential character with others' (cited in Mol, 1976). He describes an: 'implosion of cultural differences, where the collision of cultures... [does not cause further divisions]... but scattered fragments inwards, into the body of colliding cultures' (Eriksen, 1994).

Although concepts discussed thus far refer to the individual's interaction with society (and, in Erikson's case, 'other' unspecified entities possibly extending *beyond* society), Hutnick focuses upon the influence of the individual's membership to social groups and how the latter contributes to shaping the former's perception of themselves within society (Hutnick, 1985: 298). This particular observation is important within the context of the present research as recent literature suggests Muslim membership to Islamic groups and organisations have been contributory factors towards politicisation and polarisation towards extremism (Husain, 2007). Beckford et al. provide evidence in support of Hutnick's concept when discussing ethnic groups and communities (Beckford et al., 2005). Their research provides evidence of immigrant minorities regrouping in particular industrial cities throughout the UK as a result of socio-economic factors such as housing, employment, immigration laws, etc. Chain migration accelerated the grouping together of people from similar regions or indeed villages. Migrants from the Indian subcontinent are cited as examples in this instance. These groups were then able to acquire greater salience and visibility in areas where they had settled, enabling them to interact to varying degrees with wider society. Policies began to evolve promoting 'ethnic community paradigms' and groups were increasingly referred to as 'ethnic minorities' as opposed to 'immigrants', (Beckford et al., 2005: 46–8). When summarising his observations on this particular point, Beckford identifies three successive modes of group identification related to New Commonwealth immigrants from a Muslim cultural background following their arrival in the UK:

1. their initial classification under a framework for the 'race relations' paradigm,
2. their subsequent organisation and redefining of themselves as 'ethnic minorities', and
3. their current differentiation on the basis of religion (Beckford et al., 2005: 55).

Castells chose to widen identity as a construct beyond the parameters discussed so far (Castells, 1997). He considered identity to be an amalgam of elements constructed by components of history, geography, biology, collective memory, power apparatuses and religion. His assertion was that individuals, social groups and societies process amalgams and reconstruct their meanings according to the prevailing social context of that period (Castells, 1997: 7). Renani postulates, from Castells' concept of the social interactions perspective, that one's identity is situated among a series of social relations, thereby categorising individuals as social objects. He concludes by summarising his findings, stating:

> Identity, as a relative concept, should be seen as a combination of individual experience with association of several factors such as historical roots, geographical environment, educational and political systems, economic consumption, religious understanding, practices and beliefs.
>
> (2001: 16)

Britishness – an (r)evolving identity?

The issue of British Identity continues to be an area of focus and political debate, not only in regard to the Muslim community, but the British population in general (Paxman, 1999: 8–11; Marr, 2000). Such debates raise questions as to whether, and to what extent, distinctive characteristics of British identity remain in today's society.[1] Since the terrorist attacks in London on 7 July 2005 when British Muslims committed a series of suicide attacks, defining British identity has never been so important (Malik, 2006: 14).

In fact, it is against this background that Muslim identity continues to be negatively constructed. It is, as Ansari highlights, 'evolving as an identity of "unbelonging" in a "culture of resistance" and in contest with hegemonic British identity' (2004: 9). He makes historical reference to the prevailing conditions in the late nineteenth century and asserts that Muslim identities were shaped by negative attitudes and assumptions to a greater degree than those experienced in the twentieth century. This assertion can arguably be countered when considering the rise of extremist/terrorist tendencies and acts that threatened and affected western societies and their security during the mid- to late twentieth century.

The concept of Britishness, according to Colley, originates from the establishing of the nation 'Great Britain' as an entity in 1707 when the parliament of Westminster passed the Act of Union, effectively amalgamating Scotland with England and Wales (Colley, 1996). Colley argues that, despite this amalgamation, the 'new nation', so to speak, retained existing regional and local identities, i.e. English, Welsh or Scottish, and that these remained stronger than the sense of 'Britishness' (Colley, 1996: 13). Renani asserts, while commenting on Colley's observations, that the British identity became increasingly prominent with the rise of Protestantism and the establishment of the British Empire; as these two forces grew, so did British identity (Renani, 2001: 203). However, since the end of the Second World War, the distinguishing characteristics of this identity have steadily declined as the factors required for forging a British nation have disappeared (Renani, 2001). In fact Paxman, when considering the concept of 'Englishness' observed that the English 'metropolitan elite' has more in common with Parisians and New Yorkers than it does with rural or suburban England (Paxman, 1999: 264). From this, Renani concludes that if the concept of Englishness is unclear, the notion of Britishness is all the more obscure and therefore: 'the task of defining British Muslim identity will be even more elusive' (2001: 246).

His research also examines the effects of *globalisation* on British Muslim identity and in generality its impact on remaining aspects of British identity. In this vein he asserts that: 'with the impact of globalization, whatever was left of British identity is in the process of gradually exhausting itself ... [and] the fact remains that the concept of 'Britishness' is undergoing severe strain' (2001: 246).

He further asserts that it is now difficult to discern particular characteristics of Britishness from that of many other western cultures and societies, with the exception of geographical and linguistic differences. While the subject of globalisation is not within the scope of this particular research, it is necessary at least to acknowledge its effects on British Muslim identity. Also, although the purpose of this chapter is not to enter into further exploratory discourse on identity, some discussion is required regarding the difficulties of defining it in today's (r)evolving climate. This will then serve to highlight how the issue of British Muslim identity has to date focused primarily on second/third generation British-born Muslims to the oversight of British converts and the latter group's significance within wider British society.[2]

Multi-ethnic Britain: Different perspectives on multicultural identity

The Runnymede Trust raised the question of Britain being 'reimagined' as a post-nation in a multicultural context in its report *The Future of Multi-Ethnic Britain* (Runnymede Trust, 2000: 36). Unsurprisingly, the report ignited a general debate among academics and the media, not to mention the Muslim community, with each section adopting similar stances. The main feature of the debate was the prevalence of declarations that Britain and Britishness were, and remained, inherently multicultural. Such declarations were made in defiance of the report's suggestion that any reference to Britishness did in fact carry racial connotations (Fortier, 2005: 559–60).

Response to the report signalled a substantial paradigm shift in what it actually meant to be British: Britishness being conceptualised as inherently multicultural – even hybrid (Fortier, 2005: 560). Tribute to Britain's multicultural society continued to be made five years after the above mentioned report, with some media sources hailing London to be:

> possibly the most cosmopolitan city in the world: 300 languages, 50 non-indigenous communities with populations of 10,000 or more, with virtually every race, nation, culture and region able to claim at least a handful of Londoners. Almost a third (30%) of the city's residents were born outside England (2.2m) with many tens of thousands more who are second or third generation immigrants.[3]

From an academic perspective Modood maintains multiculturalism still offers attractive and worthwhile political dimensions and that society can beneifit even more owing to the present climate (Modood, 2005). Similar sentiments are shared by former Tory leader, William Hague, who believes British identity in the twenty-first century is one where the capacity to assimilate and absorb other cultures is celebrated.[4] This contrasts with debates commencing almost a decade earlier in the 1990s concerning the influx of immigrants presenting an 'assimilation' of all other cultures that were being forced upon Britain, resulting in a threat to British identity (Fortier, 2005). It also opposes the avalanche of criticism charged against multiculturalism post 7/7, with some academics and media citing the four British bombers responsible for the attacks as being 'a consequence of a misguided and catastrophic pursuit of multiculturalism,[5] [and that the bombings have] smashed the implicit social consensus that produced multiculturalism to smithereens' (openDemocracy, 2005).

Clearly, events such as 7/7 and subsequent revelations about minority communities' lack of integration and/or assimilation into majority society have caused further polarisation between advocates in favour of a multiculturalistic British identity and their opponents campaigning for minority communities' *assimilation* into British society.[6] One of the problems regarding multiculturalism could be in its contrasting definitions for both majority society and ethnic minorities. For example, Sander identified the Swedish understanding of multiculturalism to mean: 'equality between universal individuals regardless of culture, ethnicity, race, religion and gender'; whereas the Muslim minority's interpretation was that of 'an equal right to freedom of choice, which becomes a request for rights pertaining to religion, ethnicity and cultural expressions' (Sander, 1992).

The question of British identity (r)evolving is supported by academics such as Fortier (Fortier, 2005). When examining her classification of 'multiculturalist nationalism', this being 'the reworking of the nation as inherently multicultural', she indicates a progression from monoculture to multiculture. Indeed, her perspective is not entirely new and can perhaps be illustrated further when considering Halstead's perception of 'cultural pluralism', this being, 'the acceptance within a society of differences in the beliefs, values and traditions to which members of that society have a commitment' (Halstead, 1986).

Among the principles of cultural pluralism is the right of each group (or community) to retain its distinctive culture provided it does not conflict with the shared values of society as a whole (Baker, 1998). Other established theories like Halstead's, supporting a multiculturalistic evolvement, exist. 'Cultural relativism' is one such theory and has definable 'weak' and 'strong' parameters relating to its effective functioning within society (Feyerabend, 1978). The applicability of these theories should however be considered within the present context as their relevance today is questionable, particularly in view of significant changes to the political landscape post 9/11 and 7/7.

Renani highlights the usefulness of actually defining the meaning of 'nation' first, before attempting to explain what constitutes a nationalistic identity (Renani, 2001: 139). He cites Castells' definition of nations as being, 'cultural communes constructed in people's minds and collective memory by the sharing of history and political projects' (Castells, 1997). Castells points to a nationalist resurgence due to the pace and deemed threat of globalisation with nation-states viewing the latter as a threat to their respective societies. This resurgence is witnessed 'in the widespread (re) construction of identity on the basis of nationality, always affirmed against the alien' (Castells, 1997: 27 and Renani, 2001: 139) .

Fortier's 'vision' of a (new) Britain and the iconoclastic 'other', further illustrates the need to debate redefining British identity today, (Fortier, 2005: 568). This said, the question still remains; what actually defines *existing* British identity and, therefore, culture – be it multiculture (as assumed by Fortier, above) or otherwise? Ramadan's discourse endorses the above mentioned debates and theoretical perspectives of a British identity *evolving* and *incorporating different cultures*, stating that:

> The presence of Muslims has forced British culture to experience an even greater diversity of cultures. A British identity has evolved that is open, plural and constantly in motion, thanks to the cross-fertilization between reclaimed cultures of origin and the British culture that now includes its new citizens.
>
> (Ramadan, 2005)

The emergence of a British Muslim identity

Unfortunately for the Muslim communities, but understandably, the issue of identity places them firmly in the spotlight with serious questions being raised about their ability or inability to integrate into today's established multicultural society (Abbas, 2005: 16). Questions have arisen, however, and doubts echoed about the fairness of burdening Muslim communities with an issue such as defining their own identities, expecting them disproportionately to bear the burdens of a nation during these challenging times. Concern has also been expressed that integration is in reality a euphemism for assimilation (Birt, 2006: 9

and Modood, 2005). Placing Muslim communities under scrutiny only serves to exacerbate existing tensions. Evidence of this was witnessed as recently as May, June and July 2001 in the northern towns of Bradford, Burnley and Oldham, when South Asian youth (predominantly Muslim) rioted in retaliation to the neo-fascist British National Party's (BNP) antagonistic protest marches (Bagguley and Hussain, 2005: 208). Comparisons were made between these incidents, considered to be the worst outbreak of urban violence since the early 1980s and the riots among the African–Caribbean communities of Brixton (London) and Toxteth (Liverpool) in 1981; the precipitating factor on each occasion being a heavy police presence. Having said this, other significant socio-economic factors that continued to adversely affect these communities became apparent in the subsequent reports, prepared as a result of these disturbances.[7] The parallels between the two communities (African-Caribbean and South Asian) cannot go unnoticed (Cantle Report, 2001: 210–12, 239). Today, however, the difference between the two communities is the latter's transnational solidarity with Muslim communities owing to a religious, as opposed to cultural, relativity. In this vein, the question being posed to Muslims is: 'can solidarity to the Ummah be affirmed as part of British Muslim identity, as a matter of civic conscience rather than of cosmic or geopolitical alterity?' (Birt, 2006: 9).

Birt suggests that it would be counterproductive to place loyalty to the (global) Ummah and nation at opposite ends of the political spectrum as this would suggest the emergence of a dichotomy and, by extension, conflict of cultural/religious identity for British Muslims (Birt, 2006). That said, before questioning the validity of any community's identity and citizenship, clear guidance highlighting exactly what underpins the characteristics of British identity is first required. This does not appear to have occurred in light of the apparent inability to define prerequisites of something so fundamental to an established society (Paxman, 1999: 19–21). It has even been observed that, 'members of the so-called traditional British society can, at times, doubt their own identity and are frightened' (Ramadan, 2005).

Failure, therefore, to define national identity, particularly in the political arena, is unacceptable to communities expected to adhere to intangible values and gives cause for concern when considering legislation that emanated from terrorist attacks in the US on 11 September 2001.[8] Such legislation has been commonly viewed by the targeted community as anti-Muslim. In fact, Birt questions the validity of expectations upon minority groups (in this case, Muslim communities) to shoulder 'disproportionately the burdens of nationhood' when society is itself facing erosion by commodification, devolution, globalisation, etc. (Birt, 2006).

In any event, it would be interesting to examine the emerging British Muslim identity; its development and factors that have contributed to or catalysed its evolvement. Ansari actually questions whether a cohesive British Muslim identity even exists (Ansari, 2004). This question is asked in view of the diverse historical settings of Muslims who migrated to Britain prior to the post Second World War influx of the 1950s when immigrants from the Indian subcontinent first started arriving.[9] The fact that a Muslim presence has been witnessed in Britain over the past two centuries is often overlooked, and its diversity, particularly at the beginning of the twenty-first century, provides a clear illustration that it is far from being ethnically or ideologically homogeneous. Unfortunately, generalisations about Muslim communities in Britain attribute this presence to the South Asian Muslim population; consisting of Pakistani and Bangladeshi communities (Ansari, 2004: 3–5; Abbas, 2005: 3). Ansari's observations of intersecting variables that connect and separate these British citizens are interesting insofar as issues of ethnicity, kinship, doctrinal and sectarian traditions often supersede religious issues at a localised, more regional level. The religion, therefore, is seldom considered the sole form of social and political identification, let alone the primary one. As will be seen below under the section 'Resistance identity', Islam only becomes the basis of unity among the entire Muslim community when its members perceive they are being targeted for criticism or attack. Ansari dismisses the occasions when religious identity has been the main or sole unifying factor as being a rarity in the recent past; however, this observation can be countered in view of relatively recent events (national and international) that have plunged Muslim communities into the political spotlight on the basis of their religious identity (Ansari, 2004). He does, however, correctly illustrate the struggle surrounding the establishment of state-funded Muslim schools as a significant catalyst to galvanising British Muslim consciousness and therefore Muslim identity. Opposition to this type of school was voiced among members of the Conservative government at the time, as well as leading figures in the Anglican Church, on the premise that such schools would pose a threat to the 'stability and cohesion of society as a whole' (Ansari, 2004: 9–10). This position reflected the double standards witnessed by Muslim communities, especially in view of the fact that other faith groups enjoyed government support for their schools (Baker, 1998: 18–20). Muslims viewed their campaign as a symbolic challenge to the hegemonic culture and:

[t]he more the campaign was resisted, the more British Muslims saw it as a denial of their equal citizenship and of their identity since in their view Muslim schools were precisely where a distinct sense of Muslim identity could be constructed.

(Ansari, 2004, p. 10)

Significant to the context of this area of discussion is the fact that the individual responsible for raising public awareness of the campaign for Muslim schools was a British convert to Islam: Yusuf Islam (formerly known as the singer, Cat Stevens).[10]

General classification of identity

At this juncture it is necessary to highlight some of the existing classifications of identity before considering alternative models of identity constructs. Renani (citing Castells) refers to three modes of identity which accord with the scope of this particular research. It is, therefore, summarised in brief and compared with other academic discourses related to the subject. The same chronology as that of Renani has been used at this stage. Discourses on typologies of Muslims and their identity in the UK will therefore follow but will draw on recent research unpublished at the time of Renani's study. Castells distinguished between three modes and origins of identity formation:

1. Legitimising identity – that which is introduced by the dominant institutions of society in order to extend and rationalise their domination [through] social actors.
2. Projective identity is formed when social actors build a new identity that redefines their position in society and, by doing so, seeks the transformation of the overall social structure, on the basis of whichever cultural materials are available to them.
3. Resistance identity – the dissolution of former legitimising identities that used to constitute the civil society of the industrial era as giving rise to resistance identities which are pervasive in the network of society (Castells, 1997).

Legitimising identity, so far as it (initially) related to Muslim minorities in the UK, was considered an alien concept, especially when considering the secular (as opposed to religious) nature and character of the social institutions (Renani, 2001: 137). Upon consideration of such circumstances, Renani questions the applicability of this type of identity to Muslims in the UK.

Projective identity is, according to Castells, the product of the attempt to 'project' an alternative lifestyle in the direction of a transformative society. He cites oppression of identity as a possible cause for the emergence of a Projective identity (Castells, 1997). His observation in this instance is supported by Modood, who states the importance of a group being able to define itself based on its 'mode of being', which is distinct from its 'mode of oppression', 'as it is best equipped to resist oppression by those dimensions of its being from which it derives its greatest collective psychological strength' (Modood, 1992).

Resistance identity emerged as a result of globalisation, according to Castells. Those who develop this type of identity have their own communicative channels among themselves and operate within a network society. Communication with the state is on the basis of pursuing their specific interests and values (Castells, 1997: 356). In support of this assertion, Malik cites an example of first-generation Pakistani immigrants from Mirpuri who, having moved to Britain in the 1960s, still maintained the cultural systems – Baraderi (brotherhood) of their homeland which, theoretically, should have disappeared owing to their receiving social benefits from the state. However, such systems/traditions served to preserve solidarity in such migrant communities (Malik, 2007: 32). Ansari points to Islam becoming the main or sole identity for many British Muslims, especially when they experience perceived criticism or attack from the majority society (Ansari, 2004: 5). Renani also supports this position and suggests that resistance identity emanates from the insecurity experienced by Muslims when facing an alien culture – western culture in this instance. He cites the black 'Muslim' uprising under the banner of the Nation of Islam in the mid-1960s as an example of resistance identity, which emerged in response to the castigation of the black community *and* the profanities directed by society against everything considered sacred in religion (Renani, 2001: 240). Spalek further endorses this position and attributes the evolvement of such identities to the erosion of a societal sense of 'belonginess' caused by severe social and economic changes (Spalek, 2006). She illustrates the fact that subcultures may be established upon resistance identities generated by actors who are in devalued and disempowered positions. 'Trenches of resistance and survival' are therefore constructed and are established upon 'the basis of principles different from, or opposed to, those permeating the institutions of society' (Castells, 2004).

Jacobson cites young Pakistanis as examples in this instance, arguing that they experienced an array of contradictions between values instilled in them from a familial and community standpoint and those from a modern, secular society. This, in turn, propelled them to adopt a religious identity since Islam provided answers to such conflicting values and ambiguities. It also provided moral parameters within which to function among both family and society (Jacobson, 1998). Joly supports the latter observation but distinguishes between religious boundaries and ethnic ones, suggesting that society's boundaries were more porous and could not, therefore, provide the security and clarity that religion affords in an uncertain social environment (Joly, 1995). Spalek makes an apt observation at this point of the discussion concerning resistance identities: it is important to consider other, more recent catalysts to the development of such identities, i.e. reactions to 9/11 (and, more specifically for British Muslims, 7/7). The subsequent attacks on Hijab-/veil-wearing Muslim women, men and mosques only served to exacerbate existing sensitivities and increase the emergence of resistance identities among a small but significant part of the society (Muslim communities), as did the impact of anti-terror legislation (Spalek, 2006). Roald equates early Jewish communities which settled in Europe with those of Muslim community settlement in Europe (Scandinavia in particular), wherein she highlights the former's preservation of their identity by residing in 'segregated' areas and refusing to submerge themselves into the 'melting pot' of the wider, fast growing Christian society. She suggests that Muslim communities' refusal to adapt to the norms of majority society result in resistance identities being developed (Roald, 2004: 760).

Hopkins and Kahani-Hopkins observe that theories continue to develop in relation to foundations of solidarity, reflecting 'essentialist' assumptions about identity constructs. In countering this essentialism is, they claim:

a growing recognition that identities should never be analysed outside the conditions of their making and remaking. Indeed, awareness of the contingency of identity upon context has resulted in a recent interest in the historical and geographic variation in the meanings of Muslim identification.

(Hopkins and Kahani-Hopkins, 2004: 44)

The findings highlighted in their data are of particular significance to this discussion as indeed it points to 'the importance of recognising the constructed and contested nature of identity' (Hopkins and Kahani-Hopkins, 2004). This contested nature is discussed in more detail below in view of its relevance to British society as a whole and not exclusively the Muslim community. That said, it is however necessary to review existing literature pertaining to classifications of Muslims in the UK.

Typology of British Muslim Identity

Renani further divides the three modes of identity aforementioned into eight distinctive subcategories. He then juxtaposes them alongside Castells' analysis, highlighting each classification from a sociological standpoint (Renani, 2001: 136–138). Nielsen provides a typology consisting of six categories in his research of young Muslims in the UK and focuses on social factors adversely affecting them in particular (Nielsen, 1997). Additional typologies include those of Shepard, who provides a classification of five *ideological* orientations, and Ramadan whose focus is largely on *religious* categorisation (Shepard, 1987: 307–36). Each typology will now be highlighted and discussed below:

Renani's typology

1. *Nationalist Identity/Nationalism* – Renani refers to characteristics such as nationalistic patterns of behaviour, i.e. maintaining a particular dress code, subscribing to particular social etiquettes that are distinct from the majority society, and adhering to values inherited from forefathers. This type of substrata considers nationalist identity to be of paramount importance and thus accords with Resistance identities aforementioned (Renani, 2001: 139).

2. *Traditional Identity/Traditionalism* – 'This group constitutes a high proportion of the elder generation' whose lives are based on the cultural norms imported from their countries of origin. This group can also be classified under the Resistance Identity in view of their conservatism and, therefore, opposition to change. They are similar to the following category (Islamist identity) in that they place emphasis on religion; however, unlike the Islamist identities, they avoid politicisation of the religion. Renani acknowledges the complexity and multiplicity of factors which effectively render these classifications ambiguous. Nevertheless, he provides a definitive conclusion regarding their applicability stating that they should be considered as a platform for developing a more comprehensive typology of British Muslims (Renani, 2001).

3. *Islamist Identity/Islamism* – The religious fundamentals and socio-political aspects of identity are significant in this regard, under-pinning Islamic integrity. Religion permeates every aspect of this identity and separation between secular and religious practices is rejected. Political aspects of Islam permeate the individual and social spheres of life. Among the objectives of adherents to this identity is the desire to establish an Islamic state in which the Sharia (Islamic Law) governs all aspects of social life. This group accords to the Resistance Identity.

4. *Modernised Identity/Modernism* – This group includes individuals who attempt to adapt to prevailing/dominant cultural and social environ-ment/conditions. Modern interpretations of religious concepts are often sought to reconcile some of the disparities between faith and social dictates. Some of their characteristics include: i) aspirations to modernise the Muslim community and religious understanding, ii) concern about pluralisation of Islamic understanding as opposed to monopolisation of religious knowledge by Muslim scholars, and iii) concern with the legitimisation of social relationships within civil society. They fall into the categories of Legitimising and Projective identities.

5. *Secular Identity/Secularism* – Here, reference is made to the expansion of secularisation in Muslim countries, citing Attaturk who secularised Turkey in the 1920s (Niyazi, 1964). Groups possessing this identity attempt to rationalise and, therefore, divorce religion from politics and the economy. Religion is, thus, practised on an individual, pri-vate basis. Although Renani does not place this group into any of the three defined modes, it probably fits, like those in the fourth typology, among both Legitimising and Projective identities.

6. *Anglicised Muslim (Westernised Muslim)/Anglicism* – This entity includes those who have assimilated to British culture and have fully immersed themselves into the norms, celebrations and customs of society. Their original language and culture is lost, hence the inabil-ity to communicate with parents or first-generation family members in their original mother tongue. In short, British culture is more familiar to them than that of their parents. This often causes con-flict among such individuals leading them to what can be described as Undetermined Identities.

7. *Hybrid Identity* – Renani describes the main characteristic of this group as such that there is an absence of any distinct identity. Individuals in this category are primarily influenced by two major factors: religious and cultural roots alongside the newer more general

environment into which they have been placed. This category largely consists of new immigrant communities.

8. *Undetermined/Vagrant Identity* – Renani suggests this group consists of a young generation that is not inclined towards any particular identity, irrespective of whether it is cultural/traditional or modern. This group is not confused by its identity; its adherents are, however, disordered in the unpredictability of their behaviour so far as loyalties are concerned (Renani, 2001: 138–45).

Nielsen's typology

1. *The random retaliation option*: Socially marginalised Asian youth whose adherence to Islam is merely symbolic and their activities increasingly fall close to the margins of the law. In this instance, Nielsen posits the emergence of gang culture and activity among these youth as a response to racism.
2. *Collective isolation*: 'Quiet entrenchment within family and community concomitant with loyalty to community norms' (Nielsen, 1997: 135–287).
3. *Limited participation*: Academically successful individuals who are active within the wider economy; however, they maintain a separation between home and community.
4. *High profile separation*: Participants in organised Muslim activities campaigning for socio-political legislation and policies that facilitate their expression of cultural and religious values.
5. *High profile integration*: Muslim youth who develop new cultural norms while establishing methods of constructive participation among the wider society.
6. *Aggressive action*: Radical Islamic political action, first through propaganda, in an effort to provoke change towards a more Islamic ideal/environment (Nielsen, 1997).

Beckford, upon commenting on Nielsen's six social typologies, identifies the common thread among them; namely, the separation of traditional values, i.e. cultural influences and affiliations with countries of origin, from perceived religious essentials, e.g. Islamic identity and practice (Beckford et al., 2005: 58).

Shepard's typology

Shepard's first three ideological orientations (Secularism, Islamic Modernism and Radical Islamism) are, according to Renani, influenced largely by modernity in that they avoid absolute monolithic interpretations of Islam. Shepard's two remaining categories, Traditionalism and Neo-traditionalism, provide a contrast to the first three as they are orientated towards Islamic totalism. Totalists are defined as those who hold Islam to be an all encompassing faith, providing solutions for all aspects of life (Renani, 2001: 133–34 citing Shepard, 1978: 307–36). Shepard considers 'modernity' to encapsulate specific Muslim ideals where specific emphasis is upon material technology and the utilisation of such for social organisation and mobilisation. The impetus driving the latter two categories is, according to Smith:

> the fundamental malaise of modern Islam [being] the sense that something has gone wrong with Islamic history... [and] the fundamental problem of modern Muslims is how to rehabilitate that history.
>
> (Smith, 1957: 47)

Renani questions Shepard's categorisation of traditionalism being, in essence, Islamic totalism, and refers to the difference between this type of identity and the Islamists as that expounded upon in his own typology (Renani, 2001). He concludes that Shepard's typology cannot be aligned to existing characteristics of Muslim identity owing to the exclusive ideological orientation of his analysis. His argument is that such exclusivity fails to take account of the diversity and differentiation of Muslim communities in terms of ethnicity, intellectuality, culture and environment. Formulation, therefore, of a general typlogical schema is difficult without refining the specific requirements of particular subordinate or super-ordinate groups within society. Surprisingly, despite providing his own typology Renani concludes at this juncture, when discussing Shepard's orientation, that, 'Muslims cannot be forced into a single typology, which can be indiscriminately generalized throughout the Muslim world (Renani, 2001: 134).

Ramadan's typology

1. *Scholastic traditionalism*: Central to the distinguishing characteristics of this group is adherence and reference to religious scriptural texts, in particular the Qur'an and hadeeth (plural: ahadeeth).[11] Dependency is upon scholastic explanation and interpretation as codified between the eighth and eleventh centuries.
2. *Salafi traditionalism*: Adherents to this particular traditionalism ascribe themselves to the first three generations of the Muslim era

(salafus salih, i.e. the pious predecessors). This group can be distinguished from the first group by its literalist understanding of sacred texts.

3. *Salafi Reformism*: This group is very close to the traditionalists with the exception of their insistence upon ijtihad.[12]

4. *Political and literalist Salafiyya*: This group's orientation is towards a more radical interpretation of Islam and with a strong emphasis towards development of an Islamic state. What distinguishes them from other categories is their unequivocal opposition to any notion of collaboration with European/Western societies, holding such environments to be *Darul Harb* (realms of war).

5. *Liberal (or rationalist) Reformism*: Secularists occupy this category and the same example cited by Renani, e.g. Ataturk, is also mentioned by Ramadan.

6. *Sufism*: This particular group places a strong emphasis on spirituality and mysticism (Ramadan, 1999).

Renani asserts that Ramadan's typology is not completely workable for British born Muslims as it refers specifically to the more recent generation of Muslims prior to what he terms, 'the invention and institionalization of "instantaneous communication"', (Renani, 2001: 136). He reiterates a similar argument to the one posed against Shepard in that any classification based upon religious or ideological orientation restricts the scope of research and thus excludes categories such as secular, westernised or, indeed, hybrid classifications identified in his typology of British Muslims. It would have been interesting to ascertain Renani's opinion on Nielsen's typology, discussed earlier as this classification was developed shortly after the completion of his book. Nielsen also restricts his research to socio-economic factors affecting British youth and can, therefore, only provide findings from a significant but microscopic section of the wider Muslim populace.

Part of the ambit of this particular research is to examine ideological and religious constructs among British Muslim converts in view of the current academic and practitioner focus on these areas as significant psychological proponents of violent extremism.[13] Research will seek to determine the applicability of the typologies discussed in this chapter with British Convert Muslims and whether new, more relevant, typologies are required for this group.

Ethnic categorisation

Although ethnic categorisation is most apparent in stereotypes deployed by staff in prisons, among the wider society it is determined by those choosing their identity/identities (Beckford et al., 2005: 193). For example, Bagguley and Hussain make reference to an 'ambivalence' of ethnic identities in that people do not subscribe to singular or unitary identifications; they may consider themselves British as well as being Pakistani and/or Muslim (Bagguley and Hussain, 2005: 216). This process of dual or multiple identifications can be witnessed especially among second and third generation Muslims according to Bagguley and Hussain as they, in contrast to their parents' generation, challenged the previous racialised construct and connotation surrounding British identity; namely, that it belonged to the white colonial legacy. The ability to challenge such constructs evolves from the greater freedom afforded to second generation Muslims who, unlike their parents' generation, are unafraid of socialising into their own distinct cultural and religious values against the backdrop of a potentially hostile majority culture (Bagguley and Hussain, 2005: 217).

Revisiting the context of identification processes in prisons, Beckford also makes reference to 'multi-layered' group identification and highlights prisoners identifying themselves according to specific subcategories, some of which relate to ethnic divisions among their own cultures, e.g. ethnic Kashmiris and ethnic Mipuris, etc. Surprisingly, ethnic identification was given more *exclusive* priority, e.g. Pakistani, Bangladeshi, Kashmiri, etc., whereas religious identification was often *coupled* with ethnicity, e.g. 'First Muslim, Kashmiri, or Pakistani second' (Beckford et al., 2005: 194). Interestingly, Beckford makes the following observation regarding prisoners' self-identification among British Muslim prisoners:

> Contrary to some reports of changing patterns of self-identification among young Muslims in the UK we encountered very few Muslim prisoners who would freely choose to describe themselves as 'British Muslims', although many had been brought up in Britain.... If national identification was generally rejected...they often seemed keen to affirm their local identification and attachment to where they had grown up – sometimes in conjunction with their country of origin or region of origin.
>
> (Beckford, Joly and Khosrokhavar, 2005: 195; Modood, 2000).

Beckford concludes, so far as the self-identification process is concerned, that it, combined with the prominence officially given to ethnicity and religion in prisons, helped to create distinctive behavioural patterns of sociability and solidarity among many Muslim inmates. That said, the intersection between ethnicity and religion remains a complicating factor; not every Asian is Muslim.

The theories discussed above provide frameworks for developing identity constructs, especially in the absence of clear, definable characteristics that reinforce national ones reflecting multi-culturalistic dimensions. However, this research will examine the process of identification among British Muslim converts and whether findings correlate with those discussed in this literature review. The requirement for researching British Muslim converts in this context stems from their being an entity that has moved from a salient established majority to one facing the dynamics of self-identification, some of which have been discussed in this chapter. Of primary interest is whether a new process of identification occurs after conversion; how this takes place; and whether a 'multi-layered' process of identification is the conclusive stage for converts. This is important when considering data that highlights, for instance, 16% of Black prisoners as Muslims and that they identify themselves primarily in terms of ethnicity, because of the common perception that Asian Muslims (the majority Muslim community in prisons and beyond) are prejudiced against black converts to Islam (Beckford et al., 2005). On a microscopic scale, therefore, evidence suggests that converts, especially black converts, experience negativity so far as identity/identification is concerned among the Muslim majority, who in turn have experienced this on a national scale. This can be illustrated when referring again to the response to the Runnymede Trust Report. One of the reactions was, 'the compulsion to testify; the compulsion to "speak out" and to be seen to be a proud Briton' (Fortier, 2005: 568).

Fortier goes on to question how the individual relates to the national, collective mass identification of the self-declared Briton (Fortier, 2005). She cites the example of Kelly Holmes, a black British athlete and (at the time) bronze medallist, speaking to the media about her Britishness and how colour was irrelevant to British identity.[14] Post 9/11 and 7/7 subsequent research on Islamophobia highlight the inability to ignore identity so far as religion (Islam in particular) is concerned. Existing arbitrary methods of determining identity are further illustrated when considering the observations of other 'traditionally' British citizens:

I was taking less and less notice of their skin colour and more and more of the fact that what they were saying was full of British attitudes... praising their families and talking about hard work. What is important... is less their ethnic origin than the fact of being raised in Britain.[15]

Ostensive patronisation serves only to create more of a dichotomy within an already obscure and increasingly fragile multiculturalistic environment; however, it is easy to counter this by simply highlighting the fact that fundamental ethics, such as hard work and family cohesion, are not solely exclusive to British identity and are shared by almost all nationalities. Beckford et al. are likely to assert this as another, 'typical reflection of the British race relations paradigm which is intrinsically based on skin colour' (Beckford et al., 2005: 194)

Fortier continues to address skin colour when discussing the issue of identity/acceptability of the 'other' (non-white citizens); it would, nevertheless, be interesting to establish whether similar dynamics exist when colour and ethnicity are replaced with religion; in particular Islam. Fortier's research highlights the relative ease of society accepting the 'other' on the basis of superficial, physical variants, but seldom is reference made to religion or, to be more specific, ideology.

In stark contrast to societal acceptance on the grounds mentioned above, Ansari, when referring to the religion, highlights both Western Orientalists' *and* Islamists' emphasis on *distinguishing* Islam from western beliefs in order to present its adherents (Muslims) as the 'other', (Ansari, 2004: 8). He goes on to acknowledge that the problem existing in society is a perception (albeit, to a greater extent, valid) of the vast majority of Muslims being from outside Britain. As a result, they are considered more in terms of their cultural and ethnic backgrounds as opposed to being a religious minority, thereby compounding their status as 'others' or 'outsiders' (Ansari, 2004). That said, it is difficult to see how consideration as a religious minority would alter their status as the apparent fact remains; namely, much of the Muslim population now resident are first generation, having migrated to Britain over the past 30–40 years (Abbas, 2005: 8–11).

It is necessary to cite Fortier's conclusion which extends beyond the predominantly racial confines discussed in her work:

The disembodied (silent) subject is that which has the right to dwell in the first place, and whose attachment to the nation goes unquestioned: the white Briton. The embodied multicultural subject achieves unmarked status through the injunction to speak his and her allegiance. One must be seen and heard to declare her pride in Britishness in order to achieve unmarked status.

(Fortier, 2005: 574)

The unquestioning acceptability of the disembodied, white Briton's identity is unsurprising and has long been part of 'native/authentic' British psyche. Integral to British identity in the 1980s were values encapsulating sentiments, loyalties and cultural norms, 'established over centuries by the majority community, [and that] participating in the "British way of life" required "forgetting one's cultural roots"' (Ansari, 2004: 10). To contest this belief meant one (especially Muslims, to whom this particular address pertained), 'would remain external to an essential, "authentic", "unchangeable" Britishness of which they could never become an intrinsic part' (Asad, 1990: 455–80).

Earlier reference was made to aspects of this research on self-identification/identity among black British converts in view of perceptions of prejudice from the majority Asian Muslim community. Such research will also extend to white British converts for the same reasons but with the additional examination as to whether the above-mentioned *acceptability* also extends to the white British convert after s/he has converted to Islam.

Emotional register: A British Muslim identity construct? (Part 1)

Fortier introduces an interesting dimension to the issue of establishing national identity when considering emotional register during particular events highlighted by the media, relating to matters of national interest. Fortier focuses on how resorting to the emotional register of shame, for example, affects people in a particular way: 'By tracing how shame is evoked, rejected and projected on to particular subjects, I trace how identity is linked to the process of identity formation not only of "self" but also of "other" within the national collective' (Fortier, 2005: 561). Marranci holds a similar position in his study of Muslim identity in Scottish prisons: 'Some recent anthropological studies have argued that emotions are central to the way in which we perceive our surrounding environment. (Ingold, 1992: 39-56; Milton et al, 2005; Marranci, 2006: 5)

Following the events of 7/7, possibly three categories of emotional register were, arguably, witnessed among the British Muslim community in that:

1. it collectively joined with the rest of the nation in condemning the attacks, *and* sharing its sense of grief, guilt and shame at the fact that the perpetrators were British born and raised Muslims;[16]
2. some members of the community initially remained silent, fearing that such an expression or indeed, admission of guilt and shame could result in a national expression of anger, followed by a violent backlash against Muslims from the predominantly non-Muslim society. They could, in effect, be considered 'politically passive';
3. others, particularly the youth among the community, emphasised their solidarity with the 'global Muslim Ummah', and anger against the foreign policy of the UK and its allies (Rai, 2006: 96, 103–05).

The fears held by the second community group appear to hold some legitimacy when considering Gunaratman and Lewis's suggestion regarding another scenario at the other extreme of the spectrum; namely, Britain's historically racist past, and admission of this creating the potential for expressions of anger from its non-white citizens. In other words, what was considered as threatening to the white subject, in the event of admissions of guilt and shame, was the black subject's anger (cited in Fortier, 2005). It can be argued that category ii) – the 'silent' section of the Muslim community – effectively went into denial and refused to shoulder blame over these events. This is congruent with Fortier's observation, albeit to a limited extent, that, 'the refusal of shame is also about silencing their [the subject of racism's] anger' (Fortier, 2005: 566).

Within the context of this debate, the 'subject' would be the majority society that was subjected to terrorist attacks by people belonging to Muslim communities. It would be naïve to conclude that the above-mentioned factors were the sole reason for silence or lack of action from this section of the Muslim community. Indeed, it has been argued that, 'these individuals are the by-product of colonialism and modernity that work with a siege mentality shunning other Muslims who seek to blame Muslims for acts of carnage' (Malik, 2006: 16). It is also important to consider that such an apathetic approach may have emerged as a result of the perceived failure of the same society to sufficiently acknowledge and subsequently empathise with the suffering of an extensive and transnational religious community: the 'Global Ummah' which transcends national and racial boundaries so far as it relates to Palestine and Iraq (Ansari, 2004: 7). In failing to bridge the schism between sections of the Muslim and wider communities, society is faced with:

A sanitized 'happy' multiculturalism [that] requires the eradication of unwanted unhappy subjects, including those whose anger might be justified but which can be managed and re-directed away from the nation (the collective self) and on to individualized selves.

(Fortier, 2005: 567)

Fortier goes on to suggest, in support of a (r)evolving identity, that:

'multiculturalist citizenship' requires a process of ascription of differential identities and bodies to its citizens.... oscillating between conceptions founded on the embodied muliticultural – where people in their ordinariness are the referent – and the disembodied citizen or community – the utopian moment of abstraction.

(Fortier, 2005: 572)

She also issues a word of caution by highlighting the fact that it is the actual differences of individuals which effectively establish them as alien, even as 'enemy aliens', and that must to 'acquire' the status of legitimate citizenship, i.e. being called upon to be seen publicly testifying their allegiance with the conclusion that this does not necessarily guarantee their inclusion within the political signifier.

Research indicates such disparities may even be desired by individuals or communities as a result of alienation within society. Dr Philip Lewis (School of Peace Studies, University of Bradford) concludes, from his existing research into Muslim youth that a new 'assertive Muslim identity' has been developing among young British Muslims. It is distinct from 'self-consciously' Islamic groups and not necessarily rooted in any religious belief or understanding (Rai, 2006: 97). Such youth are considered 'politically active' in contrast to their elders or more traditionally-orientated peers. These youth would invariably fall into Renani's Resistance identity mode, discussed earlier.

Significant issues have been raised at this stage of the literature review, focusing research on areas of British Muslim identity and highlighting the fact that consideration of this centres largely on the South Asian community. This results in the overall marginalisation of British convert Muslims. It is, therefore, of fundamental importance that the scope of this particular research examines whether any possible conflict exists between converts' transformations to a religious minority identity and that of a national majority one. Research will seek to ascertain whether converts, by virtue of their Britishness prior to conversion, experience similar treatment to second/third generation British Muslims at the hands of the majority/host society. It also seeks to explore whether in fact such converts are even more disadvantaged as a result of their conversion due to adverse experiences from the majority society *and* the new minority Muslim communities among whom they may have attempted to integrate. Conclusive aspects of this research will examine whether a distinctive identity exists among British Muslim converts as a result of the above, and whether such identity encapsulates characteristics and identities of both majority society and the minority Muslim community, placing them in a unique position to act as conduits between the two.

Self-categorisation theory: [An]other British Muslim identity construct? (Part 2)

Theoretical perspectives, such as the self-categorisation theory (SCT) suggest that identity can be determined by the community itself (Hopkins and Kahani-Hopkins, 2004: 42). Marranci's area of research further supports this theory when discussing the idea of prisoners going through a process of 'self-definition and categorisation': 'Concepts such as ethnicity, nationality and religion become important elements to the prisoner, who uses them to form links and boundaries within the social context of prison' (Marranci, 2006b: 4). He further elucidates, providing another theoretical framework to the process of identity by highlighting it serves two functions:

1. the effect of enabling a person to make sense of his autobiographical self, and;
2. his being able to express the autobiographical self through symbols.

Examples of these symbols, one can assume, are displays of nationality, religion, etc. e.g. respectively, waving the flag of St George or wearing outwardly religious symbols such as the Hijab, to name but a few. Marranci concludes from his research on identity that a six-stage 'Tautological Circuit' surrounds the life of every individual, and that the equilibrium of these stages can be disrupted by changes in the environment.[17] This further supports Fortier's observations regarding emotional register and how this is affected by external factors. Beckford's research also focuses on identity formation in prisons in view of the societal respect for diversity as a value that guides both principles and practices surrounding the treatment of minorities. Preference is given in their research to processes of *identification* as opposed to identity due to it conveying: 'the active, contingent and situational character of the processes whereby prisoners work out and experience their similarities with, and affinities to, other people'.[18]

This approach also enabled the demarcation of various differences. Emphasis is placed on prisoners' self-definition within the context of two aspects of their categorisation by the prison authorities themselves: the locality of the prisons, and the nature of the systems in which they have been detained. This was alluded to above when highlighting respect for the diversity witnessed in prisons, both ethnically and religiously (Beckford et al., 2005: 186).

If prisons are considered a microcosm of wider society, phenotypical characteristics such as diet, language and religious practice appear to contradict this view as, indeed, they serve more as a basis for identification within prisons than outside. Beckford further endorses this assertion by referring to society's official and unofficial attention to race and religion in prisons and that this assumes greater salience with prisoners' self- and group-identification processes (Beckford et al., 2005). Their observations concerning the porosity of boundaries between ethnicities in prisons owing to the close proximity of their respective, confined coexistence also rings true for wider society and is evidence of the multiculturalism witnessed today. It (the porosity of boundaries) is not, therefore, specific to prisons. In a similar vein, research pointing to ethnic or religious solidarity/isolation within prisons being a cause for ghettoisation, echoes the sentiments of some among the wider society and, thus, also cannot be restricted to the prison environment. In fact, religious practices such as '*al-uzlah*' (isolation) are occasionally implemented by some Muslims in western societies. However, occasional misunderstandings of the contexts within which to implement such acts have led, in some instances, to the ghettoisation of communities. Misunderstandings and indeed misapplication of such practices are possible causal effects of behavioural extremism due to overzealousness on the part of adherents to such practices. In its most extreme manifestation these acts could be symptomatic of ideological extremism. It is the combination of ideological and behavioural extremism that gives rise for concern regarding the violent radicalisation of an individual and his subsequent propensity for terrorist action. Having said this, examination of other socio-religious and or psychological factors is required before determining the precise nature of extremist tendencies (or overzealousness as the case may be). Chapter 4 explores conversion theories insofar as they relate to British converts and examines the basis of ideological identity constructs as it relates to the religion.

4
British Muslims and Religious Conversion

This chapter will examine the composition of British Muslims in order to illustrate the extent to which data collection and dissemination have relied predominantly on South Asian Muslim communities/representations (Ansari, 2004: 2). This, the author asserts in later chapters, has led to disproportional representation of minority Muslim communities, of which converts are an integral part. The chapter aims to highlight pre- and post-conversion influences that affect British converts' religious and ideological delineations.

Composition of British Muslims today

The 2001 census introduced a question on religion to 'reflect the changing nature of society and the way people want to be classified'.[1]

From a policy-making perspective this question was supplementary to existing data on ethnicity. According to the census there are 1.6 million Muslims in Britain, although more recent estimates place this number closer to 2 million (Mahmood, 2005: 6). The census produced an unsurprising statistic; namely, that 68% of the Muslim population was of South Asian origin, the Pakistani community comprising 43% of the overall Muslim population – by far the largest and most dominant individual group. This number accords with figures proffered by Abbas who estimates there are one million South Asian Muslims in Britain, two-thirds of the overall Muslim population (Abbas, 2005: 20). Reference has already been made to the number of British Muslims in Britain. Unfortunately, the census fails in one area of increasing significance: to clarify the number of British Muslim converts. Statistics relating to religion by ethnic group in England and Wales highlight the fact that the number of white British Muslims constitutes 4.1% of the overall total of white Muslims (11.6%). The actual total number of white Muslims is proportionally higher than expected: 179 000 white Muslims, of which approximately a third are defined as white British, (Mahmood: 2005: 20–1). Black or Black British Muslims consist of only 0.2% being 'Black Caribbean', with the remaining 6.8% being 'Black African' (6.2%) and 'Other Black' (0.4%) (Peach, 2005: 20). These statistics do not provide figures for white and black British Muslim converts as a separate category. Peach refers to the lack of 'provenance' when reflecting on the statistics relating to Black African Muslims but, surprisingly, fails to comment on the report's inadequacy to distinguish converts from second or third generation Muslims in Britain (Peach, 2005). Authoritative research data highlighting the demography of prisons within the UK are available and there were initial grounds for optimism that these would provide an overview reflecting society's multi-culturalistic population.[2] Unfortunately, they also fail to provide sufficient statistics relating to British Muslim converts and are not, in any event, representative of the general population in Britain (Beckford et al., 2005: 34). Kose, while estimating the number of (native) English converts to be 3–5000 strong, acknowledges the limitations of such estimates to be due to the simple fact that it is not a requirement for converts to officially register their new faith, religious affiliation or identity (Kose, 1996: 19; Nielsen, 1992: 43). Other estimates provide figures of between 10 and 50 000 British converts while Birt suggests that, based on the 2001 census, figures are closer to 14 200 or 0.9% of the Muslim population in Britain (Nielsen, 2004: 44; Winter, 2000: 102; Zebiri, 2008: 44). In the absence of official national statistical data reflecting the required information, reliance must occasionally be placed on local statistical estimates which are often difficult to verify. For example, Iqra Independent School, a private Muslim School and part of the largely convert Muslim community in Brixton, South London, provided an ethnicity profile (see Chart 4.1) which highlighted the following statistics:

- 17.9% of pupils attending the school were of Arab origin
- 14.9% of African origin
- 16.4% of Asian origin
- 44.7% of Afro-Caribbean origin (however, parents were British converts to Islam), and
- 5.9% of 'Other' origins (Iqra Independent School Ethnicity Profile, 12 October 1998).

This profile arguably reflects the school's and presumably the community's ethnicity; however, it cannot be considered an effective gauge geographically for the wider British convert community, particularly in

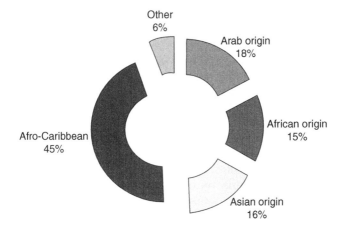

Chart 4.1 Iqra Independent School Ethnicity Profile (12 October 1998)

view of the demography of Brixton generally, and the ward in which Iqra Independent School and Brixton Mosque are situated, specifically.[3] Similarly, earlier research of Muslim converts, such as Kose's study, should be treated with an equal degree of caution owing to him limiting his research to those deemed native British by way of 'their physical features' (Kose, 1996: 3). Until sufficient research has been carried out into the demography of British Muslim converts, there will continue to be problems of defining their characteristics and determining whether their needs are similar or dissimilar to second/third generation British Muslim peers. Notably for some, this is an area of grave concern and requires immediate attention in light of the prevailing environment of violent extremism, notwithstanding the fact that attention is currently directed at the entire British Muslim community (Pipes, 2005). Nevertheless, there are promising indications that new research is beginning to address this issue and will hopefully redress the current imbalance of statistical data largely centred around the South Asian Muslim majority, to the detriment of British convert Muslims and their identity (Zebiri, 2008). For the moment, attention must be directed to existing work, irrespective of how dated it may appear, especially in the light of recent developments in Britain post 9/11 and 7/7.

The next part of the literature review will focus on discourses surrounding theoretical frameworks of conversion of British Muslims juxtaposed with research on Muslim converts from other parts of Europe (Scandinavia in particular due to the data available) in order to draw on any parallels that may be of significance to the construction of convert identities.

Conversion process

Consideration of theoretical and empirical frameworks around the conversion process is often necessary in order effectively to chart stages of development and determine the existence of any significant influences upon the convert prior to such a transition (Rambo, 1993: 5–20). Conversion is, according to Rambo's definition: 'a process of religious change that takes place in a dynamic force field of people, events, ideologies, institutions, expectations and orientations' (Rambo, 1993: 81). While acknowledging two broad perspectives of conversion, the Social Science and Religious/Spiritual Encounter perspectives, the former will be discussed and examined in more detail so as to illustrate the social and psychological dynamics that can possibly influence an individual's conversion. Having said this, acknowledgement must be afforded to the second perspective in view of its likely importance in the psyche of the new convert, as being *the* significant reason for conversion (Rambo, 1993: 10). Both conceptualisation and contextualisation of conversion is also necessary if an understanding of the environment within which conversions take place – especially in today's western society – is to be gained. This section will concentrate on *religious* conversion generally and (religious) conversion to Islam specifically. A discussion will then ensue regarding post-conversion phases and theoretical models particular to these phenomena.

Religious conversion is itself an extremely complex phenomenon and, according to Kose, comprises three experiences: i) an experience of increased devotion within the same religion, ii) an individual's move away from being irreligious to religious or iii) a change from one religion to another (Kose, 1996: 1). Although focus will be on points ii) and iii), in view of their relevance to the scope of this research, it is important to acknowledge that there are no single causes, processes or simple consequences of conversion; it is influenced by a matrix of sociological, physiological and environmental factors (Rambo, 1993: 5). In fact, Rambo prefers the term 'converting' as best encapsulating the phenomenology of the *process* of conversion as the latter term (conversion) linguistically denotes a *static* event. He goes on to propose the idea of a holistic model of conversion which includes, within its framework, cultural, social, personal and religious systems, thereby incorporating aspects of anthropology, psychology and religion. He, however, expresses preference for the former discipline (anthropology) in view of its holistic scientific approach that often tends to avoid the bias or, as circumstance may dictate, prejudices of the more parochial disciplines.

In support of this model, he refers to Lofland and Skonovd's notion of conversion 'motifs' which endeavour to combine the convert's subjective experience with the scholar's scientific perspective (Rambo, 1993: 7, 14). Kose also refers to Lofland and Skonovd's conversion patterns when analysing the responses of his interviewees (Kose, 1996: 95–110). These motifs are delineated into six categories:

- Intellectual conversion, whereby the individual seeks knowledge of religion and related issues via literature, various audio – visual and media sources
- Mystical conversion; this in effect occurring as a result of a sudden and sometimes traumatic encounter/insight or other paranormal experiences
- Experimental conversion, involving active exploration of religious options
- Affectional conversion placing emphasis on interpersonal relationships and bonds
- Revivalism; this category relies on crowd conformity to induce behaviour and has gradually diminished as an influential catalyst of conversion in the twentieth and twenty-first centuries
- Coercive conversion, such as brainwashing, thought reform, programming, etc. is considered a rare approach by Lofland and Skonovd (Lofland and Skonovd, 1981: 373–85).

Figure 4.1 shows the theoretical 'modes of response' of an individual to the conversion process.

In an effort to consolidate the multiplicity of approaches introduced to support his holistic model, Rambo proposes a further 'sequential stage model' (see Figure 4.2): 'that is multi-dimensional, historical and process orientated'. In proposing this he does, however, acknowledge that:

> No single process or stage model articulated thus far has been satisfactory to everyone, but the work of Lofland and Starkand the missiological model of Tippettprovide useful heuristic models.
> (Lofland and Stark, 1965, 30: 862–875; Tippett, 1977, 2: 203–221; Rambo, 1993: 17)

Rambo thus provides sequential and systematic stage models of the pre-conversion process which can be adjusted and contextualised according to whichever process is pertinent to the individual experiencing such change at any given time. He also places emphasis on the importance of

Active Questing: A person looking for new options because of dissatisfaction with the old ways and/or a desire for innovation and/or a search for fulfilment and growth.

Receptive: A person is 'ready' for new options for a variety of reasons.

Rejecting: Someone consciously rejects the new option.

Apathetic: Someone has no interest in a new religious option.

Passive: Someone is so weak and fragile that he or she is easily manipulated by external influences.

Figure 4.1   Modes of response to the pre-conversion process
Source: (Rambo, 1993: 59)

the religious/theological sphere of analysis regarding conversion in an effort to avoid his research becoming one-dimensional (Rambo: 1993). Roald observes that Rambo's proposed model has to be modified in order to fit the Islamic framework of conversion. She elucidates further upon this observation by stating that the differences between Christian and Muslim conversion processes (the former being the source of the majority of Rambo's research) originate from conversions taking place within the context of either majority or minority societies. In the case of Muslim conversions in the West, these occur within a majority context (i.e. the Muslim community is the minority community among the more predominant non-Muslim majority society). This important factor is, Roald concludes, rarely taken into consideration by authors thus possibly explaining the inapplicability of other general theories to the Islamic context (Roald, 2004: 79).

Stage 1	Stage 2	Stage 3	Stage 4	Stage 5	Stage 6	Stage 7
Context	Crisis	Quest	Encounter	Interaction	Commitment	Consequences

Figure 4.2   A sequential stage model pre-conversion
Source: (Rambo, 1993: 17)

Religious conversion to Islam

Kose opted to examine the childhood and adolescent experiences of individuals up until the point of conversion, comparing them with secondary data from his research (Kose, 1996: 31–46). The main objective of such research was to determine the underlying reasons for native Britons' conversions to Islam and the psychological and social foundations upon which they developed prior to conversion (Kose, 1996). Indeed, Kose's research endeavoured to establish the applicability of existing social science theories to native British Muslim converts. Here, reference can be made to Heirich's categorisation of these theories into three themes:

1. Conversion as an illusory (or fantasy) solution to stress, in which the latter dissipates due to an alliance with the supernatural or by way of redirecting one's frame of reference from the cause of stress. (Kose highlights that much of the psychological literature on religion support this perspective.) (Heirich, 1977, 83: 653–80).
2. Conversion as a result of 'previous conditioning' as opposed to catalysts as referred to above. This theme lays emphasis on social circumstances preceding conversion.
3. The third theme:

> emphasises interactions that make a different understanding of one's experience possible. It focuses upon conditions that lead one to take a particular frame of reference seriously ... [involving] analysis of patterns of interpersonal influence, whereby inputs from others become so mutually consistent and reinforcing that one begins to see things through the other's eyes.
>
> (Heirich, 1977, 83: 653–80)

Kose acknowledges that, although many social scientists focus attention on conversion being the result of a single 'causal explanation', others consider it to involve the three interaction processes referred to above, in addition to other progressive steps (Lofland and Stark, 1965, 30: 862–75). In addition to the theoretical frameworks discussed earlier in this section, Rambo also introduces a much broader typology of conversion by referring to cultural and social drivers that may actually precipitate conversion.[4] Roald instead chooses to extend her research to examine the societal role of Muslim converts among the wider non-Muslim majority and, while her main area of focus is upon the extent of Scandinavian Muslim converts' contribution to the process of Islamic change in their respective societies, she also observes the factors that influence the former's process of conversion to Islam (Roald, 2004: 13).

The concept of conversion in Islam

Conversion to Islam involves the individual making an informed decision to submit to the Will of God (Allah) and thereafter adhere, as much as possible, to the fundamental tenets of Islamic theology and practice.[5] These can be categorised as follows.

Five Pillars/Foundations of Faith

1. The *Shahada* (testimony to the belief that there is no deity deserving worship except Allah, and Prophet Muhammad is Allah's final slave[6] and messenger
2. The establishment/implementation of the five daily compulsory prayers
3. The payment of *Zakat* (a tax amounting to approximately 2.5% of one's savings/unused wealth, levied to the poor if one has such wealth and is not dependent upon it)
4. To fast in the Islamic holy month of Ramadan (from dawn until dusk)
5. To perform the Hajj (pilgrimage to Makkah, Saudi Arabia) once in one's lifetime if one is physically and financially able to do so. (Zarabozo, 1999: 179–81)

Six Articles of Faith

It is incumbent upon *all* Muslims to believe in the following:

1. The belief in one true God as Creator and Originator of the entire universe and what is contained therein, without association with other deities, nor maintaining pantheistic beliefs/doctrines
2. Belief in the angels as an aspect of Allah's creation whose main purpose is to serve Him and fulfil His commands
3. Belief in the previous Prophets and Messengers all sent with the message of worshipping Allah alone (Tawheed) irrespective of the climate or era of such message, and acknowledgement that Prophet Muhammad was the finality of prophethood and messengership
4. Belief in the divine books/scriptures that were revealed before Islam (acknowledging that these have been either lost and/or corrupted over the passage of time), and that the Qur'an is the final revelation, which contains the actual 'speech' of Allah and is immutable and incorruptible

5. Belief in Divine Decree or predestination
6. Belief in the Day of Judgement when all mankind and the rest of creation will be called to account for deeds performed in this life, prior to death, thereafter entering the abode of Paradise or Hell accordingly. (Zarabozo, 1999: 179–81)

Roald's conceptualisation focuses on the Islamic terminology surrounding conversion. She discusses the term *aslama*, the most common of Arab terminologies meaning 'submission, surrender or commitment to the Will of God' (Wehr, 1974: 425; Roald, 2004: 13). She contrasts this with the Latin word, *convertere* which means 'to revolve, turn around or head in a different direction' (Flinn, 1999: 51–72). Other less frequently used terminologies are referred to, denoting inner conviction and/or contentment; however, such meanings are seldom used among English speaking converts.

Before concluding this section, examination of another religious conceptualisation, namely, that of Freud's, is necessary in order to contrast the precise monotheistic nature of Islamic religious conversion with the somewhat polytheistic model proposed by him. Indeed, the latter model accords to Heirich's first categorisation of religious conversion – that of the illusory theme, resulting from a stressful or traumatic experience. Freud's assertion in this regard is that such illusion distorts the reality of the human condition (Freud, 1928). The polytheistic theorisation of Freud can be established from his understanding of conversion centring on the biological father. He suggests that God is 'endowed' with features that humans attribute to their own father during childhood, and any subsequent relationship with God is always modelled on that initial relationship. Thus, the requirement of adopting a belief system is psychoanalytical, stemming from childhood disappointments in parents (primarily the father) and resulting in the belief in an omnipotent God. This 'adoption' or, to be more precise, conversion enables the convert to ignore (or avoid) his/her own psychological and sociological failings. The monotheistic basis of conversions to Islam has been highlighted during discourse on the pillars and articles of the religion and thus, requires no further elucidation to demarcate the stark differences with Freud's conceptualisation.

The context of conversion

'Context is more than a first stage that is passed through; rather it is the total environment in which conversion transpires. Context continues its influence throughout the other conversion stages' (Rambo, 1993: 21). Unlike Gration's emphasis upon objective external context of conversion, Rambo expands this to incorporate the more subjective internal aspects also, as to ignore one 'is to truncate our understanding of conversion' (Rambo, 1993). The scope of this research, however, is to focus on the external context in order to determine whether prevalent climates, so far as Islam was concerned between the 1990s and up to 2007, influenced conversion to the religion and, if so, the extent of such influence. It therefore differs from the earlier research into British Muslim converts, conducted by Kose in the early 1990s, as his focus was primarily upon the more subjective, internal and emotive precursors to conversion (Kose, 1996: 31–67). Roald maintains the thread of her research regarding majority societies versus minority communities when addressing the limitation of previous research on Muslims in western countries. She observes that such research is restricted to examining Muslims in isolation, ignoring the nascent awareness of the role majority societies play in shaping and reshaping immigrant identities (Roald, 2004: 17). Part of this research intends to examine how far *convert* identities are already shaped or, as the case may be, reshaped within the context of a majority society already familiar to them. In similar vein, Roald suggests European Muslim converts can, by way of pre-existing traditions, establish a frame of reference through which to interpret Islamic sources. This would result in new Muslim converts acting as a revolutionary force or, effective conduits between majority societies and Muslim minority communities (Roald, 2004: 86). Due consideration of such interaction between the two entities mentioned is necessary in order to determine the effects of specific external factors that emanate from majority society and adversely affect the minority community. These factors are subsequently considered catalytic to some British Muslims' path towards violent extremism and terrorism. The case study of Richard Reid will endeavour to shed light as to whether external factors were the primary cause of his apparent susceptibility to extremist propaganda which culminated in his attempted terrorist act in December 2001. Rambo defines this particular phenomenon as being the 'macrocontext' within which an individual undergoes the process of conversion. It includes such elements as political systems, religious organisations, etc. It is possible that these elements either facilitate or obstruct conversion. He also refers to the 'microcontext' which accords to the more immediate, local environment of the convert and can, in some cases, 'neutralize the influence of the macrocontext' (Rambo, 1993: 22). He cites the isolating effect of religious groups as an effective way of 'cocooning' converts from wider society, thereby encouraging and increasing the intensity of religious focus and insularity. The existence of this phenomenon may, to a greater extent, be accurate; however, Rambo does not discuss the *cause* for neutralisation of the macrocontext. Reference, in this instance, can be made to the earlier section on identity, and the discourse on resistance identities, which appear to possess the necessary characteristics to effect such neutralisation.

Post-conversion

Roald correctly highlights the multiplicity of Islamic views and, indeed, variations in ideological beliefs and practices once an individual converts to the religion (Roald, 2004: 112). She also gives due consideration to a convert adhering to an extreme movement, asserting that this is coincidental to the early phase of the new Muslim's conversion process. Her reference to convert adherence to extreme movements can perhaps be tempered by observations that new converts may possess radical views, which in themselves are not extreme (Rambo, 1993). Social scientists refer to phases or stages of conversion, often placing emphasis on pre-conversion as opposed to post-conversion. This research aims to address post-conversion stages in an attempt to identify external, societal drivers that shape converts' ideological development.

Figure 1.2 in Chapter 1 describes interviewees' development post-conversion. This figure, adapted from Hudson's model reflecting the strategic life cycle of management boards, is perhaps an effective mechanism of examining the post-conversion process (Hudson, 1995: 45). An explanation of the 'Founding Phase' in this model (Figure 1.2) has preceded in the discussion on pre-conversion. The 'Youthful Phase' can be understood according to Roald's summation above; however, with reference to the convert adopting *radical* as opposed to *extreme* views. Interviews will seek to establish whether this particular phase is indeed formative: where the convert gathers knowledge about the new religion and begins socialising and meeting Muslims, possibly for the first time. The 'Adult Phase' possibly reflects the consolidation and implementation of the knowledge and experience gained during the previous phase. Finally, the 'Mature Phase' indicates a period of reflection since conversion, a possible modification of practice and perhaps, ideology. Research will examine whether correlations exist between the 'Youthful Phase' (Figure 1.2) and the 'Active Questing', 'Receptive' or 'Passive' modes of response to conversion (Figure 4.2) in relation to an individual's perceived susceptibility to violent extremist tendencies.

British Muslim converts

Ansari illustrates the fact that white British converts to Islam do not experience the conflict and issues surrounding identity as is witnessed among their Muslim contemporaries, (Ansari, 2004: 14–15). However, they have to employ essential dynamics in an attempt to effectuate equilibrium between both 'British' and 'Muslim' aspects of their identities. When examining these efforts historically, the pattern that emerges is not one of making Islam indigenous but, instead, reconfiguring Islamic ideas and making the religion more conducive to British religious norms without severe compromises to the former. For example, the first mosque established in Britain, the Woking Mission, built in 1889, was referred to as a Muslim church and those running it often highlighted the compatibility of Islam with Britain and western culture. William Henry Quilliam (Abdullah Quilliam Bey), who converted to Islam in 1887, conducted 'services' in his mosque (based in Liverpool), according to Christian dictates and procedures (Ansari, 2004: 82 and Gailani, 2000: 30).

The familiarity and established practices of British Muslims today has invariably led to the progression towards a more distinctive identity. Converts no longer have to mitigate religious practices in an effort to gain acceptance as their predecessors had done. In fact, Roald indicates the sphere of influence is such that converts' attitudes and ideas from majority society also enters and possibly affects minority communities, despite their having to adjust their 'indigenous cultural traits' in order to fit into the framework of the new religion (Roald, 2004). She makes reference to a 'transcultural identity' in which they 'move freely in majority society as well as in the various subcultural communities'. Interestingly, she also equates convert experiences to those of second-generation Muslims, both being 'defined by the overlap and interaction between Western and Muslim society' (2004: vi).

Zebiri also echoes this view based on second/third generation Muslims moving away from their parents' cultural understanding of Islam to a more progressive, universal understanding (Zebiri, 2004: 47). Interest is raised insofar as this research intends to explore similarities or perceived differences between converts and second/third generation Muslims, highlighting the notion that the latter's *cultural origins* continue to influence/shape the very essence of their 'Britishness', whereas the initial cultural influence of the convert is solely his/her Britishness. Some of Ansari's observations in this regard give credence to this notion owing to the inability of second/third generation British Muslims to 'jettison' their identity, 'because of being seen as such by others, because of their Muslim family background ... [and] because of their origins in a predominantly Muslim country' (Ansari, 2004: 17–18).

Additionally, their 'Britishness' is usually 'pragmatic' in terms of 'legal entitlement' and rarely extends to emotional or cultural bonds shared with the predominantly white, secular and Christian majority. Acknowledgement is, however, given to the fact that a weak affiliation with Britishness does not automatically mean strong cultural bonds with countries of origin. Gardner and Shakur's findings reflect the fact that Bangladeshis, while proud of their cultural heritage and Bangladeshi identity, consider the country (Bangladesh) itself to be a largely alien world (Gardner and Shakur, 1994). Exploration of the above-mentioned notion is expected to yield more data surrounding the main research questions; namely, whether the 'migration' of an individual from a majority identity construct to a minority one (Muslim in this instance) causes an initial 'chasm' making him/her vulnerable and, by extension, susceptible to violent extremism or, as result of this period of change, a more comprehensive understanding of his/her environment, and the dynamics surrounding both the society and new found religion, enables him/her to counter such extreme radicalisation and effectively act as a medium between the two communities.

Ideological affiliation and practice

Assertions of Sufism being the main ideological affiliation of Muslim converts continue to be made by authors such as Levtzion, Gerholm and Kose (Levtzion, 1979: 1–23; Gerholm, 1988, 263–77; Kose, 1996: 142). Kose cites 33% of his respondents' affiliation to Sufism to substantiate this assertion. Clearly, this represents one-third of his research group and, although significant, does not reflect the preponderance of Sufism among British converts. Zebiri acknowledges that although a disproportionate number are attracted to Sufism, the task of determining the extent of ideological affiliations for converts is complex. Seven of her target group (23%) clearly had an affiliation to Sufism (Zebiri, 2008: 46–8). However, this is far from conclusive evidence to support any assertion that this particular branch of Islam is the most popular among Muslim converts. Roald's findings tend to support the author's observation in this regard. In her discussion about extreme movements (of which Salafism was categorised as one of them), she discovered that Scandinavian converts' ideological affiliation was to such 'extreme' movements and not Sufism (Roald, 2004: 141). This correlates, to some degree, with Wiktorowicz's observations that, 'The Salafis constitute one of the fastest growing Islamic movements and enjoy a global reach in virtually all countries' (Wiktorowicz, 2006b).

Part of the scope of this particular research is to establish the validity of such observations and reasons behind Salafism's attraction among British Muslims. Academic references regarding ideological affiliations to Sufism (Birt, 2007) are more established than discourse of the same subject on Salafism, the latter of which has only gained increasing attention since 9/11. Irrespective of this, Zebiri observes that, to date, no research has been conducted to quantify ideological affiliations among converts (Zebiri, 2008: 46). Claims of converts' ideological trends being in preponderance in any particular branch or group in Islam are therefore, at this stage, premature and unsubstantiated from a social science perspective. This is not to ignore the fact that ideological *trends* exist; Roald dedicates an entire chapter to this subject where she discusses Swedish convert patterns that include ideological persuasions. She highlights the complexity of Islam in Sweden and the fact that, 'New Muslims are faced with a multiplicity of Islamic views... In search of "truth", they tend to look for the "pure sources" instead of settling for one of the many cultural expressions born Muslims term "Islam"' (Roald, 2004: 113–14). Zebiri also acknowledged that British converts reflected the diversity of religious and political trends in the UK (Zebiri, 2008: 46).

Roald's general typology of Scandinavian converts' ideological affiliations and practice is interesting and can perhaps form the platform on which to develop further research in quantifying converts' and/or indeed, second/third generation British Muslims' ideological persuasion compared with the earlier immigrant population (Roald, 2004: 113–61). Precipitating factors that have led to an increase in more violently radical or extreme ideological affiliations could be examined in a study of this nature and shed light on the process of politicisation of British Muslims. Wiktorowicz, in his study of Muslim extremism in the West, observes that, 'Thousands of young Britons are attracted to the panoply of radical Islamic movements with bases or branches in the United Kingdom, including Hizb ut-Tahrir, Supporters of the Sharia, and al-Qaeda' (2005: 5).

He also questions why individuals choose to engage in radical Islamic activism but fails to address the ideological affiliations that may act as precursors to such activism. The author suggests that this is necessary before addressing Wiktorowicz's questions which, in the event, become secondary. It is important to note that Roald's typology selects specific ideologies and movements that are not entirely representative of every

Muslim entity to which converts subscribe. It would prove too exhaustive for the remit of discourses focusing generally on European Muslim converts to discuss each ideological influence in view of the plethora of variations in Islamic understandings and practice. Nevertheless, discussion will now ensue regarding Roald's classification of convert trends with specific focus on ideological affiliations and paradigms. This particular typology is discussed here as opposed to the previous chapter (where typologies were generally discussed) because of one distinctive characteristic: its focus on Muslim converts' ideological influence/s and trends. Reference will only be made to ideological affiliations and trends relevant to the British context as some of those mentioned by Roald are not applicable or indeed seldom practised among British Muslims, not to mention converts.

Aptly, in the introduction of her chapter on this subject, Roald cites an established hadeeth (sayings, tacit approvals or actions of Prophet Muhammad) that contextualises the relevance and significance of ideological affiliation in Islam:

> The Prophet said; 'The Jews divided into 71 groups (sects), the Christians into 72 groups, and my Ummah (nation) will divide into 73 groups. Of these 73 groups, 72 will be destined for Hell and one will go to Paradise. This (group) is the Jama'aah,' (meaning the group that adheres to the Prophet's teachings, understanding and practice of the religion).
>
> (Roald, 2004: 113)

Cultural Muslims

Reference is made to individuals who, on conversion, adopt their partners' understanding and practice of Islam. This occurs particularly among female converts, although it is not uncommon for male converts to also adopt their wives' 'brand' of Islam (Hermansen, 1991: 188–201; Roald, 2004: 115). Often, it is easy to discern the type of Islam practised by converts falling into this category. For example, if a convert marries an individual of Pakistani origin, s/he usually adopts one of the more prevalent branches of faith practised in that region. In the case of UK-based Pakistani Muslims this is likely to be Deobandi or Barelwi (Zebiri, 2008: 19).

The 'rational' post-ikhwan trend

Reliance upon the intellect is one of the main features of this particular branch of Islam. Logical and rational approaches to Islamic beliefs and legislature provide the foundation on which to interpret and understand the religion. This said, many of the movements that have promoted this 'trend' have a clear 'Ikhwani' mandate and, according to Roald, orientation to Salafism (Roald, 2004: 120).[7] In order to define the above-mentioned ikhwan ideology, a historical summation of this movement's evolution is necessary. It originally evolved with the establishment of Al Ikhwan al Muslimoon (the Muslim Brotherhood) in Egypt during 1928. Its founder, Hasan Al Banna, established what is considered by some to be the prototype of today's contemporary Islamist movement (Kepel, 2005: 20). The 'Ikhwani' ideology is, according to Roald, 'a largely "rational" understanding of Islam, and a "return to the Koran and Sunna" in matters of jurisprudence, and politics is prominent' (Roald, 2004: 120).

This ideology and movement shall, in any event, be discussed in more detail later in the book where it will be compared with Salafism and takfeerism/violent extremism. In any event, Roald suggests that converts have adopted the rational post-ikhwan ideology as a result of their being exposed to literature propagating these beliefs. Additionally, she further suggests that converts are generally orientated towards this type of popular discourse, with Tariq Ramadan (coincidentally, the grandson of Hasan al-Banna) being considered a proponent of this ideology (Ramadan, 2004). It is unsurprising that converts would develop an affinity for this type of ideology/school of thought in view of their search, prior to Islam, for a fundamental truth and way of life that is easy to understand, logical and practicable. Roald cites one of her respondents who clearly illustrate this position, 'I am one of the "logical, rational Muslims", as logical and rational arguments were important reasons for my conversion to Islam' (Roald, 2004: 122).

Shia converts

According to Roald, it is difficult to differentiate between Shia and Sunni Muslim converts' 'rational' approach to the religion. She cites Shia literature, Imam Khomeini in particular, highlighting that it is 'saturated' with 'rational' ideas on the existence of God and Islamic politics. Her interviewees included six Shia converts whose reasons for embracing Shism included the apparent logic and rationale attached to it. One of the other recurring factors for choosing Shism was the issue of leadership. Historically, the Shia branch of Islam first emerged from a group in opposition to those who did not recognise Ali, the Prophet Muhammad's cousin, as his rightful successor. The predominant Sunni branch of the religion accepted the decision of the counsel that presided over deciding on the successor to the Prophet after his death. The determining factor in their decision was not lineage, which was in stark contrast with those who gave preference to Ali. This example is considered to be a political difference according to Roald's interview sample of Shia converts. Roald proceeds to acknowledge Shism as a distinctive branch of Islam in view of fundamental differences with the Sunni branch and she presents further examples to illustrate this, e.g. Shism's promotion of temporary marriages (Mu'ta) which was abrogated according to the Sunni branch. Other examples include the different interpretations of Quranic references to 'Ahl ul Bayt' (the family of Prophet Muhammad). This is one of the main lines of demarcation between Sunni and Shia branches. Roald is successful in highlighting areas of marked differences between Sunni and Shia branches, and the apparent reasoning behind converts' affiliation to Shism (Roald, 2004: 12634). However, she does not explore significant ideological variations of Shism which, in actuality, would be expected to act as contributory agents to converts' ideological affiliation. These variations are equally, if not more, significant than the examples cited above.[8]

Traditionalists

It is sufficient to quote Roald's summation of converts' ideological affiliation to this trend:

> Traditionalism, or adherence to one of the Islamic law schools (Hanbali, Maliki, Hanafi, Shafi'i) is often linked to Sufism. Many of the new Muslims who promote traditionalism also tend to regard themselves as Sufis.
>
> (Roald, 2004: 134)

Birt attempts to address the issue of traditionalism, suggesting that the question of its terminology, use and applicability to any one branch of Islam is itself, a perennial one. Contemporary reference to traditionalism can be, according to Birt, used in a:

> normative sense, [referring] to that approach which allows for authentic perpetuation and embodiment of the Islamic tradition and that contains a collective system of ongoing self-correction and refinement.
>
> (Birt, 2007: 2)

His observations accord to Roald's so far as historical reference and adherence to the Islamic law schools are concerned, however, he highlights an important consideration; namely, that:

> It has always been clear that no one group of trained scholars among the ulema (body of recognised scholars) can claim to embody [traditionalism] absolutely without the correctives of other trained scholars should that prove necessary.

(Birt, 2007:3)

References to traditionalism and Sufism being synonymous are relatively recent and, in the author's opinion, threatens to isolate significant sections of the Muslim community who also consider themselves in the same light historically, especially from the perspective of adherence to the four main schools of jurisprudence/Islamic law. In support of this opinion an additional question to Birt's about what constitutes traditionalism, can be posed in this instance: should not Salafism, by virtue of its subscription to the first three generations of Islam (which incorporates the four main schools of jurisprudence) also be considered traditionalist? In contrast to this suggestion is the exclusion of Salafis from the traditionalist debate. Birt recognises that, 'what is more often referred to in the West today as traditionalism is a particular and recent manifestation' (Birt, 2007: 3). He continues by stating, 'a set of scholars in the West attempted to defend traditional Islam against the polemics of the political Islamic movements and the Salafis' (Birt, 2007:2).

Salafism is, therefore, considered by such scholars, outside the parameters of traditionalism and, in fact, the antithesis of it. Their purported defence of traditionalism assumed significance in that an alliance was formed with proponents in the 'war on terror' in attacking Salafis and Islamists. In view of contemporary traditionalists' perspectives in this regard, it would be correct to postulate their position as affirmation of Roald's observations that Salafis and Islamists are extremist entities. Discourse on the final two typologies will now highlight her findings. Her assertion that Hizbut Tahrir and the Salafi trend are extreme is based upon her observation that, 'Their ideologies differ substantially... from those of mainstream Muslims. They are all exclusionist movements' (Roald, 2004: 41).

Roald's arguments in support of this assertion will be examined shortly. However, it is interesting to note there is no mention of or consideration given to other groups considered to be extreme by mainstream Muslims, such as a branch of Sufism; namely the

Naqshabandiyyah order of Shaykh Nazim and the Murabitun and its founder, Abdal Qadir al Murabit, which are fairly established in some parts of Europe. Academic discourse on Islamic movements or groups seldom makes reference to some branches of Sufism being from an extremist realm (Haadee, 1995: 19–22). This is probably due to the preponderance of academic authors' focus around radicalisation and violent extremism post-9/11 and 7/7. Additionally, Muslim academics and authors involved in discourse relating to this subject are, by and large, sympathetic to the often non-contentious, introspective approach of Sufism. In fact, Kose provides an entire chapter on conversion to Sufism and extensive insight into one of the Naqshabandi and Murabitun orders respectively without so much as an indication that these movements are considered extreme (Kose, 1996: 142–88).

Hizbut Tahrir

Roald provides a historical account of the group's establishment in 1948 in Jerusalem. The impetus behind its foundation was its leader's belief that all existing contemporary Islamic and nationalist movements had failed to achieve their collective objectives to raise the intellectual, political and social awareness of Muslim societies following the demise and dismantling of the Turkish Caliphate.[9] The re-establishment of the Caliphate became the ideological mandate for the group (Husain, 2004: 142). Roald identified the group's three stage ideological objectives: i) members receive their ideological education, ii) propagatory activities to disseminate the group's ideology and objectives, and iii) the re-establishment of the Islamic Caliphate. The success of the group in attracting Muslim converts is due to its founder's 'primacy' to revelation as opposed to the 'rational' trend in Islam and the group's adaptability to different social environments and political contexts. The 'rational' trend approach is considered to subordinate revelation in preference to reason/intellect whereas Hizbut Tahrir's methodology is to equate the two in the dissemination of knowledge (Roald, 2004: 145). The eclectic approach of combining both revelatory sources and intellect is appealing to converts as it protects against modern interpretations of Islam being corrupted by modern ideologies such as capitalism and socialism. Roald subsequently refers to the group's diversification so far as its understanding and application of the 'rational' approach 'It might be said that al-Nabahani (the founder) has a tendency to follow the historical example of the strict Zahiri school of thought which was perceived as 'rational"', (Roald, 2004 citing Taji-Farouki, 1996: 57–63).

It is important to note that the Zahiri school of thought was actually renowned for its literal dissemination of Islamic legislature and sources and was not, therefore, rational in any of its approaches. Surprisingly, Roald goes on to acknowledge the literalism of the Zahiri approach in her subsequent footnote (Roald, 2004: 7). She then draws a comparison between Hizbut Tahrir's ideology and the Salafis in their beliefs that Prophet Muhammad's example should be adhered to *in toto*. While this observation may be correct, it can be misconstrued because of the context under which Roald is discussing Hizbut Tahrir and Salafis, namely, as extremist movements. The reality is that Muslim communities also subscribe to this belief as it constitutes a fundamental tenet of Islam. In addition to this, such parallels pose the risk of aligning two movements that are in fact diametrically opposed ideologically in the same way that the Ikhwan, Takfeeri and Salafi ideologies have been misassociated. It is not within the ambit of this study to elaborate on Hizbut Tahrir as a movement; however, suffice it to say there are many to support Roald's observations of their extremist tendencies and practice. Having said this, it is important to define terminology around extremism and the author suggests that this be addressed within the parameters of violent radicalisation and extremism, to which the group has been associated (Wiktorowicz, 2005).

The Salafi trend

An immediate comparison is made to Wahhabism, the latter of which purportedly originated in the eighteenth century in what is now known as Saudi Arabia. Roald asserts that Salafi 'ideas' emanate from this movement. She also makes a distinction between the reformist Salafiyyah movement of Jamal al-Din al-Afghani and Muhammad Abduh in the nineteenth century. Roald points to the Salafi ideological reference to, and understanding of, the first three generations ('As-Salaf us-Saalih: the Righteous Predecessors'). However, she observes:

> They reject the Law-school system (four main schools of jurisprudence) entirely, and, on every single fiqh (jurisprudential) question, they look for the strongest evidence (dalil) in Koranic verses and the Sunna, thus searching for 'one single judgement.'
>
> (Roald, 2004: 151–2)

Therefore, according to Roald's research on Salafis in Jordan and Europe, they display intolerance for multiple views in jurisprudential matters. Roald acknowledges that despite apparent ideological and jurisprudential rigidity, Salafism is increasingly impacting upon converts. She has witnessed strong footholds in European countries like France, Britain and Holland, not to mention the Scandinavian countries. The success of this trend is attributed to the influx of financial support and resources from countries like Saudi Arabia who are supposedly renowned for their purported support of Salafi/Wahhabi institutions, (Husain, 2007: 236–7). Ideologically, Salafism is considered non-integrationist; however, recognition is given to the fact that some Salafis are, according to Roald's summation, becoming more moderate in their approach towards Western society (Roald, 2004: 152). The author proffers the view that Salafis are now actually *engaging* with governments and statutory agencies in an attempt to address the issue of home-grown violent extremism. As for the reasons why an increasing number of converts' preference is to affiliate ideologically with Salafism, Roald suggests that their socio-economic backgrounds are contributory factors. Zebiri, citing Kose, also highlights socio-economic circumstances as being influential to converts, but refers more generally to black converts as opposed to Salafi converts (Zebiri, 2008: 76). It is interesting to note Roald's perspective on the factionalism that occurred among the Salafi movement following the first Gulf war in the early 1990s. She identified four areas of division between Salafis; two of them supported the Saudi Arabian religious and political system. However, one 'trend' supported scholars linked to the government irrespective of whether the latter supported or criticised the state. The other 'trend' was linked to Shaykh Rabi'a al-Madkhali who advocated unequivocal support for the government. The third 'trend' supported scholars who openly criticised the government and were subsequently imprisoned as a result. The third trend, according to Roald's observations, possessed a 'jihadic' approach that completely opposed the Saudi Arabian system. Osama Bin Laden's ideological affiliation was to this 'trend' (Roald, 2004: 153–4). Roald then proceeds to provide the prevailing post-9/11 narrative about the Salafi-Jihadi ideology and its doctrine to regard all other Muslims as disbelievers who do not practise Islam. In this regard, reference is also made to Abu Hamza al Misri as being of the Salafi–Jihadi trend. In support of this assertion, Roald quotes Abu Hamza's reference to other Muslims as being disbelievers:

Jihad in Checnia and in Saudi Arabia is the same. Islam does not see the difference between a blue-eyed kafir and a brown-eyed kafir. Islam is the same. The first kuffar the Prophet fought against were his own uncle and his own people. Now we defend Islam itself against our

own tyrants. We even place our families among the unbelievers to
protect them against our own kind.

(Roald, 2004)

The following chapters will address Salafism and Takfeerism in more
detail in order to highlight the stark differences between the type of
rhetoric above, which is more akin to the Takfeeri ideology than that of
Salafism.

At this juncture it is appropriate to address Roald's conclusive perspective on Salafi converts in Scandinavian society. She states that adherence
to extreme movements often coincides with the early phase of a convert's conversion process and that their beliefs tend to modify at a later
stage of their development, to the extent that they either adopt Sufistic
or 'rational' ideological affiliations. She proffers the view that Salafi converts are often segregated from the wider convert community as they
hold it to be ideologically ignorant or 'astray' (Roald, 2004: 159–61).

Conclusions

In view of what has preceded, the author suggests that typological analyses in ethnographical studies of Muslim communities and groups are
often undermined by a subjectivity that can prejudice data extrapolated,
which in itself threatens the validity of subsequent findings. The extent
of this problem is heightened when considering the outsider perspective
and secondary data relied upon to extrapolate such findings. Because
of this, it is recommended that insider perspectives and related data
be obtained in an attempt to validate secondary findings. Invariably
this would, it is suggested, avoid the use of new and often inaccurate
terminologies and typologies that not only serve to obscure the phenomenon under examination but also fails to contextualise it. While
saying this, it remains necessary to examine the typologies discussed
in this and the preceding chapter in order to ascertain their relevance
and/or applicability to this study.

5
Methodology

This chapter discusses the research methodologies employed and the applicability of the data extrapolated. It discusses why qualitative methods were selected as the more viable approach, as opposed to quantitative, for the scope of research required in this study, although the latter method is utilised to a limited extent concerning data relating to background, ethnicity, social status, etc. Among the objectives of this research are to determine the validity of the typologies regarding British Muslim identity, drawn from the literature review, and whether they encapsulate subsequent findings that affect the formation of Muslim convert identities in relation to their ideological affinities and practice. Reference will be made to the theoretical frameworks referred to in Chapter 1 (Introduction) in an attempt to address the primary research questions and examine their respective contexts and validity in light of research findings. This data is expected to provide unique insight into the Salafi (Salafist) convert community in the UK, especially Brixton, South London around which this research is centred. Such findings will determine how far the identity construct of converts is influenced by the surrounding socio-economic and socio-political climates. Ideological influences are also examined to establish whether they form the basis upon which converts develop their perceptions of the wider society and, as a result, their subsequent behavioural patterns. Similarly, it aims to clarify whether their abilities to actively participate and contribute as members or conduits of the wider, majority society are adversely affected in the process of their ideological development.

The background and upbringing of many of the converts interviewed in this research are that of working class, second/third generation African–Caribbean males who are a part of, or have been exposed to, the prevalent gun, gang and knife culture in and around London, especially the south. Part of the remit of this research is to establish whether a correlation exists between the level of criminality mentioned and violent extremism in view of the focus of extremist propaganda in this area and the author's first-hand experience of tackling this phenomenon since the early 1990s. This particular area of research is essential in that it is expected to shed light on an area of Islamic ideology hitherto under-examined from an insider perspective so far as western academia is concerned; namely, the Muslim's ideological transition into a mindset of his host society becoming '*Darul Harb*' – an Abode of War. This concept/classification is in fact the main driver behind extremists' legitimising terrorist attacks on western soil, citing non-Muslim governments' positions against Muslims and the Muslim world as evidence that war is being waged on all fronts. The research aims to examine this and whether, under such classification, justification can be provided for the criminality, highlighted above, across a spectrum that can lead to terrorist attacks on a predominantly non-Muslim host society; Britain in this instance.

Practitioner/researcher

The book provides an insider account of a convert community that has experienced violent extremist propaganda and its protagonists first hand, to the extent that a few members were influenced and subsequently attempted to commit terrorist offences on a scale and magnitude previously unheard of in the western world. The author's position as a member of the community since 1990 and his position as chairman of Brixton Mosque between 1994 and 2009 places him in a unique position to provide a historical narrative of developments and factors that helped to distinguish the mosque as one of the few in the UK that has been successfully combating violent extremism for almost twenty years.

This book also relates to Lambert's parallel research: 'The London Partnerships: an Insider's Analysis of Legitimacy and Effectiveness' (Lambert, 2009). Both studies are worth cross-referencing by future authors in the field as later studies may be informed by correlations between the research which may illustrate and possibly validate the different perspectives and experiences of both practitioners. Therefore, both studies examine similar phenomena from different vantage points:

- Lambert's research examines police relationships with community leaders and the skills the latter possess in combating violent extremist propaganda at a grassroots level.

- As mentioned above, this study investigates a particular insider perspective of British Muslim converts' encounter at grassroots level with extremist propaganda and the resultant effects, if any, upon them.

In any event, future studies should take both studies into account. Robson provides an accurate description of the author's role in this instance, 'The practitioner-researcher is someone who holds down a job in some particular area and at the same time carries out systematic enquiry which is of relevance to the job (Robson, 1993: 446).

Having presided as Chairman of Brixton Mosque and Islamic Cultural Centre for 15 years, the author considers himself ideally placed to embark on research into the Salafist convert community in Brixton, South London. The specific target group is increasingly considered to be of key importance and interest to fellow practitioners and authors (i.e. police authorities, political/religious activists and academics) due to potential socio-religious/economic factors that may contribute to the violent extremist mosaic. This area of interest became even more of a focal point during the author's tenure as chairman owing to events culminating in, and arising from, the 9/11 and 7/7 attacks respectively. An academic approach of examining drivers behind violent extremism in the UK, particularly from a grassroots perspective, is now required in order to provide veracity to existing practitioner-based insights which, up until quite recently, have been marginalised. Existing and developing research lacks the essential insight required at grassroots to obtain data considered essential to examining this phenomenon. Up until recently, academic research and statutory practitioner theoretical approaches concentrated largely on top-down methods of tackling violent extremism. In contrast to this approach, therefore, the practitioner-researcher role from an insider, bottom-up perspective is invaluable within the context of the grassroots connectivity essential for the type of data required. Connectivity involves various levels of engagement with a selected group deemed 'hard to reach' by statutory bodies and is an essential component to the practitioner-author relationship with his/her group. For example, a particular local government's Youth Offending Service (YOS) has entered a contractual agreement with a grassroots organisation that engages with Muslim youth who have completed prison sentences, recognising the need for them to engage with peers they can relate to or 'connect' with and trust.[1] Strong affinities and trust are established between these youth (in this instance, young Muslim converts) and those considered to have an established credibility and respect among the Muslim and wider non-Muslim communities. The ability to relate to this type of audience, due to similar socio-economic and religious backgrounds, is another essential feature of the practitioner-researcher role. As a British Black Muslim convert, the author's experiences before and indeed after conversion provide a foundation of familiarity upon which the selected audience can engage and participate freely with the research conducted. In view of the author's ethnicity and social background, i.e. of African–Caribbean origin from a predominantly working-class family, he also shares common social and economic variables with many of the Muslim convert community in Brixton. Resonance can be found between the author and the group owing to similar pre-conversion experiences and factors that led to the resultant gravitation of many converts towards Brixton Mosque. This included factors such as institutional racism (wrongful arrest and incarceration in some cases), poor educational opportunities and lack of job opportunities and/or training. It must be noted that these existing factors also resonated with immigrant communities such as North African/African Muslims, i.e., Algerians, Moroccans and Somalis who also gravitated towards the mosque (not to mention a small but significant percentage of white converts from working-class backgrounds). Arguably, some of these pre-conversion variables resulted in a natural distrust of statutory agencies and contributed to shaping the psyche of Muslim converts. An understanding of, as well as the experiencing of, the same or similar factors that contribute to the convert's 'psychological mosaic' are an essential component of grassroot connectivity. In simple terminology, s/he must have street credibility and respect as an individual capable of representing and, where necessary, defending the target group in front of various entities whether it is the police, grassroot rivals, etc. at different levels and types of engagement. This occasionally involves high risk and sensitive forms of engagement. To shirk such responsibilities or to display apparent fear and weakness during such engagements is to risk the loss of credibility, respect and, in some extreme instances, life. In view of this, connectivity at this level must be from one familiar and comfortable with the territory, so to speak. To reiterate, academics and statutory bodies are not, therefore, able to extrapolate the necessary data from this particular field. This said, one of the most significant areas of possible demarcation between the author and the chosen target audience is generational. It is, therefore, acknowledged that some of the socio-economic and religious factors which may have previously affected or influenced the author may be different from those facing the target group today. Additionally, it must be acknowledged that the degree of access to this group could inadvertently result in a bias towards particular data because of the author's oversight and/or lack of insight in areas where possible assumptions are made. The model of research to be embarked upon accords more with the 'real world' or field style of investigation which identifies the phenomenon or area of concern, (i.e. the threat of increasing home-based terrorism among British Muslims) before providing analyses of the context in which it actually occurs. This contrasts with the more traditional model of research which requires the selection of an area of investigation, a subsequent literature review, followed by the formulation of hypotheses. Only the initial stages of both methods have been referred to, for the sake of brevity;[2] however, it is important to distinguish between the two styles, considering the current socio-political climate within which the research was conducted. This study considers UK home-based terrorism an unfortunate new reality and, based upon this premise, research is focusing on the actual context within which it has been and is being nurtured.

Research methodologies

Tesch provides a complex but useful typology of qualitative analyses in which she distinguishes 26 approaches to qualitative research (1990: 371–89; Robson, 1993: 371–2). Four basic categories emerge from this typology constituting, 'a progression from more to less structured and formal, the final grouping "reflection" being one whose proponents is particularly resistant to any systemization of their analytical process' (Robson, 1993). The author's involvement and position among the intended research group provides a unique opportunity to examine: 'a particular phenomena within its real life context' thereby enabling data extrapolation via participant observatory methods, case studies, interviews and primary documentary analyses (Robson, 1993). Undoubtedly, the 'phenomena' in this instance are the socio-religious drivers that affect the research group. This mixed method research approach is supported by Bevir and Rhodes and considered an effective mechanism for cross-referencing and the triangulation of data for purposes of validation or invalidation (Bevir and Rhodes, 2002: 131–52). Each research method used will be discussed, highlighting its intrinsic advantages and disadvantages. In any event, the triangulation of such data will also take place. Triangulation of data is considered an effective means of testing one source against the other as correlation between sources provides cross-validation and validation of the methods as a whole.

It is one method of exploring the discrepancies between actors' and observers' accounts (Adelman, 1981). If discrepancies appear among gathered data sources, the research conducted may actually explain the phenomenon of interest, indicating the need for further, more extensive studies. Robson asserts that in many cases the by-products of triangulation are as useful as its primary purpose in validating information, 'It improves the quality of data and in consequence the accuracy of findings' (Adelman, 1981).

Quantitative research

The research environment was not, on the whole, conducive for this particular approach and would have been counterproductive with the research group for the following reasons:

- A significant number of the interviewees had either a background of crime and/or negative encounters with police authorities before conversion and were, therefore, suspicious and reluctant to participate in much of the conventional methods required by this type of research.[3]
- Quantitative data does not provide the required illustrative or narrative detail required for the scope of research conducted in this particular study and does not equate to the quality of 'undeniability' which provides verisimilitude to reports, (Smith, 1975: 135, 208, 370).

Quantitative research was utilised to capture a specific area of data related to background, ethnicity, age of conversion, etc. This enables a general profile of converts to be recorded and accordingly mapped against Hudson's adapted theoretical framework of conversion (see Chapter 1, Figure 1.2).

Qualitative research

This method enables the 'individualistic' approach to collecting data by way of direct contact with interviewees (Renani, 2001). Such interaction on a personal scale provides the author with realistic accounts, providing rich data, contrasting the 'thin abstractions of numbers' provided by quantitative research (Robson, 1993: 370–1). Indeed, qualitative data is often used to supplement and illustrate quantitative data obtained, allowing the latter type to 'live' and communicate to the reader through quotations or narratives. Renani's choice for using qualitative research in part accords, to an extent, with this particular study in that, 'The more deep-rooted aspects of Muslim Identity and their interaction with (the conversion process) call out for deeper analysis' (Renani, 2001: 146). This is achievable through face to face interviews.

Participant observation/practitioner–researcher

The author's position as chairman of Brixton Mosque between 1994 and 2009, during which period the majority of research was conducted, provides the unique opportunity for participatory observation as one approach to researching the phenomenon of interest. In fact, one of the key advantages of this particular approach is the author's pre-existing knowledge and experience of the environment within which its inhabitants operate (Robson, 1993: 447). The position itself enabled a duality of roles in that his position and relationship with community members alleviated the process of familiarisation and acclimatisation. Infiltration of the target group, concealment from them as to the purpose/s of participation, etc. are therefore unnecessary as measures of extracting required data (Festinger et al., 1956: 196). Kirby and McKenna's position against adopting covert or manipulative perspectives similar to those mentioned appears to be the existing trend regarding participant observation, 'It is essential that as a participant who is also a data gatherer, the author recognise(s) the obligation to inform those in the setting about the research (i.e. what sort of research it is, for what purposes, and who is involved)' (Kirby and McKenna, 1989: 22, 196).

Lambert, cites Hamm's assertion that rich life experience is beneficial to the extent that it often enables the author to provide an illustrative historical insight to the area of research being conducted (Lambert, 2009; Hamm, 2001). This in turn enables the possibility of ascertaining how sequences of events, behavioural developments or influences, etc. contribute to existing effects on environment and context among which the target group is observed. While acknowledgement must be given to possible conflict between roles as observer and participant, the author has previous experience of such duality and how to minimise its effects (Baker, 1998: 22–4). During research into the possible effects of state funding for Muslim schools in the UK, the author was also chairman of one of the schools' board subject to his final dissertation and case studies. The duality of roles involved the development and strategic direction of the school alongside acting in the position of an observer to that process. In fact, the position of participant and observer provides opportunities for the *active* collection of data. Robson cites examples such as schools and hospitals as effective platforms for employing the participant observatory style without adversely affecting the phenomena of interest. Students and patients usually perceive authors in such settings to be part of the respective institutions and do not therefore consider subsequent enquiries as intrusive (Robson, 1993: 197). The practitioner–researcher perspective, coupled with insider knowledge and experience, also provides the author with the opportunity to highlight the extent of his specialised expertise about an environment that has yet to be penetrated by external academics and practitioners alike (Sommer and Wicker, 1991: 131–49). Acknowledgement is also given to the possibility that the author can affect the area of investigation by his presence, thereby altering the outcome of the research (Whyte, 1981: 147, 197). This said, the existence of positive counter effects should not be completely disregarded as the author's participation or observation may actually precipitate the target audience becoming more analytical and reflective about aspects of their own environment and circumstances (Robson, 1993: 197).

Due consideration is given to the unstructured and unsystematic approach of a participant observatory method. As a largely narrative and, thus descriptive, technique it lends itself to criticism from a quantitative research perspective. The author's long-standing position as chairman, coupled with the established relationship with the target group may impact negatively upon the objectivity of the findings in this regard. In other words, there is a risk of perceptual selectivity; namely, the author concentrating on particular aspects/characteristics of the target group to the detriment of others. An example of this risk can be seen in the author's knowledge of the current climate around the gun, gang and knife culture of the target audience and societal concerns surrounding this phenomenon. One of the initiatives that has emanated from societal requirements to address violent radicalisation and extremism among young Muslims (STREET) has identified a possible correlation between gang, gun and knife crime and violent extremism.[4] Knowledge of this developing area of research poses the risk of the author steering the target audience, during interview, towards this particular tangent, thereby affecting the nature and brevity of the data originally intended. This accords with Robson's observation of 'insider' problems faced by practitioner authors who 'may have preconceptions about issues, solutions [etc.]' (1993: 447). The author is, therefore, aware of the challenges of differentiating between research led and voluntary practice led procedures in order to avoid the 'we knew that already' type of data (Robson, 1993: 448). In other words, the 'research process must demonstrably offer something over and above [the] pre-existing level of understanding' (Winter, 1987: 34).

In order to counter these potential risks reliance will be given to triangulating the applied research methods. The array of concepts, theoretical frameworks, etc., expounded upon in Chapter 1, serve to avoid such risks by way of the reflexive approach employed while disseminating data. Lambert highlights the fact that few precedents exist ethnographically for the level of dual involvement required in this instance as practitioner–author (Lambert, 2009). Acknowledgement is given to the fact that further analysis is therefore required from both quantitative and qualitative research perspectives.

Case study

This method intertwines the other approaches of research applied in this book. It acts as, 'an umbrella term for a family of research methods having in common the decision to focus on inquiry around an instance.

The advantage of this approach, according to Akbar, is that it allows the author to concentrate on a specific instance or circumstance and attempt to identify the various interactive processes at work. These processes, he suggests, may otherwise be ignored or hidden in much larger scale research (Akbar, 2003). Four individual case studies are the focus of this research. Each case study adopts a chronological, historic and descriptive approach in order to examine the formative stages of socio-religious or socio-political drivers that contributed to their present ideological convictions and, therefore, present circumstances. Yin, when referring to chronologically structured case study designs, highlights the additional explanatory and exploratory components which serve to further illustrate causal sequences that may have occurred linearly over a specific period (Yin, 2009: 176–7). The chosen case study design also accords to the theoretical framework (see Figure 1.2) used to determine stages of each subject's religious development. In essence, a single case study design is adopted for the purposes of this research, although cross case-reports and conclusions are made at the end of the respective studies.

Zacarias Moussaoui

Zacarias Moussaoui was convicted in 2006 for conspiracy to commit acts of terrorism relating to the 9/11 attacks. As the descendant of Moroccan parents who emigrated to France in 1965, Moussaoui is not a convert in the conventional sense (Moussaoui, 2002: 4). Although a Muslim by birth, he did not become aware of his religious identity until adulthood. Up until that period, he grew up as a French citizen largely indifferent to religion. Moussaoui can, therefore, be considered a 'revert' to

Islam.[5] The case study illustrates his path towards Islam and the factors surrounding this 'reversion'. Participant observation, again, forms an integral part of the study, alongside the use of primary and secondary sources. Reference is made throughout to a detailed account of Moussaoui's upbringing and youth prior to his 'reversion'/reawakening to Islam by his older brother, Abd Samad Moussaoui (Moussaoui, 2002). Other primary sources include the author's transcript of the character reference provided for Moussaoui as a defence witness during his US trial in 2006.[6] Secondary sources include media reports following Moussaoui's arrest, trial and subsequent imprisonment.

Richard Reid

Richard Reid is more commonly referred to as the 'Shoe Bomber' who attempted to blow up a transatlantic flight en route from France to the US in December 2001. This study will examine Reid's development from childhood prior to his being imprisoned at Feltham Young Offenders Institute. Secondary data such as media reports and interviews with parents and academic institutions form the basis of examination in this regard. His release and assimilation into Brixton Mosque and its community immediately thereafter is the subsequent area of examination using Participant Observation methods to expound on the detail surrounding Reid's development in this instance. The author's interaction and direct involvement with Reid at this formative stage of his development as a new Muslim is illustrated at this juncture. The conclusive phase of the study relies on secondary sources of data in view of the extensive reporting of Reid's attempted terrorist attack, this being the first of its kind since 9/11. Such data also include media interviews with the author providing a profile of Reid as a new convert and the influences that attracted him to violent extremism.

Trevor William Forest

Trevor William Forest is more commonly known as Abdullah el Faisal. El Faisal was found guilty of soliciting murder and spreading religious hatred. He was subsequently imprisoned in 2003 and, upon release, was deported to his country of origin, Jamaica, in 2007. The approach to this particular research follows the pattern of the Moussaoui and Reid studies; however, a more vivid narrative can be provided via participant observation due to the various avenues of interaction between the author and el Faisal. For example, both worked in Islamia School, North West London, during the years 1993–94. This particular environment was completely different to that of the mosque or private study circles where el Faisal was to begin expounding erroneous and subsequently extremist teachings. The former environment was regulated by statutory bodies (i.e. OFSTED) as the school was a flagship institution applying to become the first state-funded schools for Muslims (Baker, 1998: 34–8, 49–60). El Faisal's parameters for teaching school children were, therefore, clearly defined and monitored. This is in stark contrast to the closed, insular surroundings of mosques and study circles which provided secure platforms from where extremist ideologies could be expounded to unsuspecting, susceptible young Muslims. The varying dynamics caused by these different environments is described throughout this case study. Arguably, it is settings like those intimated above that adversely affect the psyche of young converts, propelling them towards violent extremism. Primary data includes literature and transcriptions of cassettes of el Faisal as well as official court documentation relating to his appeal of sentence (Faisal, 1997).[7] Additional primary data also includes refutations of el Faisal's extremist ideology and practice (Salafimanhaj.com, 2007). Secondary data consists primarily of media reports on his upbringing prior to his conversion to Islam and his subsequent arrest, trial, imprisonment and deportation from Britain.

Sean O'Reilly aka Abdullah

(This is an alias so as to maintain anonymity.) This is the single case study of a young white Muslim convert who, prior to conversion, experienced the street culture of South London. This culminated in his being convicted and imprisoned for a violent assault. While awaiting trial, he converted to Islam and married a British national of Muslim origin. Subsequent to his eventual release from prison, he was exposed to the violent extremist teachings of Abu Hamza al Misri at Finsbury Park Mosque and other more clandestine gatherings. His encounter with some of his peers who had converted to Islam and were attending Brixton Mosque led him to visit the centre and review the teachings he had then received and adopted, among which was that suicide attacks (so-called martyrdom operations) were not only permissible, but necessary on British soil. This case study examines how Sean progressed from violent extremist teachings and embarked upon a more structured, less emotive impetus of learning, making new associates in the process. This case study is based primarily on one-to-one interviews.

Each case study relies upon the author's narrative from a participant-observer perspective in view of former relationships with three of the cases and existing association with one of them. The primary aim of such first-hand knowledge is to provide a unique insight of the prevailing environment and events that precipitated each individual's attraction and gravitation towards extremist tendencies. Miles and Huberman support the need for: 'some familiarity with the phenomenon and the setting under study' which the author brings to this particular study as a whole (Miles and Huberman, 1984). The theoretical frameworks introduced at the beginning of this research will be referenced in each case study, providing a consistent benchmark against which to chart the social and ideological development of each case. Such an approach is likely to illustrate, and possibly contrast, secondary data sources (e.g. media reports, etc.) In view of the methodology being applied in this instance, a holistic, narrative-led approach to case studies can be considered appropriate within the context of the research being conducted. Profiles are emerging which suggest possible causes of violent extremism; thus theoretical understandings of this phenomenon are now becoming clearer (Rai, 2006: 21–48). The above-mentioned case studies aim to eliminate existing ambiguities surrounding causes behind Muslim converts' paths to extremism. The non-trivial set of circumstances surrounding their transformations could, in the event, provide possible predictors to the violent extremism to which they ultimately gravitate.

While it is acknowledged that these four case studies cannot provide a comprehensive conclusion which explains the rise of UK home-grown violent extremism or contributory factors behind it, they at least serve to illustrate a microcosmic phenomenon of radicalisation (whether violent or otherwise) that is possibly affecting some Muslim communities today.

Interviews

Interviews of British Muslim converts are significant to the scope of this research in that they provide supplementary data from 'live' primary sources, gathered during interactions between the author and target audience. Unlike the above-mentioned methods, which are largely dependent on observation, primary and secondary *documentation* (as is elaborated upon under the 'Documentary analysis' section that follows), the interviews provide a rich and current source of data. In view of the sensitivities surrounding the target audience's perception and mistrust of authoritative or even educational reasons for engagement, interviews are semi-structured. This type of interview is intended to avoid the obstacles experienced by Wilson when trying to obtain co-operation from interviewees; namely, reluctance and lack of co-operation (Wilson et al., 1982: 367–80). Semi-structured interviews enable a flexibility and adaptability conducive to both author and interviewee considering the personal and sensitive nature of questions being asked. Questions can be modified based on the author's, 'perception of what seems most appropriate in the context of the "conversation"' (Robson, 1993: 231).

For the purposes of this particular research Powney and Watts' typology, which distinguishes between 'respondent' and 'informant' interviews respectively, is applied, (Powney and Watts, 1987: 228–42). The respondent interview style is adopted in view of it allowing the interviewer to maintain control over the direction of the interview while facilitating the semi-structured approach. This contrasts with the informant interview approach where the primary concern is about the interviewee's perceptions within a particular context. It is largely led by the interviewee and is akin to the unstructured interview approach (Robson, 1993: 231). Interview questions are designed to extrapolate information surrounding environmental factors that may have precipitated the interviewee's (hereinafter referred to as the respondent's) interest and eventual conversion to Islam. Considering the time period over which extremist ideologues have been active in the UK, the main areas of focus upon converts has been between the early 1990s up until 2009; although, while attempting to interview two cohorts of converts falling between these two periods, i.e. early to mid-1990s converts and post-9/11, the author found the younger, newer converts to be more accessible. Reasons behind this are varied; from work and family commitments which inevitably caused less frequent attendances at mosques and social gatherings, to a reluctance to relive or recapture past experiences which have been consigned to the distant past. Consideration was also given to socio-political events during this period which affected the Muslim and Arab world. Questions were structured to determine the identity construct of the converts and whether this altered over time. Factors which might have effected such change may have emanated from within Muslim communities as opposed to any socio-political events that contributed to conversion in the first place. For example, the literature review highlighted the convert's dilemma of eschewing one identity (British in this instance) for a more Islamic one, only to encounter prejudice from Muslim communities s/he has attempted to assimilate into. Such an experience may have caused some individuals to redefine their identity, reverting back to some of the traits and characteristics more familiar to their pre-conversion phases of life.

Acknowledgement must be given to the counter arguments that question the effectiveness of semi-structured interviews. For example, in some cases researcher bias may exist in that the respondent is unsuspectingly led in a direction in order to provide specific information that accords with the researcher's *desired* results or conclusion. As far as this study is concerned, bias towards one gender in particular could be argued to be due to the focus being exclusively upon Muslim male converts. However, this type of criticism can be countered by highlighting the fact that the present phenomenon of interest remains around the threat of British male Muslims resorting to violent extremism. To date, not a single British female Muslim has attempted any type of terrorist attack. While there is a need to research female British Muslims and establish whether similar factors affect their respective psyche and identity constructs, the scope of the present research is limited to the existing male phenomenon, for the reasons described above. Indeed, this study may provide a basis for conducting further research around British Muslim females.

Interview methodology

Muslim converts were divided into two broad geographical categories coming from north and south London respectively; however, it is important to note that many Muslim converts associate with mosques according to ideological affiliation and practice as opposed to geographical location. This explains why some converts reside in areas and boroughs quite far from Brixton Mosque: examples include Germaine Lindsey (one of the 7/7 bombers), who visited Abdullah el Faisal in London despite living in Aylesbury, and Richard Reid and Zacarias Moussaoui who both resided in south London but congregated regularly in Finsbury Park Mosque during Abu Hamza al Misri's tenure there. A further subdivision was made according to age and the period during which they converted to Islam. These categorisations were done so as to compare socio-economic and socio-environmental drivers that may have affected their process of conversion. The first group of convert Muslims (Convert Group A [CGA]) lived in and around Lambeth, south London, an area known for its high uptake of new convert Muslims between the ages of 16 and 30. They are predominantly of African–Caribbean origin and from what could be described as socially deprived backgrounds. Educationally, many of the respondents in this particular group had underachieved and were unemployed.

Convert Group B (CGB) came from other surrounding areas of Lambeth, e.g. Croydon, Streatham, etc. In some instances, the localities of some of the respondents from this group are considered more upwardly mobile, both socially and economically. Therefore, this group tended to be in employment or higher education. This group is also predominantly of African–Caribbean origin.

The subdivision among these groups demarcated a few older, more established converts with a larger proportion consisting of newer, younger ones. For research clarity and purpose, any respondent who converted prior to 9/11 is considered to be an older, more established convert, whereas young/new converts are those who converted post-9/11 to date. The reason for making such a distinction is because of the perceived impact on converts' psyche post-9/11 and its subsequent effect on socio-political and socio-ideological environments throughout society. Arguably, and the interviews intend to highlight this, older convert identity constructs were already established pre-9/11 whereas in contrast, newer converts' identities were actually shaped by this and other similar and subsequent world events like the 7/7 attacks, and so on.

Limitations of interviews

One of the limitations of the research was the fact that many of the CGA respondents came from disaffected backgrounds, which made it problematic to get them to comply with the research. Many of them felt that the interview questions reflected government concerns and this became an influential factor towards their reluctance to participate. This was followed by the perception that they would be 'selling out' if they participated. Another contributory factor to their reluctance to participate was their negative perception of the authorities. This developed as a result of their experiences of discrimination at the hands of such authorities.

As a result, despite reassurances that the scope of research was indeed academic and not at the behest of any governmental department, participation from this group proved somewhat problematic. Some respondents were reassured by the fact that 'one of them; a man from the street' was interviewing them in an effort for their voices to be heard. In any event, the anti-institutional sentiment expressed at the outset of the interviews, i.e., that the government, police, education sector were anti-Muslim and, from pre-conversion experiences, racist, provided an even stronger impetus to interview the respondents. In addition to this, they believed that the government's foreign policy in Iraq and Afghanistan was a reflection on their eventual statutory agenda against Muslims in the UK. Indeed, such views would be considered by some as a starting point for violent radical extremism. Leaders of violent extremist organisations have been able to use this rhetoric to recruit new Muslims to their ideological way of thinking. Abu Hamza al Misri is a good example of an extremist preacher able to attract a significant number of angry black converts in a deprived area of north London (Finsbury Park) towards an extreme and violent version of Islam. Reference should be made to Lambert's research in which a case study of Finsbury Park Mosque is given. In addition to the above-mentioned limitations with this group, difficulties were experienced concerning a few respondents' understanding of the interview questions (Lambert, 2009). They were unable to understand and, thus, provide comprehensive answers to some of the questions. This could, more than likely, be attributed to the level of education received by the respective participants, as will become evident in the research findings.

In comparison with CGA, CGB respondents were easier to interview, although an issue of confidentiality seemed to be more of a common theme among this group. Many of those interviewed also constructively answered the interview questions, making more of a political debate of the questioning. This was in contrast to CGA who provided shorter answers, without any dialogue or discussion. The older, more experienced convert Muslims, despite an initial apprehension that reflected both CGA's and CGB's concerns, were more elaborate in answering the questions. This was anticipated in view of the level of education received and their experiences since conversion.

With hindsight, if research of this nature were to be conducted again, the author would recommend establishing an informal forum or arrange focus group discussions over a period of weeks which could be divided into thematic areas of questioning around identity, extremism, etc. This would enable a more focused interview procedure which could yield specific answers from the different groups examined. Groups like CGA could, therefore, arguably provide more effective data for detailed analysis if the area of research was disseminated thematically. Additionally, both groups could be questioned together in an informal setting. The likely outcome would prove interesting ao far as ideological and social influences are concerned.

Documentary analysis

This is an indirect form of research on documentation produced for reasons other than that of conventional research. As an unobtrusive method, it cannot affect the actual processes of development; however, it can provide structured information on hard data, countering to an extent the somewhat unstructured approach of the participant observation method. This area of research will concentrate on the following documentation:

1. Court transcripts and documents related to the trials of three of the case study subjects
2. Counter terrorist agencies' literature, research and reports on Salafism
3. Academic and media reports on Salafism as a threat and proponent of violent extremism
4. Expositions from Salafist writings as to the origins of Salafism and its distinguishing characteristics from extremism.

Analysis of the above-mentioned documentation will provide the necessary insight into the socio-political and socio-religious environment that currently affects young British Muslims. Such data is intended to illustrate the extent of the risk posed by conflicting/contradictory studies and reports around similar phenomena (i.e. Salafism in this case) which plays directly into the hands of extremists who then exploit such conflict among the target audience. While 'every effort has been made to ensure that documents' are representative of the totality of relevant documents, the inevitable bias or indeed distortions will continue to permeate such data due to the fact mentioned earlier; namely, that many of the documents were prepared for reasons unrelated to academic research and study (Lambert, 2009).

Presentation of conclusions: Research findings and analysis

Reference has already been made to triangulating the mixed method approach. Because of the predominantly qualitative nature of the research, this approach aims to highlight the rigorous process through which data has been critically examined and extrapolated according to established social scientific methods. Credibility of the methods employed also serve to reduce concerns over the reliability and validity of the data obtained. Triangulation also aims to highlight existing common variables between the subjects of study and establish whether any newly identified factors influence the convert's path towards violent extremism. The findings are also compared with earlier existing research conducted on British and other European Muslim converts to determine whether common variables or indeed similar shortcomings/limitations were experienced by the authors.

6
Case Studies

This chapter will examine three case studies relating to UK-based Muslim individuals who resided in the UK in the 1990s during which there was significant conflict and upheaval affecting the Muslim world, e.g., the first Gulf war, the Balkans Conflict, Palestine, Kashmir, Chechnya, etc. These events, together with the tense political climates in other Muslim countries like Saudi Arabia were arguably precipitating factors in the extreme radicalisation of the three individuals in question.[1] The fourth case study examines a younger Muslim convert who, while not experiencing the socio-religious and political conflicts of the 1990s, nevertheless experienced the aftermath of the 7 July 2005 London bombings. Case study number four is the only study which discusses the gravitation of an individual away from violent extremism. The remaining three studies describe gravitations towards it.

It should be noted that two out of the four case studies are not British; however, the platform upon which their extremist ideas fomented were inextricably British based.[2] For example, as will be seen from the two non-British case studies, manifestations of their combined ideological and behavioural extremism surfaced after being exposed to extremist propaganda and its sympathisers in the UK. Up until that point, both individuals had assimilated into a socially conservative, Salafist community and were actively engaged community members. Additionally, both individuals continued to use the UK as a point of reference and, indeed, focal point from where to propagate and further develop their violent extremist objectives. It is for these reasons that the author has included Moussaoui and el-Faisal who, although not British, sought domicile in the UK as it became their preferred place of residence.

The case studies will be examined in light of earlier discussions in Chapter 3 which discussed typologies relevant to European and, more specifically, British Muslims, to determine whether the former can be accurately classified according to the latter classifications. Such examination is necessary in view of the generality of the typologies and the somewhat secondary nature of some of the research conducted therein and will be addressed at the conclusion of the four studies. Insider research therefore seeks to ascertain the validity or otherwise of the typologies discussed earlier. Ensuing discussions around issues of the case study subjects' identities will also inform on Chapters 3 and 4 both of which expounded upon identity in detail.

The final collective ambit of each case study will be to illustrate the extent of their respective ideological and behavioural development against the theoretical frameworks introduced at the beginning of this research. Such illustrations will be juxtaposed with the historical, ideological and behavioural characteristics that define violent extremist tendencies. The objective in this instance is to provide a platform upon which to develop new and existing frameworks in order to provide a more critical tool against which to measure or determine the degree of an individual's radicalisation and possible extremism. The author's insider perspective of each case study is, therefore, intended to inform existing models of radicalisation.

Categorisation of Islamic terminology on extremism

Introducing and describing Islamic legislative terms is important at this stage in order to enable the identification and, subsequently, contextual examination of the forms of extremism that are to be illustrated in this chapter. The potential for misunderstanding some of the religious terminology used is then, hopefully, diminished. Al-Mutairi, in his comprehensive discourse on religious extremism, categorises extremism according to Islamic terminology (Al-Mutairi, 2001). He makes an important observation which should not be ignored by western academics and practitioners alike who have often attempted to develop theories around this subject (religious extremism in Islam) from an isolated platform away from Muslim scholarly and historical input. He asserts that Sharia (Islamic Legislative) expressions and terminology are essential if one is to understand violent extremism and terrorism enacted in the name of Islam (Al-Mutairi, 2001: 56–83). Despite religious extremism not being a new phenomenon in the Arab and Muslim world, western academia has either largely ignored or indeed failed to reference the readily accessible array of experience, knowledge and expertise in this area. Al-Mutairi supports his observation regarding the Sharia's importance by citing the famous Muslim classical scholar and jurist, Shaykhul Islam, Ibn Taimiyyah:

> Knowing Arabic ... helps in understanding the meaning ... Similarly, understanding the manner in which the words express their meanings [is also very helpful and important]. Most of the misguidance of the heretics was due to this reason. They interpreted ... words according to what they claimed such words indicated, while in reality, the matter was not so.
>
> (Al-Mutairi, 2001, citing Ibn Taimiyyah, 7: 115)

Categories of extremism (Lexical meanings)

1. *Al-Ghulu (Extremism)*. This can also be described as excessiveness, i.e., a person going beyond the limits in any given matter. Shaykh Salih Ali-Shaykh explains 'Extremism means to go beyond the permissible limits in any issue. So, anyone who goes beyond the limits of the Sunnah, he is guilty of extremism.' Lane defines the term as exceeding the proper due or common limit; being excessive, immoderate, or beyond measure. Ali-Shaykh also describes behavioural manifestations, these being harshness, strictness, or rigour in religion (Ali-Shaykh, 2009).

   Another definition suggests: 'Extremism in the religion is going beyond the limits Allah established, expanding on the domains of the religion and that are demarcated by those limits' (Al-Meedani, 2001: 228).

2. *Al-Tatarruf (Radicalism)*. Linguistically, the Arabic derivation of the word refers primarily to boundaries or parameters that are established or set, i.e. 'the utmost edge or limit of something' (Al-Mutairi, 2001: 65). Its legislative connotation refers therefore to someone who is immoderate.

3. *Al-Tanattu' (exhorbitance or extravagance)*. This category is clear and refers to exhorbitance, etc. whether it emanates from speech or action.

4. *Al-Tashaddud (strength, rigidity and inflexibility)*. This type of extremism relates to overcoming or overpowering something and/or someone by being forceful and inflexible.

5. *Al-Unf (harshness, sternness or meanness)*. As in the case of Al-Tanatta (3) the meaning of this is clear.

Al-Mutairi's conclusive summary of these terms highlights the similarities between the linguistic definitions of at least two of the terms,

Al-Ghulu and Al-Tatarruf, while illustrating the excessiveness of the two. The remaining categories are simply manifestations or 'expressions' of Al-Ghulu, this being the most serious and severe classification of extremism in this instance. Al-Mutairi confirms this in his summation:

> The extremist is characterized by taking to his religion in a very strict and severe manner (Al-Tashaddud). He is also characterized, in his relations with others, by harshness and incivility (Al-Unf). He is also characterized by going deeply and beyond the needed limit when it comes to actions of the religion. All of these words, save Al-Tatarruf, have been mentioned in the texts of the Sharia.
>
> (Al-Mutairi, 2001: 67)

The above mentioned classifications provide a more discernable context around which to identify the nature of radicalisation in the following case studies (i.e. ideological or behavourial). They also provide specificity regarding the characteristics or traits of such radicalisation.

Case study 1: Zacarias Moussaoui

With the exception of mitigating factors cited as evidence in Zacarias Moussaoui's trial in March 2006 for conspiracy to commit acts of terrorism in the US on 11 September 2001, details of his upbringing and past remain limited. To date, the most authentic account comes from his older brother, Abd Samad Moussaoui, by way of a biographical description illustrating Zacarias's formative years (Moussaoui, 2002). Later accounts, provided by Abd Samad, describing his brother's process of radicalisation can be validated and, in some instances, challenged by other primary and secondary sources of evidence that developed during Zacarias's domicile in the UK. These sources, i.e. participant observation and documentary data, constitutes the majority of evidence relied upon for this case study. Documentary evidence inlcudes data and exhibits submitted as evidence in defence of Moussaoui.[3] It is important to note that Abd Samad's account of Zacarias remains the only insider perspective to date. However, this is restricted to his interaction with his brother in France; he is unable to provide an insider account of Zacarias's environment, social interaction, etc., in the UK and relies upon secondary information provided to him by his brother during the latter's visits to France. The subjectivity of some of these second-hand accounts is therefore unreliable. Abd Samad's insight of the visible behavioural changes in Zacarias are invaluable; however, the significant precipitating factors that caused these in the UK are absent. In order to obtain a more comprehensive understanding of Zacarias Moussoui's gravitation towards violent extremism, an insider perspective that covers the UK element of his radicalisation is necessary. This particular case study aims to provide that perspective.

The significance of Zacarias's formative years as a child cannot be ignored in view of the summation of the jury when deciding against the death penalty in the above mentioned case.[4] The decision, handed to Judge Brinkeman who was presiding over the trial, stated, 'We the jury do not unanimously find that a sentence of death should be imposed on the defendant'.[5] In fact, the majority of jurors (nine out of 12) accepted his: 'unstable childhood, home life without structure and emotional or financial support' as well as his father's 'violent temper' as mitigating factors that supported their final verdict.[6] Doctors Jon and Benjamin Cole refer to family conflict as key features in the personal histories of many individuals influenced by violent extremist propaganda (Cole and Cole, 2009: 29). They also refer to existing narratives which suggest that extremist recruiters prey on such individuals because of the latter's estrangement from family and, therefore, susceptibility to extremist propaganda.[7] Further elucidation of Moussaoui's trial is given later in this study; however, it is first necessary to provide a contextual platform of his childhood and upbringing as a second generation immigrant in France during the 1970s and 80s.

Upbringing, social background and identity – the formative years

Zacarias Moussaoui was born on 30 May 1968 in St-Jean-de-Luz, France. He was the youngest of four children to his parents, Omar Moussaoui and Aicha El-Wafi.[8] His parents, of Moroccan descent, married in November 1960 when Aicha was 14 years old. Aicha was born on 29 August 1946 and came from a relatively wealthy family according to local standards in Azrou, Morocco. She was one of five children and attended school from the age of eight until she was married.[9] Omar's exact date of birth is unknown; however, legal documentation suggests he was born in 1938, making him at least eight years older than Aicha at the time of their marriage. He came from a family of 12 children, of whom only two (including him) remained alive by 1972.[10] The family circumstances appear to have been straitened as Omar worked throughout his childhood while attending school at the same time. He appeared to settle into the profession of tiler by the age of 13 up until his first marriage at the age of 16. This only lasted for three months. He subsequently met and married Aicha in November 1960.[11] Initially Mr and

Mrs Moussaoui resided in Morocco with the latter's mother. They had four children: two girls and two boys – Nadia, born December 1963, Jamila, June 1965, Abd Samad, January 1967 and Zacarias. The two girls were born in Morocco and the boys in France. According to Abd Samad's account, the family immigrated to France in 1965 to search for better employment opportunities (Moussaoui, 2002: 1–4). However, the Social Worker's report (M.J. Burckhard) cites the year of immigration as 1966.[12] They initially moved to Handaille, France and resided there until the end of 1968[13] before relocating to the south-western city of Bayonne where Omar Moussaoui found employment in the building industry (Moussaoui, 2002: 1–4).

In 1970 disagreements began in the Moussaoui household.[14] Arguments between Zacarias's parents became more frequent and these were increasingly punctuated by violence against Aicha.[15] Further evidence highlights the deterioration domestically as early as 8 January 1970 when Aicha reported her husband to the Bayonne police for violence against her. He was subsequently charged for 'light violence' committed against his wife.[16] Medical reports were to be submitted later that year as evidence of the continuing physical assaults meted out by Omar Moussaoui.[17] Unsurprisingly, on 19 May 1971 Pierre Alquie solicitors issued a Spouses' Non-Reconciliation notice on behalf of Aicha against Omar. This order expressly authorised that: 'Ms. Moussaoui … reside separately' and ordered 'Mr. Moussaoui not to disturb his wife in her separate residence, otherwise, authorised the above-mentioned woman to call on the assistance, if need be, of the police'.[18]

Aicha and Omar on divorced on 28 June 1971.[19] The divorce had a devastating effect on Omar and he suffered a nervous breakdown shortly after the separation, divorce and final departure of Aicha and his children.[20] Zacarias's mother, now with four children in tow, remained in France, initially relocating to Dordogne and subsequently the city of Mulhouse in Alsace where she found employment (Moussaoui, 2002: 4). In addition to the traumatic experiences of divorce and relocation, the children were, according to Abd Samad's account, immediately placed in the local orphanage, because of their mother's stress in parenting them while attempting to maintain suitable employment. He recalls that particular period of he and his siblings' lives as 'grim childhood years'.[21] His recollection of this traumatic experience is vividly captured in the legal documentation authorising such action.[22] However, it is evident from these documents that the Moussaoui children had been placed in custody on a few occasions.[23] One such occasion was as early as 24 June 1968 shortly after the Moussaoui family had arrived in France. A decree for admission to the local Childhood Welfare Services was issued for the children to be placed under the charge of a Miss H.J. Bennett, 'in St. Jean de Luz, for the duration of the stay of the mother [Aicha] at the Maison St. Odilein Bellere'.[24]

The Moussaoui children would have been too young to recollect this event, with Abd Samad and Zacarias being aged approximately one-and-a-half years and one month respectively. Little information exists as to why they were temporarily placed in the charge of a third party so soon after their arrival in France. It was certainly not the last time that they would be placed into care. Nevertheless, after the temporary care order was issued, the Moussaoui children were visited by their mother on a weekly basis for a little under one year until she applied for an order to cease placement into care and a return to her custody.[25] Aicha reunited her children in a new family home on the Rue des Chataigniers (Moussaoui, 2002: 7). Despite the experience of parental abandonment, the children initially viewed their mother in a heroic light due to their new found circumstances and slightly improved conditions. The improvement in the family circumstances at the time owed itself to the fact that one of Aicha's line managers (who eventually went on to assume the influential position as city mayor), sympathised with her predicament, i.e. a single parent with young children, and was therefore charitable towards the family. However, these favourable conditions were to deteriorate with relocation to a 'problem neighbourhood' where the Bourtzwiller estate was located. This estate consisted largely of North African families in similar circumstances to that of the Moussaouis (Moussaoui, 2002: 8–10). In light of some of Zacarias's experiences during these formative years, it is probable that they were not, perhaps, too dissimilar to those of other children growing up in single-parent families living on housing estates in the UK and other parts of Europe during similar periods. However, as will be witnessed, issues pertaining to identity and a sense of belonging began to surface early as a result of the racism Zacarias and his family experienced. His initial family visits to his homeland, Morocco, in 1974 and 1977 were to leave lasting impressions that would further demarcate his identity as a child growing up in 1970s France where he was perceivably considered as the alien 'other' during this and later periods of his life (Moussaoui, 2002: 5–15).

At the age of 12, Zacarias moved with his mother and siblings to the southern city of Narbonne. This particular relocation unsettled Zacarias in view of his attachment to their previous home and environment in Mulhouse. He had acquired a skill for handball in Mulhouse and was playing in the local district and, subsequently, Alsace championships by the time he relocated to Narbonne. This was, according to his brother, a hobby he excelled in and to which he dedicated much of his time (Moussaoui, 2002: 18–20). When considering the type of environment Zacarias had to familiarise himself with, it is unsurprising that he dedicated himself to and indeed excelled in this sport. For instance, he continued to witness deterioration domestically owing to continuing tensions between his mother and sister, Jamila. This resulted in Jamila being dispatched to boarding school. Abd Samad was to accompany her, leaving Zacarias and Nadia with their mother. With his favourite sister and only brother absent from family life, coupled with increasingly volatile confrontations between him and his mother, Zacarias had little alternative but to seek distractions away from family life (Moussaoui, 2002: 40–3). Abd Samad observed the effect of the move to Narbonne on Zacarias. He was the only member of the family attached to Mulhouse:

> After the ordeal of the orphanage, that move to Narbonne was another great wrench for him. It meant the end of his dream of becoming a professional handball player and then perhaps a coach ... from that moment on, something in Zacarias changed. There was a sort of uncertainty about him ... an edge of bitterness and rancor.
>
> (Moussaoui, 2002: 119–20)

Regional and racial differences caused the Moussaouis to stand out in their new city; their accents and dark skins were a cause of attention from many of their peers and surprisingly, teachers in their schools. The derogatory use of the term 'blacks' was a cause of consternation for Zacarias caused by the inability of the indigenous French to differentiate between his Arab origins and those of Africans or Caribbeans. The Moussaoui children felt humiliated and unsettled by not being identifiable at first sight and having to explain or describe their ethnicity. The degree of racism experienced by Zacarias and his family continued up to adulthood, experiencing this at local, peer-group and institutional levels. His first serious relationship with Fanny, an indigenous French girl, was troubled by racism emanating from her father. Solidarity was inevitably sought with peers of similar ethnicity and backgrounds. Such affiliations would gather increasing momentum and take on religious undertones as global events, such as the first Gulf War, the Balkans conflict and Palestine acted as catalysts to unite North African Muslims in France whose perceptions of these events were synonymous with much of the Muslim world; namely, Muslim persecution at the hands of the West (Moussaoui, 2002: 20–7, 59–63, 76–9).

His education

Initial impressions of Zacarias's educational ability were witnessed while he was still in kindergarten. He was described, alongside his siblings as being 'intelligent and well behaved' without 'any specific difficulties'.[26] His brother's observations about their early education also supported the above observations in that they both 'did pretty well at school without much effort'. (Moussaoui, 2002: 25). From a participatory–observatory perspective, the author, while studying at London South Bank University between 1995 and 1997, encountered Zacarias on a regular basis, both at university and Brixton Mosque. Discussions occasionally ensued regarding progress of the respective Masters Degree programmes that were being attended.[27] Zacarias never indicated that he had any difficulty on the course. However, the only exception to this was when he approached the author to seek assistance in compiling his final dissertation. He expressed concern over his level of English language proficiency and required the assistance of a native speaker who was conversant with the language requirements at Masters Degree level.

His focus on academia could, perhaps, be attributed to his earlier socio-economic circumstances. His brother alludes to this when describing his fear of 'delinquency' and the threat it posed to 'all young people on housing estates living in difficult conditions'. Despite this concern Zacarias and Abd Samad had to leave their initial school (Montesquieu) and join Jules-Ferry Secondary School because of their 'lack of discipline'. The new school was notably different from the previous one in that its attainment levels were higher as was the socio-economic status of the students (Moussaoui, 2002: 25–6). Upon closer examination of Zacarias's school report cards it is evident that he was an average student; however, his academia was punctuated by behavioural problems, such as restlessness, absent-mindedness and occasional poor conduct.[28] In fact, the first and second trimester class teachers noted in his report of 1978/1979, 'Improved conduct would undoubtedly lead to better grades', and also, 'Results remain average . . . Please pay attention to your conduct!'[29] In Jules-Ferry Secondary School Zacarias's academic performance continued to remain average. The teacher evaluations and recommendations illustrated his increasing disinterest or, possibly, lack of focus in his lessons. Comments such as, 'Talkative, fools around – Work very inadequate . . . Interested but has tendency to fool around' and 'Little work done. Lab work catastrophic . . . Talks too much . . . Could do better if he fooled around a bit less' typified his earlier reports.[30] Despite these disruptive behavioural tendencies, some teachers acknowledged, particularly in the later years, that he was making some progress.[31] It appeared that Zacarias had settled in Jules-Ferry. However, at the end of the fourth year, Zacarias suddenly requested to transfer to a vocational school to embark upon a Certificate of Technical Education course in order to become a mechanic and fitter.[32] This came as a surprise to Abd Samad who had witnessed the immediate and apparently positive change in his brother's existing social circles. However, he eventually ascertained that Zacarias had developed an inferiority complex among his peers because of his social standing and origins. In his own words, Zacarias would decry, 'I was all on my own' (Moussaoui, 2002: 30). Nonetheless, his reports steadily improved at the City Technique College and his commitment and hard work were noted in various teacher evaluations and recommendations.[33] He went on to complete his studies, graduating first with a vocational diploma from City Technique followed by a baccalaureate and then an advanced vocational certificate (Moussaoui, 2002).

At this juncture it is important to note that, although Zacarias's academic work and, on the whole, his behaviour in class had dramatically improved, his interactive skills in team activities continued to be an explosive issue. For example, as far back as 1980 he was being described as 'agitated' and 'insolent'.[34] In yet another report from Jules-Ferry School during the Second Trimester of 1983–84 he was described as possessing 'a bad character and is very vulgar towards his classmates'.[35] By the end of the first term in City Technique College he had managed to distinguish his sporting abilities from his bad temperament; however, the latter was still evident enough for an evaluation to observe, 'Too much arguing. [He] must control himself'.[36] Zacarias's argumentative and confrontational attitude was to become more notable with his academic, social and religious development over the years with it culminating, to self-destructing effect, in the very public prosecution against him for conspiracy to participate in the 11 September attacks on the US. Further evidence of his negative behavioural tendencies was witnessed in his almost violent confrontations with his mother, to the extent that his brother had to intervene in order to prevent Zacarias from hitting her. This episode resulted in him leaving home in 1986. He returned temporarily in 1988 but then left again, only to resurface eight years later in 1996 with his head fully shaven, a long beard 'and short trousers' (Moussaoui, 2002: 43, 111), apparently indicative of his new found religiosity. In fact, upon his return that year, he visited the local

Narbonne Mosque one Friday and, after listening to the sermon, proceeded to address the congregation. It should be noted that this type of approach is often considered an affront by mosque management committees as it is deemed both a challenge and a threat to their vested authority. However, from the perspective of the attendees, it is usually considered as a religious address or advice, depending on the subject matter. In any event, Zacarias apparently stated that he was going to teach the congregation about the religion. According to accounts of this event, Zacarias began to propound the 'Wahabbi' doctrine. This was immediately rejected by some members of the congregation and a heated discussion ensued until the imam entered the mosque and directly challenged Zacarias regarding his negligible knowledge of Islam. The knowledge-based challenge resulted in Zacarias losing his temper and attempting to physically assault the imam who was protected by the members of the congregation who intervened and removed Zacarias from the mosque (Moussaoui, 2002).

The type of behaviour witnessed in the Narbonne Mosque was also experienced in London where Zacarias was, by 1996, frequenting Brixton Mosque. Further discussion regarding this period of his transformation into militancy and extremism is discussed below.

Conflict of identity: Islam as a transnational/cross-cultural answer to race and ethnicity

Zacarias and his brother were never taught Arabic or, in fact, anything about their religion, Moroccan heritage or culture. Abd Samad recounts that, in addition to the racism he and his brother had already experienced societally, they also faced discrimination from fellow North Africans because of their ignorance of their culture, etc. Despite repeated requests for their mother to teach them the basic tenets of Islam when they were young, she refused to do so. The only avenue for religious knowledge was via their mother's boyfriend at the time, Saïd, whom they witnessed praying regularly. Abd Samad recalls that he was 25 when he attended a mosque for the first time. Zacarias's first attendance was supposedly when he visited London. The latter assumption is probably correct as the author recalls one of Zacarias's earlier visits to the Brixton Mosque in the mid-1990s when he was very new, clean shaven and dressed in casual civilian clothes. It was apparent that he was not only new to the city but also new to practising the religion. Brixton Mosque was ideal for Zacarias as the ethnic profile was that of convert Muslims from predominantly African and Caribbean origin and North

Africans. He was therefore able to identify more easily with this diverse young Muslim community.

His initial ignorance of religion and culture was such that in his teens, instead of participating in Ramadan, or Eid celebrations, his mother celebrated Christmas. Occasions like these only perpetuated Zacarias's conflict of identity. As a result, he neither felt North African or French. It is important to note that his teenage years were during a time of fierce national patriotism and indeed racism during the mid-1980s. Abd Samad recounts, 'We couldn't recognize ourselves either in the all-French model or North African model', thereby highlighting the confusion he and Zacarias felt at the inability to define themselves nationally or ethnically during that period. That said, cognitive openings from a religious perspective began to take shape for Zacarias following international events that proved a catalyst for solidarity among North Africans *and* Muslims of all ethnic backgrounds. As was mentioned above, the first Gulf War in 1991 followed by the Balkans conflict during the early to mid-1990s and the continuing issue of Palestine served to unite the North African communities in France for two primary reasons: i) these events were seen as an attack on Islam and Muslims and ii) discrimination increased against North African communities as a result of these issues (Moussaoui, 2002). These events occurred at a transitory period of study for Zacarias; he had to embark on additional studies in order to increase his credits to enrol on a diploma course in Economic and Social Administration at Montpellier University.[37] However, his diploma did not give him the required credits to progress further academically. The transfer from vocational courses to academic education proved difficult and disheartening for Zacarias. According to Abd Samad, he became increasingly disillusioned and demotivated. His company began to consist of Moroccan, Algerian, Tunisian, Senegalese and Syrian students, to name but a few, who frequented a cafeteria in the university hall of residence of Montpellier. These foreign scholarship students were attuned to politics and highly opinionated regarding the crises affecting the Muslim world. According to Abd Samad, they appeared, 'to cultivate an attitude of rebellion'. He unequivocally points to this company of foreign students and the political, revolutionary views that were discussed, as the cognitive opening for Zacarias's extreme understanding of Islam. His gradual awareness and 'embracing' of Islam was not a conversion in the conventional sense, i.e. choosing a new faith or way of life and then converting to it. Indeed, although he was ignorant of his religious and cultural heritage, his social roots and origins were inextricably Muslim. Evidence of this is clearly illustrated in his brother's biographical account of him, particularly when describing their earlier visits to Morocco. Therefore, his cognitive opening and subsequent practice of Islam could arguably be considered a reversion to his long-lost or absent faith. A reconnection with the religion occurred as he searched for a suitable identity that could transcend the racial constraints he had experienced at the hands of the indigenous French, alongside the cultural and religious isolation he felt from the Moroccan culture. In fact, when examining some converts' perception of reversion, Zebiri observes that:

> Those who prefer the term 'revert' feel it conveys the sense of returning to something which is innate, and also reflects the belief that all people are born in a state of natural goodness... This ties into the notion... of Islam as the 'natural' religion... which accords with human nature.
>
> (2008: 15)

Her subsequent observation vividly encapsulates Zacarias's circumstances, 'Many converts to Islam express the sense that prior to their formal conversion they had already, perhaps always, been a Muslim without realizing it' (2008: 15).

Abd Samad observed the negative influence of the foreign students upon Zacarias to the extent that the latter's rhetoric and style of argumentation was synonymous with the cynism and general negativity echoed by those espousing views of the Muslim Brotherhood and, more specifically, Syed Qutb. Zacarias became intent on leaving France and expressed his desire to travel to the UK in order to improve his English language proficiency and possibly increase the opportunities of employment when he returned to France. In 1991 he achieved his objective after saving accrued earnings and selling his car (Moussaoui, 2002: 84–7).

'Londonistan'

When he arrived in the UK, Zacarias was a stranger; he did not know anyone. He immediately sought refuge in St Marks, a centre for the homeless in London. He found the experience at St Marks intimidating in view of some of the unsavoury characters he was forced to interact with by virtue of the fact that they all frequented the centre. These included alcoholics and drug users whom Zacarias had never before engaged with or encountered in such close proximity (Moussaoui, 2002). His inability to communicate effectively in English during the first six-month sojourn in London left him almost in a state of paralysis, thereby heightening his sense of vulnerability. That said, Abd Samad recalls the positive change he witnessed in his brother upon his initial return to France. Although Zacarias had lost weight, his sense of pride in surviving for six months indicated he had matured somewhat. There was no obvious indication of extremist tendencies or rhetoric and it appeared that he was committed to progress academically. His commitment and perseverance was rewarded with his successfully embarking on a Master of International Business degree in London's South Bank University. This university is a short distance from Brixton Mosque, which Zacarias frequented for social and religious interaction. As intimated earlier, the author often interacted with Zacarias at both the university and the mosque as he was also studying for a Master of Business Administration (in Education) degree in the same department. Additionally, his position as chairman at the time meant that discussions would ensue regarding mosque and community affairs, etc. Interviews, subsequent to Zacarias's trial in the US, highlight the extent of interaction between the author and Zacarias. Ms Anne Chapman, the Assistant Federal Public Defender for Zacarias's defence, visited the author at Brixton Mosque on 11 October 2005 after requesting that he act as a defence witness in an attempt to avert the death penalty for Zacarias. The author agreed and was subsequently interviewed. In the transcript of the interview, Zacarias was described as being, 'affable [in] demeanour...he would come and ask me questions, we'd have dialogue. We were studying together, not in the same class, but in the same university'.[38]

Interestingly, Abd Samad observed Zacarias's hardening attitude once he began to return to France more frequently. Apparently, he found Britain harsher than France and, although ethnic communities were 'tolerated', he observed that they seldom interacted with each other. In 1993 and 1994 his visits to France increased in regularity, i.e. every four months, in order to see his long-term girlfriend, Fanny. After one of these regular visits and subsequent returns to London, Zacarias approached the author animatedly indicating that he wanted to share an encounter he had experienced at the Dover border upon his return. In response to an interview question from Anne Chapman concerning any notable occasions where Zacarias became excitable about the mosque, the author's response was as follows:

> There was an occasion...when he came from France and he came directly to me at the mosque. He told me, 'I'm coming to you,' and he's really excited...I'm thinking, 'what is it about?' And when

he told me it was a cause for alarm for me, but a cause of excitement for him. [He said] 'We were stopped as we were coming across the Channel Tunnel ... We were stopped by the authorities. We were questioned for ages and they were asking us, "Are you going to Brixton Mosque?" ' So he saw I was very concerned about that. But this was a point of excitement, belonging to a place that the authorities were very concerned about ... I felt he was excited to be a part of something which would buck the trend, [that] which was a cause of concern for the authorities.[39]

On his penultimate visit to France in 1993, he visited his sister, Jamila, in Montpellier. He also visited his girlfriend, Fanny, and tried to convince her to relocate to London and live with him. She apparently refused and this was, according to his brother, a source of consternation for him. He subsequently terminated the relationship shortly after that visit. The last time Zacarias returned to France to visit his family was in 1995. Unfortunately, the next time he was seen by them was shortly after the attacks of 11 September 2001, when his picture was broadcast with news that he was implicated in those attacks. Zacarias's pattern of behaviour was consistent in that the confrontational and argumentative tendencies he had displayed when visiting the local Narbonne Mosque were also to be witnessed in Brixton Mosque. Also, the complete severance of ties with his family (whom he had, by that time, labelled as being infidels) was about to be repeated by him distancing himself from the mosque and its community (Moussaoui, 2002: 93–113). Before examining these observations, a description of the contexts leading up to these occurrences must first be given.

He had settled among the Brixton community, renting accommodation from one of the mosque elders, Shaykh Abu Bakr, and his wife at the time, Christine Abdullah. He regularly attended various religious classes that were delivered at the mosque and participated in festive events like Eid celebrations, etc. He moved out of Shaykh Abu Bakr and his wife's accommodation once he secured social benefits and was able to rent a larger two-bedroom flat in Christchurch Road, Brixton.[40] He established firm friendships with a few members of the local Muslim community and was rarely seen alone. However, it was not very long before his attitude and approach to community members, and the mosque management in particular, began to change. Abdullah el-Faisal, who had once been an imam at Brixton Mosque, was expelled before the author's appointment as chairman in 1994. His subsequent activities proved to be antagonistic and confrontational to the mosque. He established a study circle at one of the local sports facilities, the Ferndale Centre, and began advertising in the immediate vicinity of the mosque. An increasing number of his followers, many of whom were unaware and/or ignorant of the nature of his extremist propaganda, began to attend these circles, often inviting their colleagues after congregational prayers at the mosque:

> They would invite them [unsuspecting individuals] to the 'real understanding' of Islam and one of the first things they would do categorically is to denounce the Brixton Mosque because of the fact that we're convert Muslims, that we rely on scholars to interpret aspects of Islam for us to live in the society... Because they [extremist protagonists] knew Arabic... they would emphasise this point to highlight that they actually know the religion better than ourselves... that would cause confusion in the individual's mind.[41]

Zacarias was one such individual that was lured towards Abdullah el-Faisal's classes. He would return to the mosque to argue and debate with the author and anyone who opposed his understanding of Islam, Jihad in particular:

> I remember when I encountered him [Zacarias] in the canteen and I started having a dialogue with him about where he was going, what he was discussing and, in front of individuals he just became very vociferous started abusing... towards you... very abusive.[42]

His behaviour and approach towards colleagues in the mosque continued to deteriorate to the extent that he would raise his voice to proclaim his understanding of the religion. His brash and dismissive character was often ignored by fellow attendees; however, it became increasingly difficult for the mosque management to ignore such disruptive and potentially divisive behaviour:

> Initially I didn't send him out of the Mosque because I saw that he didn't know how to deal with [what he was learning from the extremists]... He was very keen to implement whatever drive was given to him for Jihad. I remember him asking me... impatiently, 'Where is there Jihad in the world, where? Tell me; show me somewhere where there is Jihad. Talk to me!' and the way he was asking, this would be like lighting... igniting something, if I'd said, 'Oh, yes, we believe in this Jihad over here, and the scholars said that...' It would

have been dangerous for me to make a statement like that at that time…looking at his enthusiasm – misplaced enthusiasm.[43]

Zacarias's path towards violent extremism was propelled by the consistency of the rhetoric he heard from the protagonists. The rhetoric he was hearing in London resonated with the discussions he had listened and participated in Montpellier University. Once again, the extremist propaganda appeared to be the only medium addressing recent and current issues affecting the Muslim world, highlighting:

> the weakness of the Muslim nation, the atrocities that were being committed – Bosnia had just finished at the time – the ineptness of the Muslims, the fact that no one was talking or calling for Jihad…[saying] 'Look at the rulers of these countries. Are they saying anything? The Muslims don't seem to be doing anything…This shows the Muslims are weak. They love America. They love the West. These are their sins. We need soldiers to go out and fight. You are those soldiers'.[44]

Up until this point, the author and Zacarias were still studying at university, however, conversations between the two had become almost non-existent. Zacarias, despite his abrasive attitude, had started to withdraw from his colleagues and engage less frequently than before. The frequency of his attendances at the mosque reduced, probably due to his affiliation with other venues as well as his preparation for his final dissertation. As was mentioned above, he approached the author, despite the deterioration in the relationship, to request assistance in completing his dissertation. This request was declined because of what was now apparent from his religious inclinations and change in character.[45]

Xavier (Yusuf)

Zacarias began to attend the mosque with another colleague and friend from France, Xavier. His parents were originally from Benin, Africa. He was, as Abd Samad accurately described him, 'physically striking'. He was a tall, attractive and friendly individual who was always seen to be smiling. In fact, he was considered by some members of the Brixton Mosque community to be a calming influence on Zacarias – where Zacarias was inflammatory, Xavier was conciliatory. Xavier and Zacarias met through Abd Samad. Zacarias had embarked on his Masters programme in South Bank and on some of his final visits to France had explained how relatively easy it was to embark on his academic course. This interested Xavier at the time and he arranged to travel to London and visit Zacarias. This occurred in 1993 and both he and Zacarias returned briefly to France following his successful entrance examination for the same course as his friend. According to Abd Samad's account, Xavier informed him of his conversion to Islam in January 1995. At this point Abd Samad's account of his final encounter with Xavier is conflicting. He states, on the one hand, that this occurred in January 1995 but on the following page he recounts seeing Xavier for the last time in the summer of 1996 (Moussaoui, 2002: 123–26). On the latter occasion he describes Xavier's religious fervour as similar to Zacarias's after the latter's experience with the foreign students in Montpellier years earlier. In any case, these conflicting accounts do nothing to detract from the facts surrounding Zacarias's path towards violent extremism. Where it was hoped that Xavier might have a calming influence on Zacarias, the opposite was unfortunately true. He became an ardent follower and 'comrade' of Zacarias; the two were almost inseperable, with Xavier being heavily influenced by his more religiously senior peer. Ensuing discussions in the mosque between Zacarias, the author and members of the management were witnessed in silence by Xavier. Where he was once jovial and amicable, he was now silent and solemn. His final visit to Brixton Mosque saw him accompany Zacarias entering the premises wearing army camouflage uniform and military style boots. They also carried rucksacks.[46] When they were confronted by the author, Xavier remained silent whereas Zacarias responded in his usual vociferous manner. On this occasion Zacarias was expelled from the mosque. Interestingly, he did not appear concerned in the slightest. With hindsight this may have been for one of two possible reasons: i) he had already established links with the extremist community with whom he was now affiliated, and/or ii) he had other imminent plans which would involve his absence in any case. Unfortunately, no definitive answers can be obtained; however, having said this, the conviction following his trial for conspiracy in the 9/11 attacks should suffice as a clear indication of his intent to participate in acts of terrorism in order to further his violent extremist beliefs. In any event, the reason for not expelling Xavier also was due to the simple fact that he had never contributed to the challenges and furore that Zacarias caused. In addition to this, it was expected that he would not remain among the mosque community after Zacarias's expulsion. Abd Samad vividly recalls the next time he became aware of Xavier and his plight:

One day in the year 2000 I was summoned by the Montpellier police. A policeman ushered me into an office and asked me to sit down. With no further ado, and in complete silence, they showed me a colour photocopy of a page from a website. On that page, there was an article about the war in Chechnya with three colour photos: three of Xavier. In the first photo, taken outdoors he was standing behind two other soldiers, wearing a military uniform and dark cap pulled down around his ears. He was smiling at the camera with the forefinger of his right hand raised. The second photo showed him sideways on, again in military uniform. He had a thin moustache and a long beard. His head was shaved. He wasn't smiling anymore but had his chin in his hand, apparently deep in thought. In the last photo, he was lying down alongside other men, with a blanket pulled up over him. His right leg was covered in blood. His eyes were closed. He looked as if he was asleep, not in pain. The photo had a caption, and the words leaped out at me, searing my eyes: 'Massoud Al-Benin, born in France, lived in London, died in Chechnya'.

(Moussaoui, 2002: 128)

Xavier died on 12 April 2000. The author saw the same pictures on the actual website which has since been banned.[47] At this juncture, a very important distinction needs to be made so far as it relates to Xavier and Zacarias. Participation in the conflicts in Chechnya were considered by the majority of Muslims, scholars and laymen alike, to have been a legitimate fight and therefore, by extension, a justifiable defensive Jihad against the Russian forces at the time. Therefore, Xavier's involvement and subsequent death does not equate to violent extremism or terrorism; on the contrary, he can legitimately be considered a mujahid or freedom fighter in this instance. Doctors J. and B. Cole's observations in this regard go some way to support the author's above assertion:

Not all of those who fight in jihad overseas return to commit acts of terrorist violence in the UK; therefore fighting jihad overseas is not an automatic indicator that an individual believes in the global jihad, or that he has been radicalised to commit acts of terrorist violence.

(Cole and Cole, 2004: 137)

Zacarias's intended actions on 9/11, on the other hand, did not, in any way, constitute any legislated act in Islam nor were there any authentically reported precedents upon which to plan such acts. His beliefs and subsequent intentions fell unequivocally under the current definition of violent extremism and terrorism. He was not seen again at Brixton Mosque; however, attendees occasionally saw him within the local vicinity. He had apparently altered his appearance, reverting to his initial style of casual, civilian dress. He had also removed his beard giving the impression that he was no longer practising his faith as fervently as before:

> After he'd left the mosque . . . he was seen locally. The beard had gone. He was back in casual clothing and we've seen that happen with some individuals in the past where they've had this fervency for their religion and they become devout and everything like that. And then you don't see them for a while and then they're suddenly not practising the religion anymore . . . I thought, 'OK, he [Zacarias] went too far into the extreme and now he's gone back in the opposite direction'.[48]

However, this apparent 'dumbing down' or backtracking in religious commitment and practice is an established decoy deployed in order to detract attention from the individual/s:

> I was surprised as . . . the last picture [impression] I had is that he'd come away from that [extremism] . . . Was that the case or was he just assuming a lower profile, which is one of the things that they're encouraged to do by their mentors, which is to remove the beard, dress in civilian clothing, don't let your identity be that obvious to the people. That's one of the extremist teachings as well.[49]

Prior to Xavier's death and before his expulsion from Brixton Mosque, Zacarias had displayed behavioural traits considered to be excessive according to the lexicographical and religious definitions of al-Ghulu (see above). These traits, in isolation, cannot render an individual a violent extremist unless of course psychological and emotional factors also exist.

Following confirmation of Xavier's death, Zacarias's whereabouts was unknown (Moussaoui, 2002: 129). He was no longer in contact with his brother and had not been seen in or around Brixton for some time. Media reports suggest that he had, by 2000, become involved with the European wing of Al Qaeda and that meetings took place between him and key members of this terrorist cell.[50] According to the same reports, immigration stamps in Zacarias's passport revealed that he travelled on 9 December 2000 from London to Karachi, Pakistan, after a meeting he purportedly had with Ramzi Binalshibh, a leading figure in Al Qaeda's

European network. He returned to London on 7 February 2001 according to receipts submitted as evidence in his trial. He then travelled again on 23 February after purchasing return flights to Oklahoma City via Chicago. Upon arrival in Oklahoma, he embarked upon flight training at the Airman Flight School in Norman but transferred to the Pan Am International Flight Academy in Eagan, Minnesota. It was at this school that he came under suspicion for his unusual interest in Boeing 747 systems and his expressed desire to fly a simulated flight from Heathrow airport to John F. Kennedy airport in New York. Flight instructors alerted the authorities over their concerns in this regard which resulted in Zacarias's arrest on 16 August 2001. His subsequent detention was, in fact, due to immigration charges as a result of visa violations.[51]

United States v. Zacarias Moussaoui: A synopsis

The following charges were brought against Zacarias:

- Count one – Conspiracy to Commit Acts of Terrorism Transcending National Boundaries
- Count two – Conspiracy to Commit Aircraft Piracy
- Count three – Conspiracy to Destroy Aircraft
- Count four – Conspiracy to Use Weapons of Mass Destruction
- Count five – Conspiracy to Murder United States Employees
- Count six – Conspiracy to Destroy Property of the United States.[52]

The trial commenced with opening statements on 6 March 2006[53] and concluded with his sentencing in May of the same year.[54] While it is beyond the remit of this research to examine this case in more detail, reference should be made to additional third party evidence in order to shed light on the extent of Zacarias's commitment to participate in what he understood to be Jihad. Sections of Khalid Shaykh Mohammed's purported testimony concerning the level of Zacarias's involvement is revealing inasmuch as it highlights the latter's problematic behaviour and the difficulties experienced even by senior Al Qaeda operatives. Khalid Shaykh Mohammed was, according to US intelligence, a 'high-ranking' member of Al Qaeda who was allegedly the mastermind behind the 11 September attacks.[55] He had been interrogated since his capture and arrest in March 2003 and numerous written summaries had been transcribed from his oral statements.[56] It is pertinent to note that, for reasons of national security, Khalid Shaykh never attended Zacarias's trial in person, nor was access granted to prosecution and defence lawyers to question him. However, the author asserts that evidence provided by him must, to a degree, now be considered with great prudence in view of recent revelations of US torture of suspected terrorists.[57] In fact, despite the official nature of Khalid Shaykh's testimony, the opening statements are sufficient to cause concern for any discerning eye, especially after the above mentioned discoveries and revelations:

> You should assume that if Shaykh Mohammed were available to testify in this courtroom under oath and subject to perjury he would have said what is contained in these statements.
>
> Although you do not have the ability to see the witness's demeanor as he testifies, you must approach these statements with the understanding that they were made under circumstances designed to elicit truthful statements from the witness.[58]

Khalid Shaykh Mohammed described Zacarias's position and intended role among his Al Qaeda cohorts. He stated that Zacarias was part of a subsequent cell that was preparing a second wave of attacks to succeed the 9/11 attempts. It was not part of the plan for Zacarias to get arrested and he was meant to remain anonymous up until further directives were given to initiate the second wave of attacks. His subsequent arrest was in fact symptomatic of the problems Khalid Shaykh experienced when attempting to direct Zacarias. Khalid Shaykh cited many examples of the difficulties experienced with Zacarias; from his self-confident and thus careless attitude regarding security matters, to his disobeying direct 'commands' and acting independently, in spite of the need to behave with a methodological, coordinative approach.[59] Khalid Shaykh even approached Osama Bin Laden and Mohammed Atif (another senior Al Qaeda operative), requesting that Zacarias be 'removed from the program'; however, the two insisted that he remain part of the team. Zacarias was eventually referred to the European Al Qaeda counterpart, Ramzi Bin al-Shibh. Zacarias's 'high level of self-confidence' and his difficulty with 'taking instructions' were significant causes of concern for Khalid Shaykh. In fact, these observations are indicative of earlier displays of stubbornness from Zacarias during his formative years in France. Suffice it to cite Abd Samad Moussaoui's observation of Zacarias during his youth, to illustrate the latter's character in this regard, 'With my brother, it's always all or nothing. When he believes in something, he does everything in his powers to reach his goal' (Moussaoui, 2002: 28).

Khalid Shaykh's observations further highlighted Zacarias's haughty and often arrogant manner of confrontation that mosques, like Brixton, became accustomed to before his expulsion. Zacarias was sentenced to life imprisonment without the possibility of release on 4 May 2006.[60] During the course of the trial possible symptoms of his deteriorating mental condition were, arguably, vividly portrayed. Examples of this could be seen in the sudden reversal of his decision to change his not guilty plea to guilty, only to request, shortly thereafter, that he revert to his original submission. He went so far as to request that his defence team no longer represent him because of his self-belief and confidence in defending himself. He went even further by offering to assist the prosecution with the case against him. He thus signed a written confession to the effect that he was supposed to be the twentieth hijacker. When asked why he had penned such a confession after denying throughout the trial that he had any knowledge of the 9/11 conspiracy, he is alleged to have retorted, 'I did it [wrote the confession] because everyone used to call me that so it was a bit of fun', (O'Neill and McGrory, 2006: 22). Expert testimonies attesting to Zacarias's poor medical condition were presented by respected doctors in the field of pyschology. Doctors Xavier Amador, PhD and Michael B. First, MD, Nancy C. Andreasen, MD, PhD and Paul Martin, PhD testified to Zacarias possessing a major thought disorder, 'most likely paranoid schizophrenia'.[61] His persistent untimely outbursts, challenges to the court and 'hate-filled' insults to family members of some of the 9/11 victims could be considered contributory factors leading one to the conclusion that he required medical attention. A question that could perhaps be posed, albeit belatedly, is whether psychological treatment should have been sought much earlier in Zacarias's youth. The author asserts that it would have proved difficult to ascertain whether such attention was required, particularly after he had arrived in Britain as there was no familial contact or reference point from where a profile or indeed, understanding of his background or socio-religious/ economic status, could be obtained. His sister, Jamila had developed psychological problems by the time Zacarias left France and had been the subject of various court and social welfare interventions.[62] Her medical records, alongside evidence regarding Omar Moussaoui's psychiatric condition, were submitted as part of the defence.[63] The defence team had clearly drawn parallels between Zacarias's father's and sister's psychological conditions and his own, suggesting that a hereditary mental illness existed. Indeed, arguments and evidence submitted in support of this summation were rejected by the jury. Additionally, in view of the lack of evidence to support his assertions that he, alongside fellow Briton, Richard Reid (aka the 'Shoe Bomber'), were supposed to be part of a group that was to hijack a fifth aircraft, the jury voted against the death penalty (O'Neill and

McGrory, 2006: 223). Other reasons for the jury's decision to avert the death penalty are discussed above in the introduction of this case study.

The author was in fact the main defence witness for Zacarias Moussaoui from the UK.[64] The rationale behind the character reference that was given in support of Zacarias's defence was to avert the death penalty on the premise that such a sentence would, by default, provide him with the objective of 'martyrdom' he was seeking. It would also elevate his status among other Muslims, sympathetic to, or worse, supportive of his extremist ideology and practices. This view was articulated in interviews following his sentencing:

> *Nasrean Suleaman*: It has emerged in the court case that Zacarias Moussaoui had offered to help the prosecution in the case against him. Abdul Haqq Baker believes that he has deliberately been trying to sabotage his lawyers' efforts to stop him getting the death penalty.

> *Abdul Haqq Baker*: It is my personal belief the reason he is doing this is because he wants that martyr status. If he receives the death sentence he believes that in the eyes of the Muslim community he will be seen as a martyr. If that is discredited in any way by questioning his sanity then he will just be locked up in prison for a very long time and that will not give him any credibility at all.[65]

Contextualising Zacarias Moussaoui's path to violent extremism within existing and new theoretical frameworks

It is necessary to try to describe the stages of Zacarias's path of reversion within theoretical parameters. This will enable a better understanding of the possible processes of radicalisation followed by violent extremist thought and/or action. The author, as Participant Observer of significant aspects of Zacarias's path towards violent extremism, is arguably better placed from an insider perspective than second- or third-hand outsider research perceptions. With this in mind, the frameworks shown in Figure 1.1 are revisited (see p. 9).

Zacarias's early, formative years were spent in relative ignorance of Islam, however, his social interaction still included many people from North African/Arab and, therefore, predominantly Muslim communities (Moussaoui, 2002: 9, 23, 44–5, 57–69). His initial exposure to Islam and interaction were, by and large, among cultural Muslim communities in France. This particular period of his life thus accorded to the 'outer circle' depicting the Muslim community in Figure 1.1. Table 1.1 (see p. 16) is also another framework that possibly supports the above observation, particularly when considering the liberal and social dimensions of his upbringing during that period. The 'liberal extreme' end of the spectrum therefore most closely depicts aspects of his environment at that time:

His subsequent interaction with foreign Muslim student groups later, when he resided in Montpellier and frequented the halls of residence at the local university, can be considered a phase of Islamisation because of the political and often 'revolutionary' nature of the discussions that ensued. Abd Samad categorised his brother's company as being from the Muslim Brotherhood (Ikhwan al Muslimeen) persuasion which in effect denoted their Islamist orientation. It is important to look back at Figure 1.2 (see p. 12) at this stage in order to chart Zacarias's cognitive development of Islam and his resultant behaviour. In the context of Moussaoui's case study, the term 'convert' can be replaced by the more precise description, 'revert'. Abd Samad indicated that Zacarias's interest in Islam began after his engagement with the foreign students in Montpellier University. He went so far as to assert that Zacarias's extreme understanding of the religion emanated from here (Moussaoui, 2002: 82–5). The author suggests that the above-mentioned Islamisation process at the hands of Islamist students commenced at the 'Founding'/cognitive phase of Zacarias's religious development.

The author further suggests that this 'Founding'/cognitive phase continued and indeed developed more emphatically after he travelled to London and interacted with the diaspora of North African and convert Muslims in Brixton. At this stage he was engaging with the penultimate inner circle depicted in Figure 1.1, namely, the Salafi community. When placing this in the context of Figure 1.2 and Table 1.1, he had gravitated across to the 'Youthful Phase' and 'Moderate perspective' of both models, respectively. Abd Samad's biographical account of the changes to Zacarias upon his regular returns to France once living in Britain reflects the initial period of the founding and youthful (formative) phases. The author concurs with Abd Samad's observations as he was present in many of the foundational classes that were held at Brixton Mosque during that period. Unfortunately, Zacarias was increasingly influenced by extremist propaganda that was being circulated around Brixton and more widely in London at that time. He still had not grasped the basic foundational and essential aspects of Tawheed, etc., and his modicum of religious knowledge and, more specifically, Salafism, placed him in a precarious position making him susceptible to extremist propaganda. This observation correlates with the nature of Muhammad Sadiq Khan's gravitation towards the 'Jihadi' constituency, discussed in Chapter 1. Unlike Khan's family, who considered his increased religiosity a positive development (Malik, 2007: 41), Abd Samad became concerned about the polemical narrative he and others often heard from Zacarias during his frequent return visits to France. It is important to note an emerging pattern that is perhaps encapsulated in Figure 1.1; namely, the 'inward' migration of British Muslims across these constituencies as their religious awareness, identity and pursuit of knowledge develops. The wider, more generic constituency (Muslims), comprised of liberal, traditional and cultural practices, is rejected for a more politicised and knowledge-filled understanding of Islam within a context that addresses current world events (Islamists). Subsequent dissatisfaction with the degree of focus upon politics, in comparison with the neglect of acquiring authentic religiously attuned knowledge, drives the individual towards the 'Salafi' constituency which satisfies the desire for such understanding. However, because of the apolitical nature of this particular constituency (i.e. the 'Salafis'), the individual recognises a void or inability to satisfactorily address the political issues considered to affect the Muslim world. The ensuing frustration causes the individual to try to reconcile religious and political concerns. However, without an identifiable context, s/he becomes susceptible to extremist propaganda which apparently addresses and provides the milieu for the political bias of the 'Islamists' constituency on the one hand and the religiously attuned knowledge of the 'Salafi' constituency on the other. At that stage, the individual's subsequent and possibly final migration to the 'Jihadi' constituency occurs. When considering the above, and the theoretical frameworks proposed, it would seem understable that Zacarias (and indeed others) could gravitate across these constituencies to the ultimate circle of the 'Jihadis' or, more accurately, takfeeri extremists.

This gravitation can be further illustrated within a wider societal context when considering the cross-section of the funnel model shown in Figure 1.7 (see p. 19). Zacarias Moussaoui gravitated toward the 'vacuum' where extremist propaganda proliferated and effectively fell below the radar. He also progressed across the continuum depicted in Table 1.1 from the 'Moderate perspective' to the 'Fanatical/Violent extreme.' The final 'barrier' between the wider, more generic understandings of mainstream Islam and the extremist is, according to this model, the Salafist community. Figure 1.6 (see p. 19) also perhaps illustrates this observation, but within a more restricted context of the Muslim community. The author asserts, in light of the above, that Moussaoui did not progress to the 'adult', foundational phase of 'reversion' (Figure 1.2) as he became distracted by extremist rhetoric at the most susceptible stage of his religious development – the 'youthful', idealistic stage. All the ingredients to launch his now extremist beliefs into action were in place. His socio-economic background, alongside the domestic circumstances experienced at home in France, and his awareness of the plight of Muslims in specific areas of the world, was now underpinned by an extremist ideology that provided a divine remedy. The final framework, which highlights the specific catalysts or drivers that led him to participate in terrorist conspiracies against the West, are shown in Figure 1.5 (see p. 17). The 'atrocity' in the case of Moussaoui was in fact an accumulation of atrocities against the Muslim world, with the actual catalyst and precursor to his thwarted terroristic attempts being the death of his friend and ally, Xavier. Following Xavier's death, the author asserts that Zacarias became even further motivated to seek what was, in his opinion, a fate similar to that of his friend. In this regard, the author was asked during a radio interview examining Zacarias's US trial, what constituted the 'tipping point' or final catalyst that caused him to attempt to get involved in the 9/11 attacks. The author provided the following reply, 'One of his friends Yusuf [Xavier] had died in Chechnya and...he was seeking a similar fate...and this was the opportunity that he could see such fate'.[66] Also, earlier in the interview, the issue of identity was elucidated upon:

> He [Zacarias] wanted a sense of belonging and there was a sense of frustration at the atrocities being committed in the Muslim world...He wanted to do something. He was actively seeking arenas for Jihad...so he was actively seeking what he could deem a battlefield.[67]

Further interviews confirmed Zacarias's search for identity, 'He wanted to revive his roots which were in Islam. He wanted to be a good Muslim, a knowledgeable Muslim, who wanted to know how to implement the tenets of Islam and make sense of the society he was living in.[68]

Subsequent case studies will examine the applicability of the same theoretical frameworks to determine whether they are accurate models around which to contextualise and map the subjects' of the studies religious influences, development and, in some instances, paths towards violent extremism.

Case study 2: Richard Reid (aka Abdur Rahim)

On 22 December 2001 Richard Colvin Reid boarded American Airlines transatlantic flight 63 at Charles De Gaulle Airport in Paris and during the flight en route to Miami, Florida attempted to detonate an explosive device concealed in his footwear. His attempted act of terrorism was quickly thwarted by members of the flight crew and passengers and he was forcibly restrained until the flight was diverted and landed safely in Logan International Airport in Boston (Elliott, 2002).

Upbringing, social background and identity – the formative years

Richard Reid was born on 12 August 1973 in Farnborough Hospital, Farnborough, Kent UK. His mother, Lesley Hughes and father, Robin, met and married in Poplar, east London in 1972 (Alleyne, 2002). Apparently, their different socio-economic backgrounds (Robin is mixed raced of Jamaican extraction and was a railway worker while Lesley is white and the daughter of an accountant and magistrate from north-east England) caused tensions in their marriage (Seaton, 2002). This coupled with the fact that Robin was in jail for burglary when Richard was born led to the couple separating in 1977 when Richard was four years old (Nzerem, 2002). Divorce proceedings were not finalised until 1984 when Richard was eleven. Up until that time, both parents had agreed to reside in close proximity to each other for their son's benefit (Seaton, 2002). Details about Richard Reid's childhood remain vague; however, a fairly accurate impression about his character can be garnered from a few friends and associates who knew him during his adolescence. During this stage of his life, he left his mother's home and moved in with his aunt, Claudette Law. Richard's independence as a young teenager developed primarily as a result of a lack of parental guidance from both parents. Robin, on his own admission, offered little or no parental guidance due to his own circumstances, 'My son didn't see his dad a lot of years because his dad was in prison a lot of the time' (Seaton, 2002). His mother, Lesley, had entered a new relationship shortly after separating from Robin, leaving little or no capacity to deal with her son (Nzerem, 2002). Richard could not relate to his mother's new partner and this exacerbated existing issues surrounding identity, 'He was trying to sort out where he was from, his roots. He wanted to find an identity – but he's got two white parents' (Nzerem, 2002: 1). This particular observation of Richard's early childhood from one of his teenage friends was to cause further conflict in his teenage years up until converting to Islam.

Education

Little information exists regarding Richard's primary or secondary education. Media sources citing secondary sources are all that are available so far as his secondary school education is concerned. He attended Thomas Tallis Secondary School in Blackheath, south-east London which, in 1989, was a predominantly white populated school. According to one of his school colleagues, Richard felt uncomfortable in this type of environment and identified more with the few African–Caribbean youth. Unfortunately, this affinity was not reciprocated by his peers and he was apparently confined to perfunctory acknowledgement. He was always witnessed walking behind his colleagues, 'bringing up the rear' (Nzerem, 2002).

Thomas Tallis Secondary School was considered a good school during the period in which Richard attended. The most recent OFSTED report in June 2007 described it as 'a good school with a number of outstanding features'.[69] Despite its reputation for providing strong, quality education, Richard failed to thrive and owing to his disinterest in academic work he was ordered to report regularly to one of the school senior teachers Ms Jane Green. She recalled him being a disorganised pupil, without so much as the basic utensils for studying, e.g., pens, pencils, books, etc. He merely attended as a 'passenger' according to her. Richard's attention became increasingly directed towards activities divorced from school and study. His chosen hobby as a graffiti artist quickly gained momentum and he began 'tagging' public transport and property. Once he had left school at the age of 16 without any qualifications, his mother relocated to the West Country leaving him isolated and without accommodation in London. He was no longer residing with his aunt Claudette and ended up living in a homeless person's hostel in Lewisham Way. In straitened financial circumstances, Richard became vulnerable to a few local gangs that compelled him, sometimes at knife-point, to commit robberies. Such acts were initially contrary to his character as in school he was considered polite and was never rude, disruptive or aggressive. However, in an effort to gain credibility and fit in he often adopted the bravado of his peers (Nzerem, 2002). It is notable that this earlier observation of Richard's character during his teenage years accord with that of the author's when describing him following the terrorist attempts of December 2001 as 'easy going, gullible' (McBeth, 2001: 2). In other reports he was also described as being 'a likeable character, amiable, affable [and] very impressionable' (Gardiner, 2001: 1). In fact, further evidence of his gullibility and search for belonging can be witnessed when comparing aspects of his adolescence with later behaviour that culminated in the above-mentioned attempted terrorist attack. Keme Nzerem, whose article is largely referenced in this particular case study, was an associate of Richard's during secondary school. He describes a particular occasion when one of his friends was robbed on a train by Richard when the latter was 17 years old:

> He [Richard] was as terrified of the ringleader of his gang as my friends were – he turned and mouthed 'sorry' as they fled up the platform. I imagined a gullible young man, confused, desperate to belong, and out of control.
>
> (Nzerem, 2002)

In subsequent media interviews following his arrest, the author asserted that:

> He was one easily led – the way the whole thing was bungled is because of his naivety... The way he tried to commit this act shows his gullibility. He was sent as a tester though he was not to know that... he was not acting alone.
>
> (Gardiner, 2001: 2)

Robin Reid also emphasised that the manner in which his son bungled the attempt to blow up the aircraft was, 'a shout for help... All he had to do was go to the toilet, sit there and then boom! Why do it in front of passengers if it's not a cry for help?' (Nzerem, 2002: 4).

Evidence that corroborated the author's observation that Richard did not act alone later emerged with the arrest and conviction of Saajid Badat, another British national.[70] Badat confessed to conspiring with Richard and others to commit acts of terrorism on transatlantic US airliners (Cole and Cole, 2009: 1–2). Tellingly, Badat told police after his arrest that he 'wanted to "get away from danger and introduce some calm into his life"' (Cole and Cole, 2009: 3, citing Jacobsen, 2008). The probable fear and compulsion that Richard experienced prior to his attempted attack is likely to be similar to that articulated by Badat. It is also a fear that he would have been familiar with from his adolescent years, albeit to a greater extent. Unlike Badat, Richard proceeded a degree too far. Unlike Badat, he did not have a home to return to.

Richard succumbed to a life of petty crime which resulted in imprisonment on several occasions. He was jailed for the first time in 1990, aged 17, for robbing an elderly person (Elliott, 2002: 2). Other reports suggest he was first convicted at the age of 14, (Alleyne, 2002). He next met his father approximately eight years later in a shopping mall. During discussion Richard highlighted his grievances regarding the racism and difficulties he was experiencing. He was, according to his father's account, depressed and low in morale (Elliott, 2002: 2). Robin's fatherly advice was that Richard should convert to Islam because of the humane treatment he would receive the next time he was incarcerated. He would also receive decent food owing to his religious identity. A few media reports cite Robin Reid as stating that he converted to Islam for similar reasons while in prison, hence his offering advice along similar lines to his son (Seaton, 2002). Robin spent a total of 18 years of his life in prison (Alleyne, 2002). Richard's arrest in 1992 resulted in his being convicted for four robberies. He confessed to a further 24 robberies, 22 thefts and one attempted theft. Unsurprisingly, he was sentenced to five years imprisonment in Feltham Young Offenders' Institution, during which particular period of imprisonment Richard developed an interest in Islam. Neil Smith was an inmate during Richard's incarceration and he recalls the inquisitiveness and changes witnessed in his colleague at the time:

> He never touched drugs and gave up smoking . . . he began to corral his intelligence and challenge the world around him . . . He wanted to know why governments do the things they do. We talked about the Iran-Iraq war.
>
> (Nzerem, 2002: 2–3)

He also sought answers from Muslim inmates regarding causes behind some of the conflicts in predominantly Muslim countries, (O'Neill and McGrory, 2006: 219). While it is almost certain that Richard converted to Islam in prison, no account exists to confirm this. Abdul Ghani Qureshi, one of the imams at Feltham Young Offenders' Institute, only alludes to Richard's conversion when interviewed, referring to 'spiritual and practical escapism' from racism as a reason for an individual's interest in Islam. His childhood friend, Marcus, also alluded to Richard's focus on God once he was in prison. Another account reports the imam as suggesting that Richard converted to avoid boredom and racial insults from fellow inmates (O'Neill and McGrory, 2006). Regardless of the reasons, Richard's commitment to become a practising Muslim occurred during his imprisonment in Feltham and was to develop further upon his release in 1996.

A new beginning: the quest for knowledge

On his release from Feltham, Richard travelled directly to London. His destination was Brixton Mosque. The fact that he met the author (who was chairman at the time) with a bin liner of personal effects, i.e.

clothing, etc. explaining that he had just been released from prison, supports the above-mentioned observation that the mosque was his first destination (Oldham, 2003). Up until the mid-1990s, Brixton Mosque had an informal policy of permitting Muslim men who had recently arrived in London from various localities, e.g., North Africa, France, Bosnia, etc. to reside overnight in its premises for a few days until they had adapted to their new and often alien environment. This service was also occasionally offered to converts, the management being aware of their vulnerability as new Muslims and the need for them to be among others of the same faith. This was especially the case where family conflicts ensued as a result of their new faith and identity. In any event, some media reports were accurate in their portrayal of Brixton Mosque as 'a place often used as a half way house for Muslims recently out of prison' (Alleyne, 2002). The author does not recall whether Richard actually slept in the mosque after his immediate release from prison but is certain of his remaining behind and engaging in extensive discussions throughout many nights with fellow attendees who did reside overnight. There was nothing unusual about these discussions in the initial stages of Richard's religious development after his release. Indeed, the regularity of his attendances at the almost daily religious programmes in the mosque suggested that he was only reinforcing what he was learning from his interaction with his new colleagues. Before long, Richard was accompanying colleagues to lectures and seminars around London. The author remarked that Richard, 'seemed at ease, relaxed. He was a consistent, committed individual – a nice individual to be around' (Nzerem, 2002: 3). Also, 'He was exuberant in his pursuit of knowledge' (Nzerem, 2002).

His enthusiasm and commitment to learning the Qur'an and Arabic were especially noted as he was witnessed, almost on a daily basis, sitting quietly in the mosque after congregational prayer, reading the Qur'an or consulting fellow attendees to ensure his pronunciation and understanding of particular verses or Arabic was correct. As Nzerem observed, 'Salafi Islam provided Richard with the guidance he had never had' (Nzerem, 2002). When he was not preoccupied with learning or revision, he proffered help wherever it was required. The author recalls requesting members of the community to volunteer to clean the mosque and remove old furniture. Richard was among the first to offer his services as a volunteer. Despite his apparent engrossment with attending classes at Brixton Mosque, Richard travelled around London and other parts of the UK for additional lectures, seminars and conferences. In fact, he initially travelled with Brixton Mosque members to Salafi-orientated events. Noticeable changes were only observed after he began attending extemporaneous study circles hosted by protagonists of violent extremism close to the local vicinity of Brixton Mosque (Boulden, 2001). Abdullah el Faisal (the subject of the third case study) was considered a significant influential figure to Richard, especially after the former's final expulsion from the mosque in January 1994. El Faisal had subsequently attracted a small but significant following who found resonance with his beliefs of takfeer. This included his derision of Brixton Mosque and allegations that its management held and supported positions that were tantamount to disbelief. The author illustrated in media interviews following Richard Reid's arrest the manner in which extremist propagandists would attract susceptible newcomers to Islam:

> What they [propagandists] do say is, 'We share the same orthodox belief as those at Brixton Mosque and elsewhere. However, those at Brixton Mosque are somewhat passive with their view [of] Jihad.
>
> They have got the understanding of Jihad wrong. In that area, they would then inculcate them with the more extreme view of Jihad, extreme, erroneous and wrong belief, and because they can see they're impressionable and wanting to be active for Islam, this is how they win them over.'
>
> Eventually, they speak against people like our center, saying 'they are government-funded, they [prop] up some of the regimes in the Middle East and this is what they're here for.' Then they [susceptible Muslims] grow to dislike us [and] our call in the [orthodox way of Islam] more intensively.
>
> They went over just in that particular area, because there's more activeness – jihad training, learning to fire guns, talking about the political situation in the world and how Muslims are being affected by so-called non-Muslim infidels of the West.
>
> (Boulden, 2001)

Unsurprisingly, Richard found it increasingly difficult to discern between the ideology and practice of Salafism and Takfeerism considering them to be one and the same. He did, however, consider the latter to resonate more with his understanding of Islam, particularly Jihad. His reference to Brixton and Finsbury Park mosques as places that shaped and influenced his religious understanding is interesting insofar as he further asserts that neither institution converted him to violent extremism/takfeerism. However, he believes they reinforced his already developing 'jihadi' ideas that were acquired through extensive reading alongside his developing perception of the world (Herbert, 2006). This world view increasingly considered US aggression as one of the countries intent on oppressing Muslims around the world. As will be seen towards the end of this case study, Richard Reid articulated his beliefs and the reasons behind his subsequent actions upon receiving a life sentence in January 2003.[71] In any event, prior to Richard's final departure from Brixton Mosque and gravitation towards extremism, he increasingly engaged in debates, some of which were heated, regarding his newly established beliefs surrounding the permissibility of suicide bombings and the killing of innocent civilians in response to western aggression against Muslims across the world. He firmly believed, according to his understanding, that Islam, more specifically, Jihad encapsulated these acts of terrorism (Boulden, 2001).

Final encounter?

The author can recall the last occasion he encountered Richard in Brixton Mosque. He was wearing a military flak jacket over a long shirt and a pair of casual trousers, (probably jeans). As the author entered the mosque, Richard descended the stairs which were directly opposite the front door. Upon seeing his attire, the author addressed him, expressing concern regarding his misunderstanding of Jihad and the attire he was wearing. It is important to stress that the address was not as explicit as indicated above; however, the import of the sentiment expressed was unequivocal judging by Richard's immediate reaction. He lowered his gaze, avoiding eye contact with the author and his shoulders dropped, possibly in resignation to his preferred path of understanding; however, he was no longer prepared to defend his perspective in Brixton Mosque – especially in front of a member of the management who undoubtedly held views that were contrary to his. Subsequent reports cite him as attending Finsbury Park Mosque which was led at the time by Abu Hamza al Misri (O'Neill and McGrory, 2006: 37–8). This mosque had become renowned for its takfeeri oratory and position during the mid- to late 1990s. He was initially viewed with contempt by other members of the congregation who were staunch supporters of Abu Hamza and was apparently keen to establish and prove himself as a worthy member. He was homeless at the time and was permitted to sleep in the mosque alongside a number of other individuals in circumstances not dissimilar to his own. Djamel Beghal, an Algerian attendee at the mosque, befriended Richard and gained his trust. He recounted many accounts of torture during the civil unrest in his country since 1992 up until 1998 (O'Neill and McGrory, 2006). Unbeknown to Richard was

Djamel's role as an active recruiter for operatives to Al Qaeda's cause. News was received later in 1998 from a few community members in Brixton Mosque that they had received correspondence from Richard who had now travelled to Pakistan in an effort to gain a more comprehensive understanding of the religion. This account accords to reports that he notified his mother of his travel to Pakistan towards the end of 1998 (Oldham, 2003). His friends and mother received occasional letters from him describing his efforts to learn the Qur'an. He made reference to the tranquillity he had now apparently achieved and the fact that he was now more certain about his understanding of Islam. There was no mention of the extremist views he held after departing from the Muslim community in Brixton. In fact, Robin Reid also made reference to two letters he received from Richard both assuring him that his son had now 'settled down' and found 'inner peace' (Nzerem, 2002). Richard's friends from among the Brixton Mosque community were quietly optimistic that his letters were indications of his being able to contextualise significant aspects of his faith, particularly in view of his apparent sojourn in a predominantly Muslim country where he could, on the whole, witness the *actualisation* of the religion. This would hopefully counter the *abstract* approach to learning and practising the religion in a predominantly non-Muslim society. Added to this optimism was the fact that a few other converts from the Brixton Mosque community had also travelled to Pakistan for reasons not dissimilar to Richard's and had returned reinvigorated and more lucid regarding their understanding about Islam.

Correspondence from Richard to his family and friends apparently continued up until summer 2001 when his mother contacted the mosque to see whether he had maintained contact. She informed the author that no correspondence had been received for most of that particular year (Oldham, 2003). After making enquiries among his friends in the community, confirmation was received that they had not received correspondence for some time also. This was conveyed to Richard's mother and it was agreed that the mosque would contact her, and she would reciprocate, if any further news was heard. Unfortunately, the next occasion when both Richard's mother and the Brixton Mosque were to receive news concerning his whereabouts and condition was via the world media following his arrest and detention on 22 December 2001. Details subsequently emerged regarding the extent of his travel.[72] It has already been established that he travelled to Pakistan in late 1998. He apparently remained there for most of 1999 and 2000 but is almost certain to have travelled across the border to neighbouring Afghanistan in late 2000 (Elliott, 2002: 4). This was confirmed in accounts of captured al Qaeda fighters who later identified Richard as a trainee suicide bomber whom they met at a training camp near Kandahar early 2001 (Cole and Cole, 2009: 5). In July 2001, he travelled from Karachi, Pakistan to Amsterdan, the Netherlands where, on the 6 July, he submitted his existing British passport at the British Consulate in exchange for a new one.[73] He then travelled on 12 July via El Al Airlines to Tel Aviv, Israel. After travelling terrestrially in Israel he boarded a bus destined for Cairo, Egypt on 22 July.[74] Another report suggests Richard then flew from Cairo to Pakistan, stopping en route in Turkey (Elliott, 2002: 4). He apparently returned to Afghanistan for a debriefing session before returning to Amsterdam once again on 9 August.

The primary purpose of his travel to Israel was for reconnaissance to determine whether there were suitable sites for terrorist attacks.[75] His debriefing session with an unnamed associate in Afghanistan was to identify Tel Aviv train station as a suitable target for a terrorist attack in view of its accessibility alongside the large number of travellers present, particularly on Saturday evenings. Richard's apparent confession to the above was corroborated by a report found on a computer late 2001.[76] The events of 11 September were to unfold a little over a month after Richard arrived in Amsterdam and there are no reports that refer to any further travel between September and December 2001. It is important at this juncture to note the US and its allied attack on Afghanistan in October, which, according to Richard's confession, formed the basis of his thwarted terrorist attack on 22 December 2001.[77] Referring back to his travel, on 5 December 2001, Richard travelled from Karachi, Pakistan to Brussels, Belgium. Two days later he changed his passport again at the British Consulate. He then travelled on 17 December to Paris, France where he reserved a seat on American Airlines Flight 63 scheduled to fly to Miami, Florida in the US on 21 December. Between the 17 and 21 December, Richard is alleged to have occupied his time frequenting the Goutte d'Or neighbourhood, renowned for Paris's Arab and African population (Elliott, 2002: 5) Despite his attempts to board Flight 63, extra security checks prompted by the suspicions of airport security, caused him to miss it and he had to reschedule his flight for the following day.[78]

'I am at war with your country'

On 22 December 2001, Richard Reid boarded American Airlines Flight 63 destined for Miami, Florida and sat in Seat 29J. By 11.45 a.m. (Paris time) the flight was almost full with 184 passengers and 14 crew.

Richard's actual seat was 29H, along the aisle. The occupant of 29J decided against making an issue about Reid mistakenly occupying his seat and simply sat beside him. Around two-and-a-half to three hours into the flight, which coincidentally rendered the aircraft beyond radio range of any land-based air traffic control, Reid attempted to detonate explosive devices contained in each shoe. A member of the flight crew, Hermis Moutardier, was alerted by the smell of sulphur and, subsequently a lighted match in Reid's hand. In the ensuing struggle which saw staff and passengers forcibly restrain Reid, the impending terrorist threat to destroy Flight 63 was thwarted. The flight was diverted to Logan International Airport in Boston where Reid was met and arrested by the Federal Bureau of Investigation (FBI). Subsequent examination of Reid's shoes revealed sophisticated explosive devices capable of 'breaching' the interior wall and outside 'skin' of an aircraft. The consequences would have been catastrophic for the aircraft and all passengers on board the flight.[79] Prosecution evidence included three emails prepared by Reid one day before his originally planned attack on 21 December 2001. One of the emails was addressed to his mother. It is necessary to reproduce this short but significant email almost in entirety, together with his comments after sentencing, as they reveal the extent of Reid's progression along the violent extremist route and his justification for the above mentioned terrorist attack:

> I have given this letter to a brother to send via the email, I hope it will reach you, I'm not sending it myself as I will not be able to do so... what I am doing is part of the ongoing war Islaam and disbelief... I know you will find many Muslims quick to condemn the war between us and the US and... I've sent you a copy of my will... (The reason for me sending it to you is so that you can see that I didn't do this act out of ignorance nor did I do just because I want to die, but rather because I see it as a duty upon me to help remove the oppressive American forces from the Muslim lands and that this is the only way for us to do so as we do not have other means to fight them). I hope that what I have done will not [deter] you from looking into Islaam, or even cause you to hate the religion as the message of Islaam is the truth, this is why we are ready to die defending the true Islaam rather than to just sit back and allow the American government to dictate to us what we should believe and how we should behave, it is clear that this is a war between truth and falsehood... this is a war between Islaam and democracy... I ask HIM [Allah] that HE guide me to the truth and cause you to understand why I've done what I've

done. Forgive me for all the problems I have caused you both in life and in death and don't be angry for what I've done.[80]

Reid's intended final communiqué to his mother highlights the attachment he has to her as much as it illustrates his commitment and perceived adherence to Islam. His perception of an ongoing war between truth and falsehood is not new and is not confined to Muslim belief alone; indeed, other established world religions also share the same view, albeit from an ideologically perceived vantage point of their faiths being the remedy against such evil. This cannot therefore be considered an indicator of his extremist ideology or practice. A clear insight into his extremist thinking *and* practice is illustrated in his comments regarding his obligation to remove 'the American oppressive forces' by way of a suicide attack or act of terrorism. While not mentioning the nature of the action he intends to commit, his hint of suicide is implicit from his mentioning, 'This is the only way for us to do so [i.e. remove the US] ... as we do not have other means to fight them'.[81]

This email highlights both Reid's belief-related and deed-related components of violent extremism that are synonymous with the ideology of takfeer and its protagonists. His final address to the court on 30 January 2003, following sentencing, confirmed his unequivocal gravitation to and preference for violent extremism as his chosen ideology and practice, as did his failure to show any remorse for his attempted actions.[82] After declaring himself a soldier[83] and extolling Allah, Reid declared:

Concerning what the Court said? I admit, I admit my actions and I further, I further state that I done them ... I further admit my allegiance to Osama bin Laden, to Islam and to the religion of Allah. With regards to what you said about killing innocent people, I will say one thing. Your government has killed two million children in Iraq. If you think about something, against two million, I don't see no comparison. Your government has sponsored the rape and torture of Muslims in the prisons of Egypt and Turkey and Syria and Jordan with their money and with their weapons. I don't know, see what I done as being equal to rape and to torture, or to the deaths of the two million children in Iraq. So, for this reason, I think I ought not apologize for my actions. I am [at] war with your country. I'm at war with them not for personal reasons but because they have murdered more than, so many children and they have oppressed my religion and they have oppressed people for no reason except that they say we believe in Allah. This is the only reason that America sponsors

Egypt. It's the only reason they sponsor Turkey. It's the only reason they back Israel. As far as the sentence is concerned, it's in your hand. Only really it is not even in your hand. It's in Allah's Hand. I put my trust in Allah totally and I know that he will give victory to His religion. And He will give victory to those who believe and He will destroy those who wish to oppress the people because they believe in Allah. So you can judge and I leave you to judge. And I don't mind. This is all I have to say. And I bear witness to Muhammad this is Allah's message.[84]

Reid's speech is illustrative in that his references and justification for terrorism identify a lack of sufficient and indeed, basic religious grounding. Arguably, it also provides ideological and political indicators of his extremism. Examples of these can be seen in the following areas of Reid's speech:

1. Reference to the perceived injustices against Muslims and Muslim countries are used as a justification and legitimisation for suicide attacks against western targets and innocent civilians. His references to the suffering of the Iraqi children and issues of torture are considered by the majority of the Muslim world to be legitimate in view of overwhelming supporting evidence that exists. However, his use of these examples to legitimise terrorism is incorrect and in opposition to the Quranic injunction which states:

   > O you who believe! Stand out firmly for Allaah and be witnesses, and do not let the hatred of others swerve you away from doing justice [i.e. committing terrorist acts]. But be just! That is closer to Taqwa [piety].
   >
   > (The Holy Qur'an, Chapter 5 Verse 8)

2. An inference is made to the excommunication (takfeer) of the leaders of Muslim populated countries that allegedly support the US in its abuse of Muslims, indicating his belief in the extremists' interpretation and proclamation of takfeer.
3. His proclamation of war is singular in its objective by way of mentioning himself alone as the sole combatant. This reflects the subjectivity surrounding his misunderstanding of Jihad as no single individual, divorced from legislative power and or scholasticism within a predominant Muslim society, can proclaim Jihad singularly or collectively.

Drs J and B Cole's observation behind some of the motivating factors behind British Muslims' decision to embark on what they perceive to be jihad is pertinent at this stage of discourse:

> Justice and injustice are powerful motivating forces in Islam. Tyranny or zulm, as the opposite of justice, has to be resisted, just as it was by the Prophet Muhammed and his followers, as well as by others over the centuries.
>
> (Cole and Cole, 2009: 116 citing Burke, 2004: 29–30)

For some, this could be driven by a simple sense of idealism generated by their social identification of themselves as Muslims and heightened by their radicalisation over these conflicts. This basic sense of injustice about the weak being oppressed by the strong can be a very powerful motivation and justification for violent action.

(Cole and Cole, 2009)

Sentencing

Richard Colvin Reid was initially charged with the following offences:

- One count of the attempted use of a weapon of mass destruction
- One count of attempted homicide of US nationals overseas
- One count of placing an explosive device on an aircraft
- One count of attempted murder of passengers on an aircraft
- Two counts of interfering with a flight crew
- One count of wilfully attempting to set fire to and destroy an aircraft
- One count of using a destructive device during a crime of violence
- One count of attempted wrecking of a mass transportation vehicle which comprises of a new offence created under the new US Patriot Act.[85]

He subsequently received a life sentence.[86] His correspondence and interviews since imprisonment largely maintain the rationale behind his attempts to commit terrorism; however, they reveal a degree of confusion whereby remorse is coupled with certainty regarding the raison d'être of the attempted terrorist act:

> I knew exactly what I was doing... of course I would have been sad to have those people die, but I knew that my cause was just and righteous. It was the will of Allah that I did not succeed.
>
> (Herbert, 2006)

Reid's comments accord with Cole and Cole's above-mentioned observations regarding the motivation for violent action and, in this case, violent extremism.

Reid's path towards violent extremism: a theoretical perspective

Reid possessed little or no knowledge about Islam prior to his imprisonment and subsequent conversion in Feltham. The only account of him being exposed to the religion was when his father advised him to convert to avoid some of the more mundane and difficult aspects of prison life (Seaton, 2002). Unlike Moussaoui, he never had the opportunity to fraternise with Muslim communities pre- or post-conversion due to the fact that he embraced Islam while in prison. The author suggests that his religious foundation and practice would have been very limited because of this lack of exposure, making him susceptible to any 'brand' of Islam that would have been presented to him. Upon his release he travelled directly to Brixton Mosque which was known for its practice of Salafism as well as it being a convert-led community. He, therefore, placed himself among McCants et al.'s theoretical 'Salafi constituency' as depicted in Figure 1.1 (see p. 9), thereby avoiding any immediate engagement with the two wider and arguably larger constituencies.

The period of time for his migration across the 'Salafi' and 'Jihadi' constituencies can be considered to be relatively short in comparison with the gradation of Moussaoui's progression into the same community. One of the contributory factors behind Reid's somewhat accelerated 'radicalisation' is possibly due to the minimal exposure/engagement he had with the wider Muslim constituencies. He was not exposed to the political inclinations and bias that proliferates the 'Islamists' constituency; however, his awareness of world events affecting the Muslim world had already developed during his imprisonment in Feltham (Nzerem, 2002). A similar climate to that of Moussaoui's therefore existed for Reid's initial frustration with the apolitical bias of the 'Salafi' constituency and his subsequent migration across to the 'Jihadi' community. In fact, this observation is concurrent with the progressive stages of his religious development when considering Hudson's adapted framework charting the post conversion process of converts (see Figure 1.2, p. 12).

The idealism referred to in Drs J and B Cole's observations above also accord with the above theoretical framework, particularly when examining the 'youthful' phase of Reid's development. As was discussed in Chapter 1, this period of growth is an idealistic stage of development based upon a predominantly basic and abstract exposure to the religion and its tenets, etc. As such, it is also a stage of significant vulnerability for converts/reverts. Prior to conversion, Reid's life had spiralled into one that is increasingly archetypal of youth from similar backgrounds in Britain; namely, a lack of opportunities owing to poor education, a dysfunctional family and subsequent congruent criminality. Excepting the fact that cross-section of the funnel model depicted in Figure 1.7 (see p. 19) refers primarily to the societal positioning of British Muslims, to some extent, it also possibly reflects Reid's pre-conversion positioning as well as post-conversion during the 1990s. Hard to reach youth, irrespective of religion or ethnicity, etc. fall below the radar of statutory agencies in many societies and the UK is no different in this regard. Reid's life, pre-conversion and his frequent incarceration attest to this observation. By the time he had converted and left prison he was already at a susceptible stage of development and positioning within society. Figures 1.7 supports this assertion as does Figure 1.6 (see p. 19).

To summarise the overall theoretical positioning of Reid after being released from prison, and provide a comprehensiveness to the frameworks referred to herein, the author asserts that he was already situated centrally in the vacuum or, void (Figure 1.7), making it easy for him to avoid the wider, more generic community of Muslims and their understandings of Islam (Figure 1.1). He, therefore, gravitated to a community whose socio-economic mosaic was not too dissimilar from his own. He was at a stage of learning, having recently converted to Islam (the 'youthful' phase of Figure 1.2) hence his susceptibility to violent extremist propaganda (Figure 1.6). Table 1.1 (see p. 16) also highlights his almost immediate positioning at the 'Moderate perspective' of the continuum after he left prison and attended Brixton Mosque. Furthermore, it provides an illustrative explanation of the accelerated pace of his gravitation towards the 'Fanatical/Violent extreme' end due to his lack of exposure to the wider Muslim community located across the entire spectrum.

Reid confirmed the catalyst for his decision to attempt to perpetrate what would effectively have been a devastating albeit innovative act of terrorism was, 'the foreign policy of the US government, which . . . had resulted in the murder of thousands of Muslims and oppressed people around the world from Vietnam to Southern Africa to Afghanistan and Palestine' (Herbert, 2006). Interestingly, his remarks regarding perceived US oppression are, for the first time, generalised to include non-Muslims. Moussaoui's catalyst for attempting to enact terrorism, as discussed in his case study above, was possibly the death of his friend Xavier. The apparent catalytic driver for Reid, on the other hand, was largely political, divorced from any personal, emotional circumstances. This is apparent from a letter written by him in October 2002 while in prison in the US, in response to a note from Neil Young, a US-based journalist from *The Firm* magazine, who asked him to explain why he felt he had been 'let down' by the British system (Knight, 2005). Reid's reply was emphatic:

> You asked me where do I feel the British system failed me... In reality my actions did not come from personal grievances but rather because of my belief that the western countries with America at their head are both openly and secretly fighting the religion of Allah (Islam)... As for those who wish to condemn our means of warfare, then we did not drop a nuclear bomb on Japan nor do we fund the torture of our opponents, nor do we place sanctions on a people for the crimes of a tyrant whom we placed in power [i.e. Iraq].
>
> (Knight, 2005)

Drs J. and B. Cole's research supports the above observation regarding specific catalysts behind radicalised British Muslim's acts or attempted acts of terrorism:

> Although the 'war on terror' was not the catalyst that started the radicalisation of the dataset, it can be viewed as a trigger for these individuals to either engage in terrorist violence or to redirect their violence towards terrorism in the UK.
>
> (Cole and Cole, 2009: 116 citing Burke, 2004: 130)

Figure 1.5 (the cycle of violence model – see page 17) provides an illustrative setting against which Reid's terrorist attempt is more avidly discerned. The consistency of Reid's position and the cogency of his replies reflect the extent to which politicised Islam and takfeeri/violent extremist propaganda were embedded in his psyche. Both belief-related and behavioural-related components have been illustrated in Reid's speech and attempted actions reflecting the degree of his inculcation into the takfeeri, violent extremist ideology. These characteristics are arguably concurrent with observations that both traits (ideological and behavioural extremism) combined contribute to the portrait of a potential violent extremist and, therefore, terrorist. A question may be posed concerning the possibility of Reid progressing to a more 'adult' phase of understanding Islam and eventually eschewing his extremist beliefs. At present recent media reports suggest the contrary, and although he is ardent in his pursuit of religious knowledge, his learning remains abstract (Brough, 2009). Until effective counter radicalisation programmes are implemented in prison, thereby challenging his extremist beliefs, it is unlikely that the violent extremist/takfeeri ideology will dissipate. In any event, this study will continue to look at socio-religious/political factors that adversely affected such individuals, including personalities who influenced them. One such personality, currently considered among the UK's most influential ideologues and protagonists of violent extremism, arguably influenced individuals like Reid. He is the subject of the next case study.

Case Study 3: Trevor William Forrest (aka Abdullah el-Faisal)

This particular case study departs from the focus of the preceding studies and examines manifestations of extremism limited to el-Faisal's rhetoric alone. While there appears sufficient and incontestible evidence illustrating his support and advocacy for violent extremism, none exists so far as any attempts by him to enact terrorist actions. El-Faisal was one of the more significant and influential ideologues and protagonists of violent extremism in the UK during the mid-1990s up until his arrest in February 2002 (Cole and Cole, 2006: 163). This is because he is considered to have influenced a significant number of British-based Muslims who attempted or conspired to commit terrorist acts against western societies and/or their respective interests. These individuals included the likes of Richard Reid, Dhiren Barot, Mohammed Hamid and Germaine Lindsay.[87]

Upbringing, social background and cognitive openings

Details of el-Faisal's upbringing are vague, save for his being raised in a Christian family in Jamaica. His parents, Merlyn and Lorenzo Forrest, were Salvation Army officers.[88] He was born Trevor William Forrest and brought up in the farming district of Point in St James Parish, located on the western coast of the island near Montego Bay. He was among four children to his parents (Lister, 2003b). As a child, he was never considered by his mother to be either difficult or one who was ever involved in familial or peer group conflicts (Plunket, 2008). Media reports suggest that he converted to Islam at the age of 16 after one of his high school teachers introduced the religion to him. Details relating to his academic education only extend as far as the name of the school he attended – Maldron High. His teachers, particularly the one who allegedly introduced him to Islam, remain unknown. Conflicting reports regarding el-Faisal's immediate post conversion development suggest he first emigrated to the UK and thereafter Saudi Arabia where he embarked upon an Islamic studies programme for seven or eight years. Other reports suggest he first travelled to Riyadh, Saudi Arabia and then the UK.[89] Most reports, however, fail to make any reference to his initial visit to Guyana, South America, where he first embarked upon an Islamic studies course. It can be assumed that this course of study whetted his appetite to study the religion in more detail and from there he decided to apply for an accredited Islamic studies programme in Imam Muhammad bin Saud University in Riyadh (Addae, 2007: 4). Apparently, following the completion of his studies in Guyana, el-Faisal migrated to the UK and applied to the above-mentioned university. Again, scant detail exists about his studies in Guyana except that he concentrated on Arabic and Islamic Studies.[90] It is therefore difficult to establish the level of religious discourse or education he obtained at that stage. In the absence of such detail surrounding his formative years as a new Muslim the following areas pose a problem for the author so far as obtaining empirical data to establish the initial part of el-Faisal's ideological profile:

1. Ascertaining the type of religious and ideological education and/or influence he was exposed to prior to embarking on studies in Saudi Arabia
2. Establishing whether his religious education in Guyana adversely affected the 'founding' and/or 'youthful' phases of his early development as a Muslim (in accordance with Figure 1.2)
3. Identifying the type of Muslim community he interacted with during this period, i.e. whether they were from among the general Muslim, Islamist, Salafi or 'Jihadi' constituencies (in accordance with Figure 1.1)
4. Determining the extent of his religious development and understanding and whether he was exposed to extremist propaganda or teachings prior to migrating to Britain and subsequently travelling to Saudi Arabia (in accordance with Table 1.1)

The inability to determine these factors creates a vacuum in being able to identify potential catalysts or drivers that may have contributed to possible violent extremist leanings in el-Faisal's formative years as a convert. This difficulty contrasts with the preceding case studies in that they both provide preliminary secondary data which highlight either the socio-economic or socio-religious drivers that affected both subjects' early religious development.

Nonetheless, it is clear that he graduated from Muhammad Ibn Saud University in 1991 having acquired proficiency in Arabic and obtained a first degree. Upon graduating he returned to the UK. The author and his colleagues were introduced by Brixton Mosque management as new converts to el-Faisal and he was invited to conduct classes for the group. However, it should be noted that he was first questioned by the mosque as to his ideological and religious affiliations, due to their adoption and adherence to Salafism. After receiving assurances that el-Faisal's ideological persuasion was the same, lessons commenced. In contrast to the new converts' concerns, el-Faisal's Jamaican origin was more significant to the mosque management and a notable cause for celebration among the wider community during that particular period. The reason for this could perhaps be traced back to their initial dependency, albeit reluctantly, upon the prevalent cultural and religious dominance of South Asian and Arab Muslims. Unfortunately, this religious influence was often coupled with racism towards African–Caribbean Muslims, particularly converts. El-Faisal provided an avenue through which to eschew such dependency and enable Brixton Mosque's increasing convert community the opportunity to develop a distinctive religious identity devoid of the cultural influences and racism experienced by the elders. In the event, he settled in the UK with his wife and two young children in 1992 after obtaining a Minister of Religion visa as the newly appointed imam for Brixton Mosque. During his first year he conducted a series of classes, led the Jumuah (Friday) sermons and prayers, and presided over Eid celebrations. The community appeared optimistic in view of a new sense of direction and developing cohesion between the older and younger members of the community. Unfortunately, such optimism was to be considered premature in light of the management suddenly revealing a new ideological gravitation towards Sufism, particularly that of the Murabitun movement which was not only at variance with the Salafi members of the community but the majority of other attendees also. This gravitation culminated in the first serious conflict within the mosque, referred to as 'Black Sunday – the first crisis' in Chapter 2 of this book. Prior to this event, owing to his apparent Salafist leanings, el-Faisal was informed by the mosque management that he could no longer conduct classes or provide sermons if he maintained his ideological position, which conflicted with Sufism. El-Faisal and the Salafi members of the congregation were left with no alternative except to find another venue where their classes could continue. One of the elders, Sirat Abdul Malik was sympathetic to the group's plight and invited them to continue study circles in his home.

Classes therefore continued uninterrupted for a short period thereafter. It was during this time that el-Faisal's violent extremist beliefs began to emerge. His ousting from Brixton Mosque irked him, particularly in view of the fact that it had been members of the existing management who initially invited and employed him. The content and quality of his teaching began to deteriorate and his attacks on the mosque management became increasingly polemical. The author can vividly recall the final study circle when, not only was el-Faisal requested to cease study circles, due to the extremism he now expounded; he was also opposed by the attendees who resolved to prevent him from his plan to overthrow the mosque management by using violence if necessary. Notably, prior to this final study circle and the events of 'Black Sunday' el-Faisal revealed that he was also delivering study circles in north-west London to a more committed group of students who were prepared to forcibly oust Brixton Mosque's management committee. The author and other colleagues were unanimous in their opposition to such actions, stating that they contravened established Islamic principles prohibiting the revolt against established Muslim authority. A short reprieve from el-Faisal's intended action was agreed in order to contact one of his teachers from Muhammad Ibn Saud University, Shaikh Abdullah Jibreen, a senior scholar in Saudi Arabia at the time. Suffice it to say that Shaikh Jibreen rejected el-Faisal's position. Despite this censure being conveyed to him, el-Faisal remained resolute regarding his plan. His resolve alongside other unrelated but extenuating circumstances surrounding the affairs of the mosque accelerated the 'Black Sunday' crisis. El-Faisal's position, coupled with the proclamation of takfeer upon the committee and members of the wider community provided an indisputable line of demarcation between el-Faisal and the Salafi community of Brixton.

The self-styled 'Shaykh'

El-Faisal continued to strengthen his reputation in North West London and by 1993 he was working as a full-time imam in Islamia Independent School for Girls, located in Salusbury Road, Brondesbury Park. The author also commenced work at the school in July that same year in the capacity of legal administrator for the school's trust. Although tenuous, both el-Faisal and the author's relationship remained cordial during that period. El-Faisal continued to focus on conducting classes and Jumuah prayers for his congregation which was conveniently located close to the school. However, following the election of a new chairman in Brixton Mosque after 'Black Sunday', he began to refocus on establishing a base either in the mosque itself or the surrounding area. The election of a new chairman who once attended his study circles did not lessen el-Faisal's attacks on the Brixton Mosque community. In fact, his familiarity with the new leader and management only led to increased animosity culminating in his infamous recording in which he denigrated the Salafi community in Brixton, proclaiming them to be disbelievers (Addae, 2007: 76–9). He also attempted to destabilise the new management by attending the mosque uninvited to conduct a study circle for between 30 and 40 members of his followers from around London. His attempt was thwarted by the mosque management; however, he proceeded to establish weekly study circles in one of Brixton's sports centres, Ferndale, to the chagrin of the newly-elected mosque management. He also developed relationships in neighbouring Camberwell, south-east London where he also conducted regular classes. It is important to note el-Faisal's charisma was the main impetus behind his success in attracting new audiences. Indeed, in his youth and prior to conversion, he was affectionately nicknamed 'Dictionary' because of his academic excellence (Plunket, 2008). (Similarly, Malcolm X became a renowned orator due to his charisma and encyclopaedic knowledge of the English language, acquired during his incarceration (Hayley, 1968: 41).) Further evidence of el-Faisal's oratory prowess can be witnessed in his wife's description of him:

> He was, she said, an enigmatic and powerful figure. 'I fell in love with him. It was his looks, his character, and his preaching. I knew that I should help him to propagate his [beliefs] and Islam.'
>
> (Syal, 2003)

This ability, coupled with his provocative descriptions of the alleged malaise and lack of concern of government-backed scholars, proved an effective and captivating combination of topical issues for his audiences (Addae, 2007). The author recalls the effect of el-Faisal's teachings on a few individuals who began to attend both his Ferndale study circles and the mosque. They would leave the mosque following evening congregational prayers to attend his circles. When they returned the confusion regarding ideological and political issues was evident in their behaviour. Those convinced by his rhetoric either became confrontational or gradually gravitated away from the mosque. By this time, el-Faisal had adopted the title 'shaykh' and began referring to himself as a scholar. He promoted and sold his lectures through various outlets, such as study circles and Islamic bookshops enabling him to gain a wider audience. Members of his newly-established congregation would also frequent Brixton Mosque and attempt to invite or recruit potentially interested parties. Unsurprisingly, this led to a series of confrontations in and around the mosque's immediate vicinity in the short term. The newly-appointed chairman and management committee failed to remove the discord and mistrust that had developed in the community. The strategy and approach to promote Salafism among the largely non-denominational multi-ethnic Muslim congregation was rejected due to the manner in which it was being conveyed. As mentioned in Chapter 2, a panel of arbitrators from other Muslim communities in south London were asked to intervene and preside over determining new leadership. The author was subsequently appointed as chairman on the premise that it was the non-Salafi members of the community that chose him and that he would possibly unite this section of the community with the Salafi contingent. Suffice it to say, this was accepted by the majority of the community although the latter group was initially sceptical concerning the new administration. El-Faisal visited the author at his home to express support for the new leadership. He requested that he be reinstated as an imam and this was tentatively agreed on the basis that he publicly recant his extremist beliefs with an unambiguous undertaking to recommence teaching a more orthodox and mainstream version of Islam. El-Faisal agreed to this and arrangements were made for him to address the mosque congregation. Consequently, when addressing the congregation, he reneged on the agreement. This resulted in his immediate expulsion from the mosque. It was the penultimate occasion he was to attend Brixton Mosque (the final occasion was when he attended Sirat Abdul Malik's funeral about a year later). The above event proved critical in that el-Faisal then embarked upon a negative campaign of propaganda against Salafis, adopting and promulgating the takfeeri ideology regarding the permissibility of harming or killing them on the basis that they were considered disbelievers. He stated in one of his many lectures against Salafis, 'If he is a supporter of kufr (disbelief), a Saudi Salafi, you have to kill him and chop his head off' (Addae, 2007).

The case against el-Faisal: his arrest and convictions

At this stage it is necessary to examine the reasons for el-Faisal's arrest, imprisonment and final deportation against the background of what has been discussed above. This will enable a complete contextualisation of his extremist teachings and their effect upon the young British Muslim populace in Britain today. Reference was made at the outset of this particular study to the influence of his teachings upon convicted terrorists, many of whom are British. His rhetoric attracted a captive and young audience during a period in which perceived injustices against the Muslim world were continuing unabated. El-Faisal's knowledge and experience of Saudi Arabia and his ability to juxtapose the apparent scholarly ineptitude with western, non-Muslim foreign policies against the Muslim world provided an effective and convincing portrait of collusion to 'dismantle the Sharia', thereby perpetuating the subjugation of Islam. By discrediting contemporary scholars of the religion and relying upon classical scholarly texts, the author suggests el-Faisal's intention in this regard was primarily twofold: i) to deceive unsuspecting Muslims into believing and accepting that he was in fact an authority/point of reference on Islam, and ii) to develop a personal licence to interpret legislative dictates and provide religious rulings (*fatawa*) according to his own understanding without recourse to established, traditional scholarly principles. His repeated denigration and disparagement of the majority of contemporary scholars attests to this observation (Addae, 2007).

He was arrested on 18 February 2002 after police discovered cassette recordings of him advocating the killing of 'Western unbelievers' (Lister, 2003a). This was not the first time he had been arrested; he was apparently convicted for an unrelated offence for possessing an offensive weapon in 1997 (Lister, 2003a). Upon arrest and cautioning in 2002, el-Faisal asserted, 'I do not incite murder, it's not my policy to incite murder, I only preach Islam and secondly I'm not a racist, I do not hate anyone, I only hate crimes against humanity'.[91]

Judge Peter Beaumont cited a nineteenth-century statute to convict el-Faisal of three charges under the Offences Against the Person Act, 1861 for which he was sentenced to seven years imprisonment (Lister, 2003). The trial was unusual in that it was the first in over one hundred years to evoke this statute. Additionally, it was the first time that jurors had been prohibited from presiding over a case on religious grounds.[92] El-Faisal was also the first Muslim cleric to be charged and convicted after 9/11 in the UK. More specifically, the three charges related to el-Faisal's incitement to murder Americans, Jews and Hindus, although no charge was brought for his unequivocal incitement to kill fellow Muslims, considered apostates. The nature of el-Faisal's incitement in this instance can be seen from the transcript of one of his lectures entitled, 'The Devil's Deception of the 21st Century House Niggers' (Addae, 2007: 63–70). After listening to the cassette of one his opponents and providing a counter narrative, el-Faisal asks the audience: 'What do you think we should do with this person?' The audience replied, 'Kill him!' El-Faisal retorts: 'I can't hear you!', to which the audience replies more raucously: 'Kill him!' After repeating the question once more and receiving an even louder response, he concludes: 'OK, that makes sense' (Addae, 2007: 68–9). This pantomimical exchange reflects the entertainment value of el-Faisal's lectures and why he remains a successful orator, despite his ban in the UK (discussed below). Surprisingly, statutory authorities either ignored or failed to act on innumerable recordings of this nature which were directed solely against Muslims. This leads the author to conclude that such incitement, so long as it is confined to Muslims, is considered insignificant. In any event, el-Faisal was also found guilty and sentenced for the following offences: i) using threatening and insulting words for which he received a 12-month sentence to run concurrent to the first charge and ii) using threatening and insulting recordings for which he received a two-year sentence to run consecutively with the first charge (Lister, 2003). The judge recommended that el-Faisal serve at least half his sentence before deportation from the UK upon his release. During the trial at the Old Bailey, el-Faisal asserted that he had been misrepresented and that he had only made reference to the Qur'an. In fact, he argued that the Qur'an was in fact on trial, not he (Ryan, 2003). After sentencing, his defence lawyers, Saunders & Co. Solicitors, filed for an appeal. On 17 February 2004 the Court of Appeal considered el-Faisal's appeal against conviction on counts 1, 2 and 4 which all related to soliciting murder. Consideration was given to the defence that developed el-Faisal's:

> assertion in interview that all he was doing was elaborating and interpreting the teachings in the Quran, and that, when he spoke of killing, he was speaking only of killing in self-defence, his references to the killing of non-believers having been misconstrued by the prosecution. In elaboration of this, he highlighted the various passages in his speeches where he had referred to killing in or on the 'battlefield'. He asserted that, however the individual tapes of his sermons might be interpreted by the prosecution, it was the case that none of them meant or was intended to mean that killing could be indiscriminate. Any killing was to be done on the battlefield and was aimed at those who oppressed, persecuted and murdered Muslims.[93]

El-Faisal further expounded;

> I deliberately use that word, 'battlefield' so that the audience would understand that acts against, for example, embassy buildings as in the Sudan or on a bus or on a train are not. I meant by battlefield where

the conflict is taking place, not where civilians would be found but on the battlefield alone.[94]

El-Faisal's explanations in defence of his statements should be contrasted with some of his lectures that were not the subject of his trial. They illustrate the reality of his position regarding the west as an abode of war (darul Harb). In his lecture, 'Exposing the Hypocrites', he states, while mocking and belittling his opponents:

> Another sign of the hypocrite is that he's very pessimistic, so he says... 'how can we fight America, it's impossible let us throw the towel in the ring and give-up, we'll never fight America. We don't have the ability to build submarines and planes and tanks, tomahawk cruise missiles and patriot missiles and so on and so on. It doesn't make sense that we declare war, we don't have weapons...' this is a hypocrite speaking.
>
> (Addae, 2007: 18–19)

In a more emphatic address, he purports:

> You're allowed to take all these [state] benefits that these kaafirs give you, because everything that the kaafir owns is yours. Every single thing that the kaafir owns is yours so you're allowed to take all the benefits that they offer you and you're even allowed to have four wives and put them on benefit, so hope they give you a mansion in Hampstead Heath!
>
> (Addae, 2007: 32–3)

An established principle in Jihad is the entitlement of the victors to the spoils or proceeds of war, including property that belonged to the defeated enemy (Fawzan, 2005: 475–6). El-Faisal's reference to complete ownership of non-Muslim property and wealth is indicative of his belief that the west, Britain in this instance, is an abode of war and that its inhabitants can be considered the enemy. His belief, therefore, promotes the premise of the entire country constituting a battlefield, although the actual levels of 'Jihad' may vary from subversive (i.e. terrorism) to deceitful measures (fraud, theft, etc.), depending on the circumstances (Addae, 2007: 34). A more explicit reference intimating his understanding of non-Muslim lands being abodes of war can be witnessed in his lecture entitled 'Jihad':

Is there any peace treaty between us and Hindus and India? No, so you can go to India and if you see a Hindu walking down the road you are allowed to kill him and take his money, is that clear, because there is no peace treaty between us and him, his wealth isn't sacred nor his life because there is no peace treaty between us and him.[95]

Referring to the Court of Appeal case again, the prosecution countered el-Faisal's defence by stating that:

those explanations which the appellant gave in evidence as to the meaning of his words constituted a gloss which was plainly inconsistent with the breadth of the words actually used, in particular in the passages which we have already quoted... The words of the appellant are so general, and the nature of the passages quoted such, that the field of conflict in which the appellant urged Muslims to kill plainly extended beyond any battlefield in any sense and included acts of terrorism against Kaffars generally and in any place where, in a loose sense, there is a struggle, as the appellant saw it, between the forces of Islam and various identified non-believers such as Americans, Jews and Hindus, in the course of which the killing of non-combatants, including women and children, was acceptable as collateral damage.[96]

In summation, the judge stated the following:

We are quite satisfied that the jury were well aware of the basis upon which the Crown asked for a conviction, namely the appellant's exhortations and, in particular, the passages we have highlighted, were of a general kind which solicited killing on an indiscriminate basis in areas other than the battlefield and that they roundly rejected the evidence of the appellant as to his limited intent... The appeal against conviction is therefore dismissed.[97]

After serving four years of his sentence, el-Faisal was deported to his native country, Jamaica, on 25 May 2007 (Johnstone, 2007). He was escorted by the police to Gatwick airport where he boarded a 12 p.m. direct flight.[98] His appeal to fight deportation on the basis of Human Rights was rejected.

El-Faisal: The extremist ideologue

Evidence has already been provided to illustrate el-Faisal's oratory skills alongside the entertainment value of his lectures. For young unsuspecting Muslim youth whose religious awakening or 'founding'/'youthful' stages of Islamic development had been aroused, el-Faisal was an appealing alternative to the traditional or cultural and somewhat liberal Islam their parents or the older community espoused. Faisal's 'brand' of Islam not only addressed current affairs concerning the Muslim world, but also challenged Muslim leaders and religious scholars over their perceived ineptitude to unite the 'Ummah' and counter western aggression against their peoples. He was successful in presenting Islam as an appealing and powerful alternative to the various strands of Islam considered passive and ineffectual. In this respect, Figure 1.1 (see p. 9) is recalled to illustrate the appeal el-Faisal had across each constituency.

Arguably, he managed to attract significant numbers towards the more centrally located and extreme constituency of 'Jihadis', appealing to his audience's youthfulness, 'street culture' and frustrations which developed as a result of conflicts of identity and societal disadvantages. The author suggests el-Faisal's audience would have comprised young Muslims who had not progressed beyond the 'youthful' phase of religious understanding and development. When considering el-Faisal against the same theoretical framework (see Figure 1.2, p. 12), it becomes more difficult to gauge his own level of development.

His experience and development as a convert Muslim is such that he had the opportunity to progress beyond the first two phases. Indeed, he was able to actualise Islam as opposed to practising it in abstract during his time as a student in Riyadh due to the majority society comprising largely of Muslims. Whether he developed his extremist belief while studying in Saudi Arabia or prior to this is unclear, as intimated at the outset of this case study. However, in view of his recorded attacks against the Saudi government and the scholars in particular, it is relatively prudent to conclude that his antipathy in this regard was fuelled by his experiences as a student. His confirmed ideological foundation accords with historical takfeeri and extremist beliefs. Evidence to support this assertion can be made when examining his position on Tawheed al-haakimiyyah as a fourth category:

> There are many Muslims whose hearts are hard like the Jews, take for instance those Muslims who do not believe in tawheed al-haakimiyyah ... He [Allah] doesn't allow anyone to share in His legislation and still they say 'tawheed al-haakimiyyah is bida

[innovation].' How many types of tawheed are there? Four! Allah is the only creator, Allah alone deserves to be worshipped, Allah has ninety nine Names and Attributes and Allah is the only Law-Giver – Tawheed ur-Ruboobiyyah, Uloohiyyah, Asmaa wa's – Sifaat and al-Haakimiyyah.

(Addae, 2007: 42–3)

This contrasts with established ideological principles that confirm tawheed as three categories, with al-haakimiyyah incorporated among them. Syed Qutb was a contemporary advocate of tawheed al-haakimiyyah. El-Faisal reinforces his belief regarding this component of tawheed in repeated attempts to disparage his most staunch opponents:

Do you know it is impossible to find a Salafi book on the market, a book on tawheed and they mention tawheed al-haakimiyyah? Have you seen such a book? ... but they will never mention tawheed al-haakimiyyah because they do not want to offend their kaafir paymasters.

(Addae, 2007: 45)

Again, it is difficult to determine the stage of el-Faisal's development and understanding when considering it in context to his beliefs and statements in this regard. It is possible that he progressed to the 'mature' phase of development, albeit with unmistakable delineations towards violent extremism. Unfortunately, the theoretical framework depicted in Figure 1.2 (see p. 12) appears limited and therefore ill-equipped to explore beyond whether an extremist's contextualisation of the religion can, at such a late stage of understanding or development, be altered. Currently, there exists recently published research that relates to individual and collective disengagement from terrorism (Bjorgo and Horgan, 2009). Further examination of post-extremist/deradicalised stages of religious development could possibly form a more specialised remit of research requiring attention from a solely British Muslim perspective. In any event, although evidence presented above is inconclusive so far as applying the theoretical framework (Figure 1.2) to el-Faisal's actual phase of understanding and development, it is, the author asserts, definitive when applied to the final three models illustrated in Table 1.1 (p. 16) and Figures 1.6 (p. 19) and 1.7 (p. 19).

El-Faisal's positioning, based upon the preceding evidence, places him at the 'fanatical' extreme of the spectrum. However, his ability to attract audiences from across the 'liberal' extreme cannot be ignored. Many second/third generation Muslim youth, as well as converts, are likely to have been positioned towards the latter extreme of the spectrum during some period of their negligible/non-practising/pre-conversion stages of life. They would, to a greater extent, have engaged with their local communities and/or wider society. El-Faisal's propagatory ability is such that he could attract them across the spectrum towards the more 'fanatical' extreme. The author suggests that such attraction could, in turn, contribute to the youths' eventual disengagement from their respective communities and/or wider society. The effects, as have been seen in the preceding case studies, would be adverse, heightening the youths' receptiveness and susceptibility to violent extremist propaganda. The resultant gravitation towards a more extreme understanding of Islam and the positioning among a lower, less accessible echelon of society is almost inevitable, unless of course the negative propaganda is effectively and robustly countered in a timely manner i.e. prior to 'violent' radicalisation. The possible scenario described above is vividly portrayed in Figure 1.6.

Case study 3 conclusions

Figure 1.7 (the funnel model) further illustrates el-Faisal's positioning among the wider Muslim communities and depicts his effect on young Muslims gravitating towards a more violent extreme understanding of Islam.

El-Faisal, to reiterate, was successful in traversing the most liberal to more orthodox and extreme communities, attracting the interest and support of youth from the respective localities, 'He had no specific home base and no natural constituency. Instead, he operated as a freelance radical preacher [and] travelled the UK preaching to different groups' (Cole and Cole, 2009: 168). One account suggests that Germaine Lindsay was first introduced to el-Faisal by Mohammed Sadiq Khan during study circles in the latter's hometown of Beeston.

The final case study examines the factors which enabled a young Muslim convert, initially affected by violent extremist propaganda, to revert to a more orthodox, mainstream understanding and practice of the religion. Particular focus will be given to the stages in which this individual's 'turnaround' occurred and whether any of the theoretical frameworks referred to throughout this research accurately depict such occurrence. Consideration will also be given to Bjorgo and Horgan's psychological analysis of individual disengagement from terrorism to determine whether any parallels exist between this and the process of deradicalisation witnessed in the fourth case study (Bjorgo and Horgan, 2009). The conclusion of the entire chapter will then review the typologies introduced in Chapters 3 and 4 to determine their specificity to the existing studies within the context of what has been discussed.

Case Study 4: Sean O'Reilly[99]

This study examines Sean's conversion to Islam and the preceding socio-religious influences that provoked his initial interest and attraction to violent extremist propaganda. More significantly, it will also explore the reasons behind his subsequent rejection of this. Discussion will then ensue regarding the applicability of theoretical frameworks which, up until this point of research, have been examined from the perspective of an individual's gravitation *towards* violent extremism but not *away* from it. This particular case study is, therefore, important from the view of identifying factors behind individual decisions to reject extremism. This could then provide a possible premise upon which to further investigate deradicalisation or disengagement from violent extremist ideology and practice. Bjorgo and Horgan observe:

> While it would be analytically misleading to characterize initial, sustained and decreasing involvement in terrorism as anything but a group process, thinking about individual issues represents an important step in working towards a comprehensive multi-level model that describes the properties of the disengagement process. Such a model, if effective, would integrate individual, group, network organizational, social movement and cultural levels of analysis and provide a solid foundation from which policy interventions could begin to be developed.
>
> (Bjorgo and Horgan, 2009: 18)

The study relies upon primary sources of data; namely, a semi-structured interview and Participant Observation, departing from the focus of the previous three studies and their reliance upon secondary data. This approach has enabled the author to obtain a more comprehensive first-hand account of some of the causes for violent radicalisation.

Upbringing, social background and identity – the formative years

Sean is a single child from Irish parents and was born in south London in 1983. His father emigrated from Ireland approximately 45 years ago while his mother was born in the UK. The family is of working class background and has resided in south London for more than 40 years.

In fact, Sean's grandmother settled in Brixton, south London when she arrived from Ireland and her descendants continue to reside there:[100]

> I've basically lived in Brixton all my life... my mum's mum came from Ireland; we've lived in the same place in Brixton... so I mean I was born, raised in Brixton... I'm still there basically. I mean, I've always been here.[101]

Despite his ethnicity, Sean did not experience racism from his predominantly African–Caribbean neighbours and peers, although he faced occasional chastisement from sections of the white indigenous community: 'thinking you're trying to act black'.[102] His family's Irish extraction meant that, like a majority of the black community, they had experienced racism. This is vividly captured in Sean's account of racial conflict witnessed during his childhood and recalled by his grandmother:

> Yeah, I think it had an effect on, honestly, all of my family members, because a lot of them have got one-sided views. All of my friends were black, growing up, so I witnessed the difference... even my Nan, when she first came here, she came when a lot of West Indian people came as well, so she experienced the same: 'No blacks, no dogs, no Irish.'[103]

This recollection is reminiscent of similar accounts that pitched earlier African–Caribbean and Irish emigrants together, resulting in wide-ranging interaction between the two communities (Reddie, 2009: 59–63). In fact, it has been asserted that:

> A unique and curious empathy existed between the two communities which witnessed: considerable espirit de corps... between these two sets of often-despised arrivals – employment adverts frequently featured words 'no blacks or Irish' while accommodation notices would routinely expand this slogan to read 'No dogs, blacks or Irish.'
> (Reddie, 2009: 63 citing Bradley, 2001: 117).

Despite these experiences and perceptions, Sean did not consider his cultural affinity with Ireland to be particularly significant or stronger: 'I mean I still have strong respect for the struggle that people went through and I still recognize that, I still have grievances about that... not particularly cultural-wise.'[104] However, they instilled in him a sense of solidarity with his black friends. Racial issues, together with other social stigmas, such as the absence of father figures in the home (his father left the family home while he was a child) solidified the relationships with his peers: 'We didn't look at it as a white/black thing; we just looked at it as sharing the same experiences.'[105]

Sean attended local state schools in south London which were demographically similar to his neighbourhood. For instance, the secondary school he attended in Camberwell, south-east London comprised 75–80% African–Caribbean pupils. The remaining student roll comprised of indigenous white Britons, South Americans and Portugese, etc.[106] The effects of urban, inner city schooling were overwhelming positive for Sean in that his perspective and outlook on matters, as a young teenager, were expansive:

> My views were a bit more... widespread; I wasn't narrow minded because I was always around new people. I had new friends, like I had Asian friends, black friends, I had South American friends, Columbians, etc. so I had a bit more... I think that helped in the long run, especially coming to Islam. It doesn't give you such a blinkered view of the world... you don't live in a box. You actually understand there are people out there with different cultures; they're going through different problems, different things. I think it makes you respect people a bit more, being around other people.[107]

He left school with five GCSE qualifications and applied to study Sports Science at college. However, a hand injury meant that he could not complete the course and he was eventually expelled. In addition to this, he had become distracted by the surreptitious activities of his peers such as consuming and selling drugs.[108] Sean recalls the adverse effects on his morale during that period: 'Once I got kicked out of college, I didn't really... want to work too much... having started smoking [cannabis] or whatever, it kind of takes the drive away from you... I got caught up, selling weed... just scraping by basically.'[109]

Unemployed, he sought the more illicit avenues of generating money to maintain his responsibilities (i.e., he had a two-year-old son by the age of 18) and lifestyle.[110] He had become accustomed to urban street life and all that it entailed by the age of 13, although he was a relatively late starter as far as drug taking was concerned – his first experience of smoking cannabis was at 18. Familial influences were such that criminality among the male contingent was considered normal:

> A lot of my family have been in prison, served jail terms for armed robbery [and] other numerous things. So it's not like it was something

new to me ... growing up like that, it makes taking up selling drugs or robbery ... it doesn't make it such a big issue to you.[111]

Interestingly, Sean refers to his life at that time and the fact that members of his family and peers were involved in various elements of criminality in a manner that accords with the theoretical 'funnel' framework depicted in Figure 1.7 (p. 19).

> You do as you see fit. I mean, obviously, a lot of my friends were doing the same thing ... and you end up just rolling with each other, everyone from the area's going through the same things ... it was never a gang thing ... so you just get sucked into the vacuum.[112]

This 'vacuum' is practically synonymous with the above mentioned framework as it illustrates Sean's gravitation prior to conversion from commonly acceptable societal norms (i.e. located at the outmost circle) across to petty criminality (i.e. the innermost circle) where susceptibility to adverse influences is, the author suggests, at its most critical. As suggested in the preceding case study of Richard Reid, this model, subject to minor amendments to the constituencies, could also be reflective of Sean's societal position prior to conversion.

Cognitive openings: conversion

Unlike many of his peers, Sean did not approach any mosque or individual to enquire about Islam. Although he knew a number of Muslims prior to his conversion at the age of 22, his interaction with them failed to give rise to interest in the religion. As a matter of fact, he did not consider these individuals exemplars of the religion: 'They hadn't changed ... I'd never see them praying, they were still smoking weed, they were still selling drugs or whatever. So I was thinking; "it's a new thing for them".'[113]

However, while he was residing at his father's home owing to bail restrictions imposed at that time, his interest in the religion was aroused by books that a close friend had bought:

> He had a court case, and I was on bail at my dad's address. So he's living with me at the time ... he's going and getting books about Islam, and he's going and leaving them when he's going back out. So I was picking them up, reading them ... bits and pieces. Over the space of a few days I just felt ... this is something I've just got to do ... and

I mean, I didn't even really read into the fundamentals about praying and fasting... just... about science and the Qur'an and the life of the Prophet... something just clicked with me, because before I was Muslim, it doesn't matter how much money I made, how many girls I was with, what rave I went to... afterwards you just feel empty, because you think; 'alright, I've done that, now what?' There's no end satisfaction because you always want to go to the next extreme.[114]

Sean's subsequent enthusiasm to convert to Islam was unparalleled so far as any previous religious commitment was concerned. Although he subscribed to Catholicism, this was on the basis of his family's adherence to the religion.[115] He converted during the Islamic holy month of Ramadan in 2005 and immediately began adhering to foundational tenets of the religion such as praying and fasting. Initially, Sean avoided informing his family about his new-found faith. He wanted to establish himself and his new identity as a Muslim before approaching them: 'I didn't want people phoning me and stressing me out and I was just enjoying the atmosphere of Ramadan... it was something new for me, and I just felt fresh.'[116]

Reference at this point to Rambo's theoretical 'modes of response' model of conversion, discussed in Chapter 4 (see Figure 4.1, p. 68), can be revisited as it encapsulates a particular aspect of Sean's conversion. Sean's description of conversion accords with the 'Receptive' definition of Rambo's Conversion process in that he was prepared to explore new avenues. It also concurs with the 'Founding' phase of conversion as depicted in Figure 1.2 (p. 12).

The reaction of his family upon discovery of his new faith was one of concern. As intimated above, his bail conditions restricted him from residing in or near the estate where his mother lived. Despite this, he still visited her in order to inform her of his conversion. He recalls her surprise on the first visit caused by his religious attire. This, together with the announcement of his conversion was an unprecedented act in his predominantly Christian family. After all, 'It's not every day someone goes home and says: "Mum, I'm Muslim now," especially in white families'.[117]

Family concerns arose due to the prevailing climate around Muslims and negative media portrayals of Islam as a fanatical and extreme religion, etc.[118] The apprehensive reception received from his family, particularly his cousins, resulted in his distancing himself from them for a short period. Contact, however, was maintained with his mother, yielding an almost immediate positive response; she began to provide halal meals for him on his subsequent visits. He reflects on this period and recalls his mother's dilemma: 'I'm an only child, and her thing is: "What am I going to do? My only child, my grand-kids... I'm not going to abandon my son over something because people don't like it".'[119] Eventually, his cousins accepted his choice of faith and family ties were resumed.[120]

Remand and trial

Prior to conversion, Sean resided for a short period in Brighton, Sussex. He had been made aware of his grandmother's illness while living there and returned as soon as news of her decline and consequent death reached him.[121] Unsurprisingly, his main concern was his mother's health. He attended his grandmother's funeral and spent some time with his mother. It was during this period that an incident occurred on the estate, leading to his arrest:

> To cut a long story short, we were passing through, late at night, me and my cousin... a big argument ensued. Some people were stabbed, I got accused of stabbing them and it lead to a big court case. I didn't turn up for my trial because I embraced Islam while I was awaiting trial. My trial was supposed to start... I didn't turn up, so I was on the run basically, for nearly a year.[122]

He was apprehended by the police following an unrelated incident where they were searching for his brother-in-law. Sean's passport was retrieved and he was detained for questioning. Further investigations surrounding his identity resulted in the discovery of an outstanding warrant for his arrest. He was subsequently detained with former bail conditions being revoked.[123] His arrest induced a period of reflection regarding events leading up to his remand. During his six months in prison, he re-evaluated what he had learned as a Muslim and addressed the areas of conflict he had been experiencing with aspects of the religion; especially, those relating to ideology:

> Having first embraced Islam, I had some wrong views, to say the least... When I first became Muslim... obviously, you don't really know anything. So the first Muslim you're closest to, that's like your teacher, or your mentor... so whatever they're telling you, you kind of take it as it's holy – true, because you're thinking; 'he's a Muslim, he's not going to lie to me.' He may very well not be lying to you; he might be misguided himself.[124]

During interview, Sean emphasised the political and emotional focus of his Muslim peers and the fact that much of their religious development was devoid of learning the religion from authentic sources. He, on the other hand, had a 'penchant' for reading and realised the deterioration of his progress after fraternising with this particular circle of friends. His initial zeal to acquire knowledge had largely been replaced by discussions regarding political issues and events:[125]

> The group of brothers I knew was split over; 'Was this, [the 7/7 London bombings] a martyrdom operation or it's haram [impermissible]?'[126] Others asserted, 'What they did... it's good. They're martyrs, they did it for Allah.' So it's just split.[127]

He began to witness stagnation in his development, particularly in the area of religious knowledge. The author suggests that this stage of Sean's development is indicative of his attempting to cross the threshold from the 'founding' to 'youthful' phase of conversion (Figure 1.2). However, he was unaware of how best to progress to the next stage due to the limitations of his company during that period:

> Being around them and their taking knowledge from people who haven't got knowledge themselves... it normally turns to send you in two ways: to either far extremes or you 'fall off' – you come off the religion because you have no knowledge base... people can question you, and it makes you more extreme; it pushes you in those two directions. You've got no balance; because you don't know how to deal with the people around you, and the society... you can't contextualise how you're living and things that are happening... or you're getting a fatwa [religious verdict] from whichever country but you don't know how to implement it in your daily life. Being around people like that, it's a dangerous concoction if you're impressionable... which I found a lot of the people I was around, they were impressionable.[128]

He also noted the gradual isolationist attitude of his colleagues, post-conversion, to the extent that they distanced themselves from non-Muslim members of their own family. Sean realised that his peers' isolationist approach actually increased their susceptibility to extremist propaganda and ideology:

> The rights of your family in Islam, whether they are Muslim or not, you kind of come to realise the great wrongs that a lot of people do

to their family when they're trying to cut themselves off...and this is from ghuloo...100% extremism – cutting yourself off from your family, even though you have to keep family ties...you think you're achieving good [but] you're achieving evil because for one: you're giving a negative image of the deen [religion], first and foremost, two: you're gaining the displeasure of Allah and three: you're becoming an isolationist, which is a danger in itself because again, you have no balance in your life...so now you've set a benchmark for yourself to be extreme, basically.[129]

He continues by stating:

This is another issue that leads people to takfeer. They become so hyped and so involved in secondary issues when they become Muslim... [I'm] not saying the suffering is secondary but not knowing tawheed, not learning the Qur'an or anything like that. You become so involved in the politics and issues of takfeer, which you've got no right to become involved in, having been Muslim for four/five, six/seven months. You become so involved in that and so engrossed in it, that you feel doing anything less is sometimes kufr (disbelief), which is, I've heard people say, or their eeman (faith) has gone because of being in this kufaar (disbelieving) country...it leaves you open to all sorts of crazy ideas.[130]

Sean's observations are indicative, the author asserts, of the abstract understanding prevalent among many young Muslim, particularly converts, due to their apparent inability to contextualise Islam within British or Western society. The extreme referred to by Sean here can, perhaps, be accurately portrayed by the bipolar spectrum of religious extremism of Table 1.1 (p. 16) and the funnel model of Figure 1.6 (p. 19). In fact, Table 1.1 possibly highlights the *nature* and *rationale* for such extremism, whereas Figure 1.6 posits the gravitational direction of individuals described in his account.

Beyond the boundaries of the 'liberal' extreme depictions of the respective models, one should be able to easily imagine an individual renouncing or, as Sean described above, 'falling off' the religion and reverting to former pre-conversion practices/lifestyles, etc. The susceptibility of young Muslims at this stage arguably constitutes part of the premise for extremist recruitment and indoctrination. Drs J. and B. Cole support this observation in their identification of four strands to the indoctrination of new recruits:

1. The promotion of clean living
2. The exploitation of identity issues
3. The exploitation of generational and cultural issues within Muslim communities; and
4. The channelling of idealism or rebelliousness through the ideology of the group. (Cole and Cole, 2009: 174)

As it relates to Sean's observations and experience, only points 2 and 4 are the most relevant. In fact, he highlights that in view of his pre-conversion antipathy towards statutory/governmental authorities, anything 'anti-authority' resonated strongly with him.[131] It is important to understand the backdrop against which such anti-establishment feelings developed:

> It [the conflict in Northern Ireland] had a big effect on me. Looking at the things that were going on and some of the atrocities that were committed on both sides. It had an effect, because when I came to Islam, I had more of an understanding of how the wars were going on and British involvement in these wars having seen how it ripped Ireland apart and the big effect it had on the people there. I see the pitfalls of foreign involvement in countries... just from my family background. My family was very, very against British involvement in Northern Ireland, so I mean I already had an inkling towards that... I wasn't their biggest fan, basically... because of their foreign policy [and] interference in foreign countries.[132]

Drs J. and B. Cole further elucidate upon the pre-conversion politicised psyche of potential recruits when observing: 'In other cases, they [extremist groups] simply build on a politicisation that is already developing within the individual' (Cole and Cole, 2009: 174). They cite Maajid Nawaz to illustrate his apparent politicisation, prior to practising Islam, via rap music because of its inherent anti-establishment message, and his subsequent attraction to Hizb ut-Tahrir's rebellious, anti-authority kudos (Cole and Cole, 2009). Sean's account and experience contrasts sharply with the example cited here as his raison d'être for politicisation extended beyond the apparent superficiality of Nawaz's affinity for the counter-culture inspired by rap music. Indeed, Bjorgo and Horgan's observations would not go amiss at this point:

> While dozens of autobiographies of former terrorists exist, there are also increasing examples of accounts by those whose involvement

and engagement amounts, upon closer inspection, to little more than peripheral activity.

(Bjorgo and Horgan, 2009: 19)

More tellingly, they note:

There is a new-found credibility in being an 'ex-terrorist', which in some cases has led to bitter recriminations and acrimony as a result of unrealistic expectations about what 'ex-terrorists' are assumed to be like.

(Bjorgo and Horgan, 2009)

They then cite a vivid example of the furore caused by one such claimant who, according to multiple media reports: 'did nothing more than stir up anti-Muslim sentiment in an attempt to confer self-legitimacy'.[133] Reference to the word 'terrorist' need only be replaced by the term 'Islamist' in order to highlight recent, similar claims of purported former extremists in the UK.

Cognitive openings part 2: Reflection

As has been discussed above, Sean was able to reflect upon and re-evaluate his learning as a young Muslim. He was now married with children, having met his wife from a new, more established Muslim community. His marriage was significant in that during the formative stages of the relationship domestic conflicts centred on both his and his wife's ideological affiliations: 'when I first got married, me and my wife had some arguments about this "Salafi/not Salafi" thing'.[134] It should be noted that his beliefs prior to marriage and imprisonment were akin to violent extremism/takfeer. He was exposed to propaganda videos related to Iraq, Afghanistan and Chechnya which imbued in him a sense of urgency to: 'fight someone...kill someone'[135] because 'that's our first instinct because of our background.'[136] In addition to his marriage, one significant factor that contributed to his gravitation from violent extremist propaganda was his encounter with another Muslim who also attended the same mosque as his wife and her family:

A particular brother used to come and sit and talk with me, in a good way as well...he just said; 'look, I know you've heard certain things from certain people, but come and find out for yourself, do you understand? That's kind of how I got introduced to Brixton Masjid, because obviously before, I've heard the usual thing; 'oh, its a police masjid, MI5 masjid, people there, they work for Saudi.' It's the same views you hear now, that I heard then.[137]

Sean's encounter and friendship with this individual is synonymous with the pattern described by Garfinkel in her study of psychological transformation from involvement in violence to non-violent activity (Bjorgo and Horgan, 2009: 21, citing Garfinkel, 2007: 186). She noted a key factor in such transformation as being the significance of personal relationships: 'Change often hinges on a relationship with a mentor or friend who supports and affirms peaceful behaviour' (Bjorgo and Horgan, 2009).

In the event, Sean visited Brixton Mosque and was impressed with the timetable and structure for religious classes. He attended many of the classes to halt the stagnation in his learning of the religion. He immediately came to the realisation that he had been reading books but not understanding the text and that the classes provided an accurate contextualisation of various religious tenets. His approach to learning the religion had been, up until that realisation, abstract.[138] His decision to eschew former peers and attach himself to the new community was emphatic:

> So once I started going to classes that kind of sealed it for me as well; hearing the knowledge and just meeting the people there. It had a big impact on me. The knowledge is probably the key thing for everyone. When you see people moving to extremism, even the people … they seem knowledgeable, but they're very emotional. So they twist things to their whims and desires.[139]

The importance of knowledge at this stage of a young Muslim's development is crucial, especially as far as it relates to ideology. In support of this, Drs J. and B. Cole identify two interconnected indoctrination and grooming processes at work in their dataset:

> At one level, they are indoctrinated with an extremist Islamist ideology, which justifies the use of violence for politico-religious objectives, but simple adherence to the ideology does not mean that an individual will necessarily prove willing to commit an act of violence.
>
> (Cole and Cole, 2009: 195)

They proceed to describe the second process as the progression to actualise violence. Sean did not make the transition towards such acts of violence at that stage. He was, however, fortunate in the timing of his decision to abandon the company he had been keeping prior to remand: 'Out of twenty of them, probably fifteen are in jail now, some for armed robbery, and... five or six of them for terrorist charges.'[140]

Sean recounts his interaction and time spent with them on what he considered recreational activities such as paintball, etc.; however, upon further reflection he acknowledged that they were probably more than mere leisure pursuits. Drs J. and B. Cole discuss how susceptible Muslims can find themselves in similar predicaments to some of Sean's former colleagues when they are targeted for socialisation into terrorist activity:

> Gradual involvement in non-violent activities in support of terrorist violence is one way of incrementally socialising an individual into terrorist violence. This was true of many Provisional IRA recruits in Northern Ireland. Initially, new recruits would be involved in non-violent activity only, but would gradually be involved more and more around the periphery of violent activity before being directly involved in an act of violence... The most common non-violent terrorist activity is fundraising, including through criminal activities... testing their commitment to the cause.
>
> (Cole and Cole, 2009: 199)

Given Sean's and some of his former colleagues' pre-conversion affinity for violence and criminality, eventual involvement in activities for which they have been incarcerated becomes consequential, especially after exposure to extremist indoctrination. It is interesting to note the effects of Sean's interim incarceration following his encounter with members of Brixton Mosque. Richard Reid, during his imprisonment, continued after converting to Islam to develop an interest in political aspects of the religion, particularly global events affecting the Muslim world. In contrast, Sean developed a balanced understanding and perspective on his life and issues that immediately affected him:

> It was difficult, but I think one thing that had helped me was that, since I'd started going to Brixton Masjid, I'd kind of got more of a balanced view of things. Even though I hadn't been going there long, I'd kind of changed my views a lot.[141]

During his eventual court trial, he was found not guilty of Grievous Bodily Harm (GBH) and released after six months with the period of his imprisonment considered as a penalty for absconding while on bail.[142]

Reversal of fortune or effective grassroots counter-radicalisation?

Sean's account and experience provide an opportunity to examine and test the validity of theoretical frameworks cited throughout this research. His apparent 'outward' gravitation between the 'Jihadi' and 'Salafi' constituencies (see Figure 1.1) and 'reflux' from the 'gravitational pull' of violent extremism towards the 'Salafi communities' (Figure 1.6) indicate the effectiveness of latent bottom-up or grassroots counter-radicalisation efforts of communities which are located closest to violent extremist entities. His disengagement, so to speak, from violent extremist propaganda was primarily psychological and can be attributed in part to a particular factor identified by Bjorgo and Horgan in their analysis of psychological disengagement; namely: 'Disillusionment arising from strategic, political or ideological differences' (Bjorgo and Horgan, 2009: 22).

As discussed previously, Sean's progression from violent extremist/takfeeri belief was as a result of his witnessing its propagandists' political and emotional emphasis on secondary issues of Islam. Additionally, he experienced an ideological vacuum caused by distorted and misconstrued aspects of the religion. Furthermore, the incongruity of the rationale behind extremist propaganda caused him to re-evaluate his own position as a Muslim convert in British society. Referring to the 7/7 London bombings, he was able to reflect on the following: 'What if that happened to my family? Would I do that to my family?[143] On further reflection since eschewing his former beliefs, Sean continues to empathise with victims and family members of terrorist attacks and is now involved with cross-cultural engagement programmes which enable constructive dialogue between such individuals and Muslim communities.[144] Consequently, his gravitation across to the 'Salafi' constituency has been embedded due to his affinity with Salafism. In view of this it is unlikely that he will continue his 'outward' gravitation at this stage of research. The Change Institute's studies of violent extremism also yielded similar results in this respect. Of the 23 interviews conducted in the UK six were Salafi, with three of them being 'former jihadists', (Change Institute, 2008: 181–2). A further two interviewees also considered themselves as ex- or former jihadists without specifying current ideological affiliations. The author cites these interviewees as further evidence of theoretical 'outward' gravitations from jihadi constituencies, and 'refluxes' from violent extremist ideology, thus providing increased validity to the models proposed in this research. Roald, in summation of her three-stage conversion theory, outlined in Chapter 4 of this research, indicated a small number of converts remain at the first 'falling in love with Islam' stage for longer periods than others. This, she suggests, is especially true of Salafi adherents (Roald, 2004: 288). In view of the observations regarding Sean, the author proffers a supplementary explanation to her observation; namely, by the very orthodoxy and/or conservatism of their practice, Salafis are in a position to eventually contextualise their religious understanding and practice within society. Admittedly, this often occurs at a slightly later stage, after realisation of socio-religious/environmental factors and the fact that they differ significantly from the regions or localities whence they derive their religious instruction, i.e. scholars residing in predominantly Muslim societies, etc.

The previous three case studies arguably illustrate the applicability of the theoretical models when used within the context of gradual radicalisation towards extremism; however, Sean's particular case study, when juxtaposed with the previous three, illustrates how the models can also be used in the same context to highlight a gravitational progression *from* extremist trends or ideologies. It is important to note that the following discussion is not concerned with the possibility of deradicalisation or disengagement – indeed, emerging research has established their respective veracity (Bjorgo and Horgan, 2009). The reliability and applicability of the theoretical models, therefore, form the ambit of discussion at this juncture. The author has tested these frameworks against the case studies in question and acknowledges, particularly in el-Faisal's case, limitations so far as the extent of applying the conversion phase model depicted in Figure 1.2. That said, each model provides a premise for testing against other similar research where an informed insider perspective can possibly challenge or, indeed, further develop the theoretical frameworks in question. In the meantime, other existing academic research can possibly continue to be applied to these frameworks in order to ascertain their validity. Drs J. and B. Cole for example, make reference to a particular process of recruitment and indoctrination which seeks to: 'focus . . . more on channelling the idealism of the recruit through the ideology of the [extremist] group' (Cole and Cole, 2009: 177). The 'idealism' described is synonymous with the 'youthful' phase of a convert's development depicted in Figure 1.2. This was arguably the stage that Sean proceeded to while on remand. His subsequent encounter with a member of Brixton Mosque was an additional factor allowing him to reconsider and rescind his more extreme views and beliefs, which enabled his gradual but progressive gravitation to the 'Adult' phase.

Post-extremist ideology and practice: Converts as conduits between wider non-Muslim society and Muslim communities

Sean illustrates the improvement to his character since converting to Islam by referring to the relationship with his mother:

> It's been a relief for my mum...because she knows she can call me, and I'm either at home, or I'm at the masjid or I'm at work. And I think it makes her proud in a sense, that she knows that I'm trying to achieve something.[145]

This change has also imbued in him a stronger sense of his British and Muslim identities, and the contributions he, as a convert, can make societally:

> The convert community is growing and I think it has got a contribution to make...we've got a big role to play because of our backgrounds...we can be role models, for one. And for non-Muslims to see: 'he's come from the same background as me but he's still the same person, he's just got his religion now.' But you're still balanced, you can still work...you just don't do certain things anymore, and that shouldn't be a barrier...[It's] how you carry yourself...some of us have good jobs, [others] need to get proactive in the community.[146]

He openly expresses frustration with the wider Muslim populace over the apparent malaise and failure to acknowledge that they also have equal, if not added, responsibilities in tackling violent extremism among their own communities:

> We need to step up to the table as Muslims, we can't just generally keep thinking it's someone else's problem...you don't get the backing sometimes, but at the same time, there's not enough people willing to step up to the plate and admit some of the problems in the Muslim community. I think we [converts] have got a contribution to make in changing those problems. First and foremost, addressing

those problems and helping the youth to understand who they are, giving them an understanding of the religion.[147]

Sean's views and concerns are significant inasmuch as they address the second part of this research's central question: are British convert Muslims best placed by virtue of their identity/ies to act as effective conduits between the majority (host) society and immigrant, second/third generation Muslim communities in understanding and effectively leading in the fight against violent extremism in the UK today? Roald's questions are of similar import in a Scandinavian context but hold equal validity in this instance:

> How important is the role of new Muslims as intermediaries between Muslim communities and Scandinavian society? Is the particular position of new Muslims who have 'one foot in each culture' beneficial for a fruitful dialogue between the two cultures?
>
> (Roald, 2004: 289)

Sean's perspectives also reflect the positions of other academic research which similarly explores the role of converts in Western societies:

> Converts may have greater empathy with non-Muslims because of their non-Muslim past and ongoing relationships with their family of origin. They often have a heightened awareness, compared to other Muslims, of how Muslims are viewed by outsiders, so there can be a strongly reflexive element to their discourse.
>
> (Zebiri, 2008: 39)

Kose's earlier research on predominantly white Muslim converts supports Zebiri's findings:

> They [converts] still regard themselves as members of their society and they do not favour isolation. On the contrary, they are fully conscious and aware of their own local environment as well as the universal aspects of the faith they have adopted.
>
> (Kose, 1996: 134)

Roald's Scandinavian context sheds further light on convert roles albeit so far as the more academically qualified concerned:

New Muslims function on various levels in society and... [those] who have a role as intermediary between Muslim immigrant communities and wider Scandinavian society are mostly highly educated. As academics they have the ability to promote a balanced view of Islam and Muslims that might be accepted by majority society. They also tend... to distinguish between 'ideal Islam' and 'Muslim practice'... By this non-Muslims might more easily understand the complexity and the problematic issues of Muslim communities in Western society.

(Roald, 2004: 295)

While Sean does not fall into this category of the 'highly educated' and his background is uncharacteristic of an intermediary role according to Roald's findings, his intelligence and 'streetwise' background have become increasingly significant within the British context, particularly post 7/7. His full-time employment with STREET UK Ltd and related community work has led him to part of a newly-established advisory wing to the government – the Young Muslims Advisory Group (YMAG).[148] The formation of this group and its advisory role to government ministers is unprecedented so far as the Muslim communities are concerned. Sean explained his reasoning behind accepting an invitation to join the group:

Being the only convert in the whole selection process, from forty on the residential to twenty-two... I kind of felt it was a duty upon me to take it up and represent my community... And I don't want it [the group] to be overrun with a daw'ah [propagation/religious call] that's like, pro-government, because I'm not pro-government by a long shot and if I think something's wrong, then I tell them... I'm not someone who's going to get star-struck by ministers.[149]

Zebiri affirms his position, citing similar examples as evidence to support converts acting as conduits between non-Muslim and Muslim communities in Britain: 'Converts might therefore feel freer to be openly critical of the host society, and more outspoken on political issues' (Zebiri, 2008: 40). She then refers to one interviewee's comments which illustrate the position of some Asian Muslims, which is indicative of the 'liberal extremism' discussed in this research:

The Asian middle class now tend to bend over backwards to accommodate people and I think that's a major problem... You stand up against oppression. I think reverts [i.e. converts] do that more and it's easier for them.[150]

In addition to this and, notwithstanding her view regarding the position of educated Muslims as the more effective intermediaries, Roald accedes that: 'On a grassroots level, however, many Scandinavian new Muslims are active' (2004: 297). She then refers to the more menial or secondary roles occupied at this level, such as kindergarten teachers, cultural workers, etc. Further discussion regarding Roald's findings surrounding the role of converts as conduits between non-Muslim society and Muslim communities appears in Chapter 8, the conclusion of this study, in order to establish the validity of her findings against what precedes in this chapter and Chapter 7 where interview data is explored.

Sean's personal and religious development, coupled with his perceived role within British society reflects the gradation towards the 'Adult' phase of conversion. Unlike the first two case studies, he did not gravitate from the wider/outermost generic 'Muslim constituency' or more 'liberal extreme' as depicted in Figure 1.1 and Table 1.1 respectively. His 'outward' gravitation and 'reflux' from extremist entities was arguably more intense and over a relatively shorter period of time than the 'inward' gravitation of both Moussaoui and Reid. As it presently stands, the period of time required for inculcation into violent extremism remains debatable; however, emerging research highlights the lengthy process of indoctrination into Islamist ideology: 'It is evident that all of the dataset were being indoctrinated with an Islamist ideology over a lengthy period, of years in most cases' (Cole and Cole, 2009: 203). More alarmingly, 'It was their final decision to engage in terrorist violence that happened very quickly' (Cole and Cole, 2009). In contrast to extreme radicalisation or indoctrination processes, research charting deradicalisation, disengagement from extremism or even the *rapidity* of each process is limited (Bjorgo and Horgan, 2009: 17).

Typologies revisited: Finding the perfect match

A closer review of the typologies discussed in Chapters 3 and 4 provides an interesting amalgamation of descriptors when attempting to apply them to each case study. For example, Castell's modes of identity are applicable to each study insofar as his third categorisation – 'Resistance Identity' relates to: 'The dissolution of former legitimizing identities that used to constitute the civil society of the industrial era, as giving rise to resistance identities which are pervasive in the network of society' (Castells, 1997).

The first three case studies related to only one of the categories developed by Renani; namely that of the Islamist identity. Another remote resemblance to his typology is perhaps the 'Undetermined/Vagrant identity' which, at most, when considering the counter-radicalisation import of this study, suggests the susceptibility of young Muslims to be due to their lack of identity and unpredictability so far as loyalties are concerned (Renani, 2001: 138–45). Nielsen, on the other hand, provides distinctive classifications for at least two of the studies. His classification of 'Aggressive action' denotes initial radical Islamic political action via propaganda (Nielsen, 1997: 135–287). El-Faisal's case study could arguably fall into this category; however, the definition of 'radical' Islamic action would have to be defined further. Nielsen's current definition, as it stands, is too broad and open to misinterpretation. In other words the *extent* of radicalism would need to be determined. His classification regarding 'high profile separation' and 'high profile integration' respectively could, to varying degrees, be applied to Sean's subsequent societal contributions and involvement with a governmental advisory panel. Having said this, the connotations of separation and/or integration can be construed negatively, depending on whether the perspective considered is either Muslim or non-Muslim. In other words, such terminology does not accurately portray the realities of Muslim participation in each instance. Ramadan's typology is, perhaps the most accurate in reflecting the position of each case study. However, his definition of 'Political and Literalist Salafiyya' is, the author suggests, inaccurate. This definition more accurately describes the *Ikhwani* (Muslim Brotherhood) or violent extremist/takfeeri constituencies among Muslim communities, particularly in view of the belief that all western societies denote abodes of war (*darul harb*) which, coincidentally, underscores Ramadan's delineation regarding this category. Nevertheless, as his typology presently stands, the first three case studies would fall under the 'Political and Literalist Salafiyya' whereas, the fourth could be posited under his classification of *'Salafi traditionalism'*, that is, adherence to the first three generations of Muslims (As Salafus Salih – the Righteous Predecessors) and the literalist understanding of sacred texts (Ramadan, 1999). Finally, brief reference can be made to Roald's typology in Chapter 4 of this study. Suffice it to mention that she considers the 'Salafi trend' in its entirety to constitute an extremist entity and, analogous to Ramadan's typology, also places violent extremist/takfeeri elements of the Muslim communities among this category.

Case study conclusions

This chapter has attempted to examine some of the possible factors behind the initial attraction to violent extremism. Particular attention has been given to ideological delineations in order to determine precise areas and periods of radicalisation into violent extremist rhetoric and/or action. The author acknowledges ideological influences constitute only part of a more diverse mosaic of an extremist's character, and that other equally important factors can contribute to catalytic drivers towards terrorism. Indeed, Drs J. and B. Cole suggest:

> For many young British Muslims looking to rebel against the traditional values of their parents' generation, the wider community and/or the government, involvement in these [extremist/Islamist] groups can simply provide a cathartic and vocal 'pressure valve' for their anxieties, frustrations and sense of helplessness. But some highly committed individuals may view the activities of these groups as 'pointless pontification and debate' and may simply bypass them as they search for facilitators through whom they can access terrorist networks.
>
> (Cole and Cole, 2009: 155)

The latter part of this observation certainly appears true so far as Moussaoui and Reid were concerned and provides a cogent explanation for the cyclical model of violence framework (see Figure 1.5, p. 17) revisited in these particular case studies. Data provided in each case study did not reveal any involvement at the precursory stage of the cycle; however, in the cases of Moussaoui and Reid, the processes of discontentment, i.e. 'anger, frustration and bitterness at own society' and the quest for 'revenge and retaliation' are easily discerned. This led to their ultimate or intended actions to commit suicide attacks against Western interests. Drs J. and B. Cole acknowledge the common presumption that their dataset were incensed by the 'war on terror' and the UK government's policy in this regard; however, they assert that this, 'cannot be seen as the catalyst which triggered the start of their radicalisation because virtually all of them had either begun the process of radicalisation, or had joined terrorist cells, prior to 9/11' (Cole and Cole, 2009: 129).

This observation certainly rings true in the respective cases of Moussaoui, Reid and el-Faisal, all of whose inculcation into violent extremist ideology were fomented during the mid- to late 1990s. Chapter 7 will examine primary data obtained from semi-structured interviews of young Muslims, many of whom converted to Islam post-9/11 and/or 7/7. Only a few Muslims who converted during the 1990s have been interviewed to compare socio-religious climates during that period to that of their younger counterparts. Additionally, the data obtained from the Chapter 7 will be further compared with the above-mentioned case studies in an effort to triangulate and validate research finding.

7
Research Analysis of Interviews

The research data discussed in this chapter is reflective of a particular sample of British Muslim converts within an identified and specific geographical context. It cannot, therefore, be considered as representative of all Muslim converts in Britain. Zebiri also acknowledged the limitations of her research insofar as the sample of converts interviewed could not be considered representative in view of the impossibility of finding: 'a random sample due to the lack of a sampling frame (there being no way of identifying all British converts)' (Zebiri, 2008: 10). Chapter 4 made reference to the Office for National Statistics' (ONS) report in 2001 which, while highlighting the percentages of white British Muslims (4.1%) and Black British Muslims collectively (i.e., Black-British, Black-Caribbean, Black-African and Black-Other – 6.8%), failed to indicate what constituted the actual number of converts in relation to the more predominant ethnicities. According to the Scottish census, also conducted in 2001, approximately one-third of converts were categorised as Black Caribbean, approximately one-tenth as coming from Asian origins and the remainder belonging to White/Other backgrounds (Zebiri, 2008: 45). Chapter 5 addressed the sample groups' ideological and social affiliation to Brixton Mosque in contrast to a geographical one, resulting in interviewees (respondents) coming from various parts of London other than the borough of Lambeth where the mosque is situated. Such affiliations are not dissimilar to other religions where members travel to congregations that reflect their socio-economic, religious or cultural status and/or preference (Reddie, 2009: 81–2). While highlighting quantitative aspects of the data extrapolated from the interviews, particular focus is placed on qualitative findings in order to compare and contrast them with evidence obtained from the preceding case study chapter. Indeed, the author would argue that the voices and experiences of the respondents will inform the relevance and, indeed, applicability of the research question. The qualitative data obtained herein could also provide a premise upon which to develop or encourage further insider-based research of a similar nature among a more culturally diverse and wider geographic sample of British converts than at present. The author acknowledges that, to date, research samples of converts range from approximately 30 (Zebiri, 2008: 9) to 70 (Kose, 1996) individuals when discussed within a British context. In this vein, he suggests that more extensive research across a much larger section of the convert community is required if progress is to be made around examining its potential susceptibility to violent extremism on the one hand or its effectiveness in countering this phenomenon on the other. Additionally, more extensive research or discussion regarding *converts'* possible roles as conduits between the wider host society and Muslim communities could possibly yield more definitive data that complements the few academic discourses available (Zebiri, 2008 and Roald, 2004).

Thirty-two interviews were conducted; 30 males and two females. However, in view of the initial difficulties experienced when attempting to interview female converts, the author opted against including data of the two women as, not only would it be disproportionate to the findings of the male respondents, it would also be unreflective from an empirical standpoint. In the event, the sample of male respondents was comprised largely of young converts between the ages of 18 and 25 (26 in number, equating to 86.6% of the sample). Only one of the respondents was aged between the 25 and 35 age brackets, with the remaining group falling between 35 and 45. These two age groups constituted the remaining 13.3% of the sample.

Identity

While the ethnic profile of the sample was predominantly African–Caribbean all respondents expressed preference to more specific delineations of their respective identities, as shown in Table 7.1 and Chart 7.1. The overall percentage of white converts (9.9% – 6.6% and 3.3% respectively) from this sample group is reflective of Sean O'Reilly's experience living in a predominantly black/African–Caribbean locality, in which Brixton Mosque is also situated. Respondent 30, Dawud George, is one of the few white converts in the sample group who highlighted the fact that his secondary school, while mixed, comprised largely African–Caribbean students.[1] He was comfortable within this environment and did not feel it had any adverse effects on his outlook

Table 7.1   Identity/ethnic background

Identity/ethnic background	Number/percentage of respondents
Black Caribbean	14 (46.6%)
Black African	5 (16.6%)
Black British	3 (10%)
Black Other	2 (6.6%)
Other/Mixed, (1 Middle eastern, 1 Dominican/Mauritrean, 1 Caribbean/white)	3 (10%)
Other/White (1 White Irish, 1 Portuguese)	2 (6.6%)
White British	1 (3.33%)

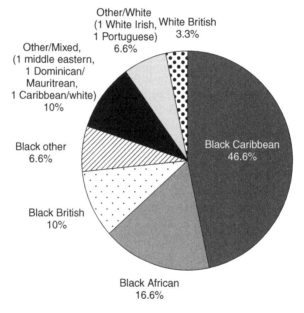

Chart 7.1   Identity

regarding racial issues, etc. pre- or post-conversion. Respondent 11, Abdullah Smith, on the other hand, was conscious of his identity prior to conversion and this affected his initial decision to embrace Islam: 'I didn't want to be white and be Muslim, because of other people's perceptions, but when I did turn Muslim, I realised it has nothing to do with your culture... and your colour.'[2]

Twenty-eight (93.3%) of the respondents confirmed they were comfortable with their British and Muslim identities; however, one explained that he had only developed confidence with his Britishness after converting to Islam. Prior to conversion, particularly in his formative years as a teenager, he experienced acute racism:

> I remember when I was growing up, I grew up through the tail-end of the blatant, obvious racism that existed in British society; so I experienced my fair share of that in my youth, in my teens. And this kind of made me feel that I wasn't accepted as a British person. I was looked at as Black first ... or people judged me based on my 'blackness' rather than the fact that I was actually born in the land that they were. But because I was black, I wasn't really English. So ... I know that that is something which subconsciously affects me and causes me to distance myself from that title of being English or British. But as I've accepted Islam, and I've found belonging with Islam ... more so than identifying with my Black culture, or my 'Britishness' ... I've found that I've identified more with my 'Muslimness' ... I'm not too bothered about being labelled British now, so it's not a problem for me. I will call myself British and I won't feel anything because of it.[3]

One of the two respondents uncomfortable with their dual identities cited a lack of societal acceptance of British Muslims as a reason for such discomfort.[4] The other respondent would not elaborate on reasons for his discomfort/conflict with dual identities.[5]

Education and social background

Twenty-seven (90%) of the sample group attended inner-city state schools with the remaining three having been educated in private (two respondents) or Catholic schools (one) respectively. Despite the large number that attended state school, 33% considered their upbringing and social background to be middle class. Approximately 57% (17) were comfortable in describing their social status as working class whereas three (10%) either did not know or simply refused to identify with any social class structure. In any event, 21 (70%) attended culturally-mixed schools. Five (16.6%) attended predominantly white populated schools with the remaining respondents' attending either predominantly African–Caribbean (3%), Asian (3%) or Roman Catholic (7%) populated educational institutions. Only one-third (33%) of the respondents progressed from secondary school education to college while even fewer (20%) had embarked upon undergraduate or postgraduate studies at university.

Pre-conversion beliefs, influence and practice

The majority of respondents held religious beliefs prior to conversion with most of them professing affiliation to Christianity (60%), albeit to varying degrees. One respondent explained how he was challenged to review his faith in view of one of his close friends' decision to convert to Islam:

> While I was at university, a good friend of mine was studying there too, and he was studying theology...I knew he was thinking about becoming a priest, or even a monk. So when he became Muslim, for me, this was very surprising. Because, for me, becoming a Muslim was a complete diversion from where he was, what he was planning to do before. So I had to question him; 'why have you decided to become a Muslim when you were thinking about becoming a priest?' And once I knew there were clear differences between our religions...only one of us could be correct...we discussed the differences and from there I saw that Islam was the truth.[6]

Thomas, on the other hand, questioned his sudden change of circumstances while in prison and decided that it was predestination that determined his shift from Christianity to Islam:

> I was locked up...I got a three and half year sentence. About ten months through this sentence, I was praying to Jesus Christ...I was getting baptised and Holy Communion through the Catholic Church, I was getting deep into that. But through the Qadr [Divine Decree/preordainment] of Allah I got beaten up while I was in the block, and that was the weekend I was supposed to be baptised, so I thought, 'well hold on, why did this happen?' and I started questioning...chatting to people...my family on the road...some of them had converted to Islam so obviously that made me question it...the more...I read about it [Islam], that's when I officially became Muslim.[7]

Another respondent, Abdul Halim was raised according to the tenets of Rastafarianism which, in itself, relies heavily upon Old Testament and predominantly Judaic teachings: 'I was, as a child...brought up as a

Rasta. My parents practiced the Rastafarian religion, which is linked to Judaism, strongly to the Old Testament.'[8]

Interestingly, a significant proportion of the sample admitted to either not possessing any religious beliefs prior to conversion or being atheist (23%). Michael simply believed in a creator; however, his beliefs consisted of either a miscellany of Christian and Muslim beliefs or no belief whatsoever.[9] Unlike Michael, Yusuf did not possess any religious beliefs. However, a traumatic experience, similar to the account of Thomas's above, caused him to reflect on his life:

> I was walking down the street where I bumped into a couple of guys...they asked me for my money...they pulled out a knife on me and they stabbed me three times...when I was in hospital, I met a Muslim guy that was sitting next to me and he was telling me about the religion...He asked me a question, and this question made me think...'where are you gonna go after you die?' I was surprised...because I never really thought of it deeply...basically I just felt attached to what he was saying to me, and I thought I can relate to it.[10]

Traumatic or violent experiences as precursors to conversion are not unfamiliar to the sample group that is the subject of this study. Having said this, not all respondents are prepared to go into detail as can be seen by Abdullah Smith's brusque reply: 'and then something happened to me, which was a turning point in my life, because I was doing wrong things...and basically, I took my shahada as soon as the thing happened'.[11]

Rambo illustrates 'crisis' as part of the sequence to conversion. In this vein, the above-mentioned accounts of traumatic experiences and/or adverse encounters arguably fit into the theoretical model produced in Figure 4.2 (see p. 68), particularly when considering them as precipitating factors to the respondents' conversions.

The premise of many of the respondents' previous beliefs appears to have been shaped, to varying degrees, by social and familial influences (see Table 7.2 and Chart 7.2). However, with the exception of some of the sample group, few of them were overly influenced by parents' religious practices or affiliations. Kose also observed in his research of native English converts that they: 'seem to have come from families where there was no strong identification with any religion' (Kose, 1996: 38). That said, it is interesting to note, when comparing his findings around similar questions of pre-conversion religious beliefs to this study,

Table 7.2 Religious beliefs prior to Islam

Religious beliefs prior to Islam	Number/percentage of respondents
Christianity	18 (60%)
Shiism[12]	1 (3.3%)
Rastafarianism	1 (3.3%)
Atheism/no belief	7 (23.3%)
Unspecific belief/s in existence of God	3 (10%)

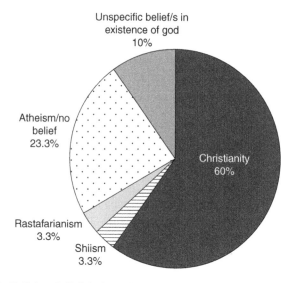

Chart 7.2 Religious beliefs before Islam

both groups possessed an intrinsic belief in God (83% and 76.6% respectively) despite many of their non-conformist approaches to traditional Abrahamic faiths.[13]

Conversion

Twenty-seven (90%) of the sample group converted to Islam during their adolescence. This data concurs with similar research among converts to Christianity whose average age of conversion was also during adolescence (Zebiri, 2008: 136). According to Zebiri's findings, conversions to Islam within European and North American contexts occur at a stage considerably past that of adolescence. She cites Kose's findings which placed the average age of conversion of his sample group at 29 alongside those of Poston who also observed 31.4 as the median age in his research; Kose's and Poston's median age groups equate to an overall average of 30 years (Kose, 1996: 37; Poston, 1992: 166). This, however, contrasts sharply with the author's findings which clearly point to a lower median age for conversion of only 17.6 years (see Table 7.3 and Chart 7.3). Indeed, only 10% of the sample group converted between 21 and 30 years of age, thereby conflicting with older theories propounded by Thouless, Lonergan, and Kohlberg who asserted religious conversions occurred among older age groups due to their moral compass and 'cognitive-development-theory of moral reasoning' (Thouless, 1979: 104; Lonergan, 1972: 238; Kohlberg, 1984: 172). When considering these theories regarding moral reasoning, it is prudent to observe

Table 7.3 Age of conversion

Age	Number/percentage of respondents
12–15 years old	7 (23.3%)
16–20 years old	18 (60%)
21–25 years old	2 (6.6%)
26–30 years old	1 (3.3%)

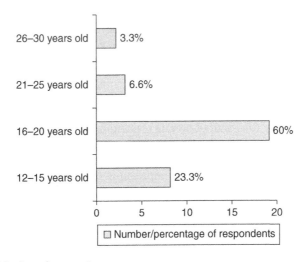

Chart 7.3 Age of conversion

respondents' rationale behind converting to Islam, particularly as it relates to their current perceptions of society. When asked what they disliked about British society and culture, some of the responses reflected some of the sample group's respective moral compass and reasoning:

> There are incompatibilities between Islam and Western culture, such as the emphasis on entertainment and lack of emphasis on intellectual thinking or reasoning... the over-emphasis on consumerism and fulfilling your [desires?]... always having to have the latest of something for you to feel important. Or the emphasis on important people being stars, whereas you have academics or intellectuals, or people that are known for research and forwarding society... they don't get the same recognition.[14]

Rahim McDonald responded to this question emphatically by answering:

> Well, in a nutshell, the culture is decadent! The culture is one which erodes the morals of society. And that's blatantly obvious. I mean, look back a few years... it was a safe place, crime was low, there wasn't the promiscuity (as it is now), there wasn't these STDs [sexually transmitted diseases], as there is now. And the culture is one fuelled by Capitalism, which is about getting more and more... being materialistic. If you're not somebody who takes the academic route to get money, then you go to crime. The morals of society have eroded to the extent that you have this drinking culture... And you have unwanted pregnancies... I mean, the list goes on and on.[15]

The above examples should suffice in contrasting the above-mentioned theories that support the basis for religious conversion among older age groups as being the result of morale reasoning, etc. One possible answer for the earlier cognitive and moral reasoning among members of this particular sample group is their exposure to varying degrees of trauma. Brief accounts of violence and or imprisonment have already been cited above. Having said this, Zebiri suggests one reason for the decrease in age relates to Islam's visible presence and accessibility via society, education and media. In any event, through her own research this trend is acknowledged with 23.5 years being the median age of conversion (Zebiri, 2008: 42). She also refers to Roald's findings among Scandinavian converts which estimated that approximately 80% of them were below the age of 30 when they embraced Islam (Roald, 2004: 109). Al-Qwidi's research, which placed the median age at 25 years, is also cited in support of this shifting trend (Qwidi, 2002: 155). It should be noted that the age of conversion for the preceding case studies (Chapter 6) fall within both the author's and Zebiri's medians.

Attraction to Islam

Accounts from a few of the respondents' more traumatic experiences have been discussed above. Although trauma or crises comprise, in some cases, major factors that contribute to religious conversion, other unrelated yet significant drivers also exist (Rambo, 1993: 44–55). It is not within the scope of this book to expound upon religious conversion theory in too much detail – indeed, aspects of this were discussed in Chapter 4. What follows in this section are accounts of key attractions to Islam from the sample group in an effort to identify and compare the findings with those of the case studies in Chapter 6.

The categories shown in Table 7.4 and Chart 7.4 are broad in their encapsulation of data related to this area. This is due to the difficulty in providing specific categories for each answer. For example, some respondents were attracted by the role of Jesus in Islam: 'A big factor was the role of Jesus in Islam'.[16] Answers of this nature were placed in the category of tawheed in view of their relativity with Islamic monotheism, i.e. Jesus being a prophet of God and not part of a Trinitarian deity as propounded in Christianity. Zebiri also noted tawheed as a common theme that attracted her interviewees to Islam (Zebiri, 2008: 57). This statistical evidence contrasts with Reddie's observations regarding black converts being more critical about practices of some of the churches as opposed to doctrinal tenets of Christianity (Reddie, 2009: 82–3). Indeed, 30% of respondents citing the Islamic concept of monotheism in preference to the Trinitarian concept of godhood indicate the ambit of where

Table 7.4 Attraction to Islam

Attraction	Number/percentage of respondents
Tawheed (Islamic monotheism)	9 (30%)
Islam as a way of life/Brotherhood	15 (50%)
No contradictions/simplicity/made sense	3 (10%)
Traumatic experience which precipitate 'soul searching'	3 (10%)

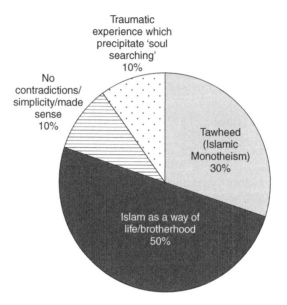

Chart 7.4 Attraction to Islam

their respective criticisms were directed. Half of the sample group were attracted to the structured practices and dictates of Islam and/or the sense of solidarity among Muslims – in other words, 'brotherhood'. It is important to note that a significant number of them either had an affiliation with gangs prevalent in south London or, at the very least, would have been exposed to gang culture. This perhaps explains, in some instances, why the 'brotherhood' in Islam proved to be a significant attraction.[17] One respondent, Thomas, recalled:

> My non-Muslim friends at first thought I was part of a Muslim boy gang called PDC [Poverty Driven Children, more commonly known as Peel Dem Crew] but I corrected them, said 'nah, I['m] Muslim but I'm still down with the Peckham boys... [It's] not like that but we're still friends... But my mum... obviously she read in the newspapers about the so-called Muslim Boys but I corrected her.[18]

Some of the respondents' answers were simple but emphatic about 'the unity...the brotherhood...the love...'[19] as strong attractions for converting. Zebiri also observes that the attraction to Islam in this regard 'sometimes corresponds to a perceived lack of these qualities [brotherhood, warmth, hospitality, etc.] in British or Western society in general' (Zebiri, 2008: 57).

Factors such as these, alongside universally shared values of empathy for Muslims facing difficulties, persecution or oppression, go some way towards explaining the immediate connectivity of new converts with the Ummah and the strong sense of brotherhood. Reference need only be made to Chapter 6, case study 2: Richard Reid, to ascertain his earlier pre-conversion gang activity and subsequent affiliation with Brixton Mosque owing to its population of converts and then his final, almost regressive group or gang-like involvement with Abu Hamza's congregation at Finsbury Park Mosque. Reid was galvanised by a sense of injustice against Muslims in Afghanistan, Palestine, Iraq and Chechnya, to name but a few places. This coupled with the apparent malaise and perceived ineptitude of Muslims in general, imbued individuals like Reid with a sense of urgency to act and effectively redress the imbalance. Drs J. and B. Cole make specific reference to their dataset's need to affiliate with peers of similar understanding and that this is either heightened or reduced depending on an individual's emotional state at any given time (Cole and Cole, 2009: 143). Three of the author's sample group (10%) converted to Islam while in prison and their cognitive experiences were not too dissimilar to Reid's. Thomas's account of his conversion is shown above when discussing pre-conversion beliefs, influence and practice. Suffice it, therefore, to recount the experiences of Abdul Halim and Ishaq Thompson respectively:

Respondent 26, Abdul Halim:
Basically, I got into trouble with the police so I was arrested. While I was in prison I had time to read and search. I began reading about religions, seeking answers. So I was given a book about Islam, and comparing it with other world religions, like Buddhism and Hinduism...Judaism and Christianity and after reading that book, it made a lot of sense, what it was speaking about, so I decided that Islam was the true religion and I became Muslim.[20]

Respondent 27, Ishaq Thompson:
When I was younger, I used to win script competitions in the Boys Brigade...memorising sections of the Bible; answering questions, comprehensions, compositions. So I had a good idea of what the Bible was trying to teach...But there was one particular verse in the Bible where it mentioned Jesus when he fell on his face and prostrated to his Lord in the Garden in the Gethsemane...I was

incarcerated at the time and I was in a cell with an African, a French-African. I was playing my music from my radio that evening, and I saw him... get up and he actually put a mat down on the floor and he raised his hands. I wondered what he was doing. I presumed he was doing some kind of ritual prayer, so I turned my music down, but all of a sudden I saw him go down onto the floor and prostrate on his face. At that moment in time, I believed whatever religion he was part of, this was the same religion as Jesus propagated! In the Christian Church, you go on your knees, you put your hands up and you sing hymns... There is no form of submission that I see when you're asking anybody... the highest form of submission is when you put your face down actually on the ground and show that you are submissive to whoever is above you. So by this movement, or this fact, I acknowledged that this was a religion that I really wanted to ask questions about.[21]

Two (6.6%) of the respondents' cognitive openings occurred while studying at university. Their experiences were similar to Moussaoui's in that they were exposed to a more diverse group of students at a higher level of education than previously. According to Moussaoui's brother, Abd Samad, his religious cognitive awakening and initial politicisation occurred during his fraternisation with other Arab/North African students in Montpellier. That said and, despite relatively early exposure to Muslims during his secondary school tenure, Uthman's interest in Islam developed as a result of his decision to study it as a module in his first degree:

I went off to university and that was where I mainly came across Islam [in] two ways: Firstly, studying Islam as part of my degree, which was very orientalist; as a non-Muslim, I didn't think it was very fair or accurate about Islam... which made me read a bit more about Islam. And also, at university, I met a lot more Muslims and it was some of these friends that basically told me about Islam in more detail and started speaking to me about the religion.[22]

Abdul Basit's university experience has already been described above. The socio-economic position and environment of these two respondents compared to Moussaoui's are in stark contrast; they both attended private schools and come from middle-class backgrounds, whereas Moussaoui was subjected to rather poor state education due to his poorer and, arguably, second-generation working class background.

Socio-political, religious and environmental factors are therefore likely to have had more inadvertent effects on Moussaoui than these two more socially privileged respondents. When examining the backgrounds of respondents whose cognitive openings occurred in prison (discussed above), it becomes evident that their experiences almost mirror Reid's. All three recipients, like Reid, grew up with their mothers in single-parent families. They did not further and/or complete their education beyond secondary school at that stage and became distracted by urban 'street' life which included elements of criminality, drugs and social disengagement. An escalation in the seriousness of the crimes for which they were incarcerated possibly indicates the degree of disengagement reached by them. This certainly rings true when considering Reid's circumstances. While far from revelatory, the above details provide a picture of the environments in which Moussaoui, Reid and members of the sample group developed and while it is easier to discern the somewhat predictable effects of some of the differing socio-economic and/or political climates, it is difficult to isolate or identify religious and, more specifically, ideological influences.

Religious delineation and educational orientation as new Muslims

When questioned about their preference for religious delineation over half of the respondents described themselves as Salafi (see Table 7.5 and Chart 7.5). Many pointed out that a more generic description would be that of the Sunni tradition, recognising the demarcation of the two main sects in Islam (the other being Shia). Just under half of the respondents preferred the generic description. The author also placed respondents who answered along the lines of 'following the way of Prophet Muhammad' among the Sunni category. The respective delineations, in particular Sunni and Salafi categorisations, arguably place respondents in the respective 'Muslim' or 'Salafi' constituencies depicted in Figure 1.1 (see p. 9).

Table 7.5 Religious delineation

Religious delineation	Number/percentage of respondents
Salafi	16 (53.3%)
Sunni	13 (43.3%)
Other/unsure	1 (3.3%)

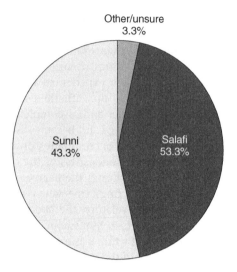

Other/unsure
3.3%

Sunni
43.3%

Salafi
53.3%

Chart 7.5   Religious delineation

However, it is necessary to exercise caution when generalising such delineations, particularly when attempting to chart the developmental stages of each respondent using Hudson's modified framework reflecting the lifecycle of converts' post-conversion experiences (Figure 1.2, see p. 12). It was established at the outset of the interviews that the sample group were ideologically affiliated to Brixton Mosque which is situated in the 'Salafi' constituency. The author suggests that, in the context of this research only, those respondents who expressed preference for the generic term 'Sunni' were at transitory stages of religious learning and development between the 'founding' and 'youthful' phases. Additionally, respondents who preferred to identify themselves as 'Salafi' were between the 'youthful' and 'adult' phases of conversion with a small number having progressed to the more reflective, 'mature' phase. That said, see Chapter 4 regarding ideological affiliation and practice among western converts and the observation that Salafism is considered among the fastest growing Islamic movements today (Wiktorowicz, 2006).

Evidence in support of this assertion can be seen in some of the respondents' answers regarding their process and methodology of learning and/or their understanding of the ideological and political issues affecting Muslims in Britain today. For example, when asked about the extent of their religious understanding and perceptions regarding the challenges faced by Muslims today, their answers ranged from the more simplistic, basic replies to detailed, well articulated responses reflecting the extent of their religious maturity or immaturity depending on the level of their religious education:

Sample answer 1:
I believe that we can overcome these challenges that Muslims are facing today by simply returning back to our religion... and if all Muslims return back to what the Qur'an and what the Prophet Muhammad, peace be upon him, came with, then we'll be alright, insha Allah.[23]

Sample answer 2:
My understanding of Islam helps to influence me a lot about the problems we face today because as Salafi people refer directly back to the Qur'an and Sunnah and how the first three generation of Islam and how they understood it and practiced it the most.[24]

Sample answer 3:
It's just the way they are innit... everyone's different.[25]

Sample answer 4:
From what I see, it's not good what people are putting Muslims through these days. Every Muslim what comes through with their face covered up... they think: 'Oh, she's going to bomb the place or something. Just cos she's got her face covered up.[26]

Sample answer 5:
The governments... they're striving for wealth, wherever the wealth is in the world. And the wealth of the world happens to be in the Muslim lands, which is, obviously, the 'black gold' which is oil. That is what it boils down to as far as I see it... I see the Muslims; you know... they need to go back to their religion... to get their infrastructure stronger in their countries.[27]

Sample answer 6:
As a Muslim, we're taught how to deal with things. For example, not getting emotional about a situation, actually looking at it rationally and analysing the situation. And turning to people who know better, people who are more aware of the situation – who are more grounded in knowledge. We're taught to turn to them, putting aside our emotion. So I find, from an Islamic point of view, it does help me deal with the current situation.[28]

Method of religious dissemination

The statistics shown in Table 7.6 and Chart 7.6 are self explanatory as regards religious instruction at the formative 'founding' phase of respondents' development. The two non-responses are perhaps attributable to a reluctance to reveal any previous extreme beliefs on the part of the two respondents. In any event, most of the group recall their initial periods of learning about Islam. Surprisingly, although none of them learnt a politicised version of Islam, a few professed that they have become more politically aware since converting to Islam:

Sample 1:
I wasn't that political...it's changed a bit now because I'm more aware of what's going on in the world and more interested in what's going on in the Middle East. So yeah, some of my views probably have changed.[29]

Sample 2:
Yes...I would say before my conversion I wasn't really into political affairs at all. Since coming to Islam, I've had to...I've been forced to study political affairs, since we're in the middle of a lot of situations. So when, for example, there was September 11th, that was probably the first time for me in which I had to kind of look into those affairs, current affairs...political affairs.[30]

Zebiri observed that social and political factors were as prominent as tawheed among her sample of interviews and considered it indicative of the 'disillusionment' factor experienced by converts to Islam (Zebiri, 2008: 57).

When comparing data between Tables 7.6 and 7.7 (and Charts 7.6 and 7.7), a correlation emerges between the area of instruction and the

Table 7.6 Initial area/s of religious instruction

Initial area of religious instruction	Number/percentage of respondents
Tawheed (Islamic monotheism)	10 (33.3%)
Politics	0
Practical aspects of Islam, i.e. prayer, fasting etc. (Pillars of Islam)	18 (60%)
No response	2 (6.6%)

Table 7.7 Source of initial learning

Source of initial learning	Number/percentage of respondents
Books – Self taught or gathered information independently	16 (53.3%)
Mosque/study circles	4 (13.3%)
Friends/religious teacher	4 (13.3%)
Other, e.g., internet, videos, various sources, etc.	3 (10%)
No answer	3 (10%)

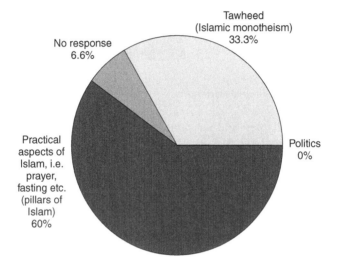

Chart 7.6 Initial areas of religious instruction

actual source from where this was derived. Over 50% of respondents gathered information independently through books, etc. This possibly accounts for the high proportion that learnt about the foundational and doctrinal aspects of Islam such as prayer, fasting, etc. While highlighting this, reference should be made to Sean O'Reilly's case study in which he described the process of religious stagnation as a result of his initial reliance upon books and failure to seek religious direction from established and reputable people of knowledge. The author, therefore, concurs that this area (namely, self teaching via books, internet in isolation, etc.) is one of the premises upon which a new Muslim at either 'founding' or 'youthful' phases of development (see Figure 1.2) could

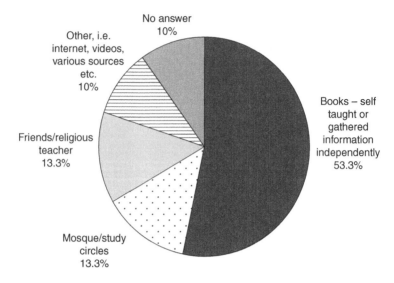

Chart 7.7 Source of initial learning

unwittingly fall prey and succumb to violent extremist propaganda (Cole and Cole: 2009: 195–9). This is not to say similar risks do not exist among the other avenues of learning shown in Table 7.7; however, these mediums often involve interaction at varying degrees, be it private or public, making them slightly more transparent and measurable than isolated approaches to gathering non-contextualised knowledge about the religion. Interestingly, apart from Uthman who embarked upon studying Islam as part of his first degree, only one respondent formally progressed along the route of developing his religious knowledge within an academic framework. In this regard, Abdul Halim is also similar to el-Faisal (case study 3) in that his religious conviction and development led to him applying to study abroad in an institute of religious education. However, unlike el-Faisal who studied in Muhammad Saud Univerisity in Riyadh, Abdul Halim opted for the University of Medina, Saudi Arabia – another renowned university in the Muslim world.[31] Additionally, and perhaps more importantly, Abdul Halim's experiences while studying further reinforced his religious delineation of Salafism whereas el-Faisal continued to gravitate towards the more fanatical and violent extremist understanding of Islam. Evidence to support Abdul Halim's Salafist delineation comes from an unlikely source which provides disparaging undertones. This comes as no surprise considering the rather obvious 'liberal extremist' inclinations of the author:

In Jeddah I arranged to meet two students, one from Brixton and another from Dublin. Their long beards, extremely short robes, and fixed gazes rendered them oddities in the upmarket surroundings... we spoke about life in Britain... They were firmly on the side of the [Saudi] monarchy and the clerics who supported it.

(Husain, 2007: 248)

Abdul Halim made the author aware of this encounter with Husain and the latter's subsequent remarks. Suffice it to mention that he considered Husain's remarks inaccurate and out of context. Nonetheless, Husain's description of Abdul Halim's general support for the Saudi Arabian establishment contrasts starkly with el-Faisal's disparagement of the regime: 'We have to liberate the scholars, liberate Makkah, liberate Madeenah, liberate Masjid al-Aqsa [in Palestine] and we say to hell with the Saudi government' (Addae, 2007: 40). Considering the fact that both graduated from Saudi universities with predominantly Salafist curricula, it is interesting to note their respective Salafist and takfeeri inclinations.

Converts and religious culture: Experiences as new Muslims

Research highlighting convert experiences among established second or third generation Muslim communities is widely available (Kose, 1996; Roald, 2004; Zebiri, 2008). This is not, therefore, a new area of discussion. Nevertheless, the interviewees in the sample group in this study were questioned about their experiences in this regard to ascertain whether any negative encounters among the Muslim communities impacted on their practice or ideological affiliation. Many of the respondents recollect being accepted and welcomed by cultural communities (66.6%) whereas only 20% recounted a negative, unwelcoming response. The remainder of the group provided various responses such as community receptiveness depending on the geographic locality of the mosque. For example, if the mosque was located in a predominantly Asian area, the potential reaction to a new visiting convert could be hostile.[32] One respondent, Abdul Basit, remarked: 'Most mosques are welcoming, although I do feel if you go to a mosque which is dominated by one ethnic people, they can be a bit cold'.[33] Rahim McDonald's response is even more emphatic:

As regards to the other community that we were a part of, the Asian community, they were very cold towards us. They were not welcoming. There were a few who did welcome us – who did realise that 'these guys have come off the street, a life of crime and hedonism, and now they've accepted the religion', which for them, they feel like it's their religion. So some people, they look at it and they think that you're coming into 'our domain' and we don't really want you ... because this is an Asian thing.' So they would give us the cold shoulder.[34]

It is interesting to note that Rahim's experiences were during the early 1990s and his encounters are different to many of his younger counterparts today. Zebiri comments on the relative ease of newer converts, observing that: 'Overall those who converted more recently seemed to have suffered less disillusionment, perhaps because they received more support from fellow converts' (Zebiri, 2008: 62).

She also highlighted the 'sense of relief' converts felt when fraternising with each other. Abdul Halim confirmed this observation, commenting:

One of the main things that I was blessed with when I became a new Muslim was coming to a community which was also made up [of a] majority [of] converts from similar backgrounds to myself: Caribbean, African backgrounds. This had a very positive impact on my development as a Muslim.[35]

Despite the overall positive encounters with the more cultural communities, many among the sample group became aware of, or experienced prejudice/cultural bias as they developed as Muslims – 43.3%, with 10% of this group citing marriage restrictions as a significant problem. Reddie's examination of Black Muslims in Britain also cites intercultural marriage as an obstacle for young African–Caribbean converts (Reddie, 2009). In the event, all of the sample group within this study felt that the negativity and indeed racism experienced at the hands of some of the culturally-led communities and mosques did not adversely affect their practice of Islam. In fact, a few became more committed to espousing the correct understanding and practice of the religion in their lives:

You know, one of the fundamental things was (which was really close to my heart) that we are one nation; it doesn't matter if we're created in different colours, different moulds, different shapes ... it's who's the most righteous. And it was clear that they [cultural Muslims] didn't study this, this verse in the Qur'an! It hasn't affected the way I practice the religion; it just makes me pray more and more that the community, the Ummah, becomes more united and they try to educate the general masses who I come across in my daily life.[36]

Roald provides an important distinction between a new convert being *received* by Muslim communities and accepted: 'When asked how they were received by the Muslim community, the great majority of new Muslims expressed that they were well received; only 5 respondents claimed to have been poorly received' (Roald, 2004: 254). She explained that the discrepancy in this particular area of her research could be attributed to 'a tension between reception and acceptance'[37] as:

new Muslims felt that born Muslims greeted them in an exuberant manner...New Muslims perceived all this as a sign of being accepted...However, as time goes by they become aware that a good reception does not necessarily mean one that is wholly accepted into that new faith community.[38]

Zebiri echoes similar experiences among her interviewees with nearly all of them experiencing difficulties with born Muslims at some stage of their conversion. Her group, like Roald's, were initially warmly received, encountering conflicts later on in their development as new Muslims (Zebiri, 2008: 61–2). These experiences are not too dissimilar to Moussaoui's experiences among the North African communities in France during his more formative years; although, it should be acknowledged that the hostility/negativity experienced by him was more attributable to his relative ignorance of his own 'inherited' or cultural religion than anything else at that stage.

Convert perceptions of British society

This area of research is significant insofar as examining the possibility of converts acting as conduits between the wider host society and Muslim communities in Britain. The sample group's perceptions are therefore important if converts are to be considered as integral to the development of policies and mechanisms whereby the prevalent climate of mistrust, discrimination and discord can be effectively addressed and tackled. Just over a quarter of respondents (26.6%) considered their new religion as wholly or partially compatible with British culture. Ishaq Thompson believed that both Islam and British culture could, to some extent, co-exist but it largely depended on 'whether the society and the government really want[ed] them to.'[39] Yusuf asserted that, 'Islam is very compatible to where I grew up. You're meant to love one another, be good to your neighbour and Islam teaches us that'.[40]

Dawud George asserted the religion's general compatibility with British culture but highlighted areas of conflict, e.g., illicit sexual relationships, consumption of alcohol, etc. for both of which Islam is explicit in its censure.[41] A slightly larger proportion of the sample group (36.6%) considered Islam completely incompatible with British culture. Although only a few respondents in this category were prepared to elaborate on their answers in this regard, the majority expressed reluctance to elucidate further. Respondent 26, Abdul Halim's answer to this question has already been highlighted above when examining the issue of moral compass and reasoning relating to ages of cognitive openings for conversion. The remaining group (36.8%) expressed uncertainty regarding this particular question. Nevertheless, combined percentages of respondents who either did not consider Islam remotely compatible with British culture or were uncertain, require further exploration in relation to the subject of *al-uzlah* (seclusion/isolation) within a British societal context. This could perhaps help to determine whether *al-uzlah* is an automatic response or reaction to the incompatibility or uncertainty felt in this instance regarding Islam as it relates to British society and culture. It is important, at this juncture, to reiterate that the linguistic definition and practical application of *al-uzlah* are not, in themselves, manifestations of extremism – the raison d'être for implementing such an act, and the extent to which it is applied, require initial examination before reaching such a conclusion.

One interview question concerning the most significant problems affecting British society today elicited a variety of answers, many of which ranged from the most basic to more detailed responses. Generally, however, many from the sample group cited liberalism and the 'anything goes' type of lifestyles that now pervade British society as a problem vis-à-vis the practice of their new religion. In the event, focus has been put on responses addressing challenges as they relate to society as a whole and not as it relates to Muslim communities, i.e. Islamophobia, etc. Again, as already intimated at the outset of this section, such focus is necessary in order to develop an understanding of convert perceptions as they relate to British society and their local environments. Respondent 17, Andre, made the following observation relating to society's overall lack of spirituality: 'The people ... don't remember God...they do not take time to contemplate...to think about God and think about death. So I think this is mainly their biggest problem. They should actually be aware of their Creator.'[42] Uthman echoed similar sentiments, also recognising a:

> lack of spirituality, a lack of religion...devoid of morality...I feel there's a void there. The churches are empty, but people are still (which is in human nature) looking for spirituality and religion. And that's why there are such large numbers of people reverting to Islam; the pace at which people are converting has risen.[43]

Reddie's recent discourse on the subject of Black Muslims in Britain certainly lends support to Uthman's observations here, especially in view of the Christian orientated perspective that he frequently refers to when attempting to explain the increase of young black British converts to Islam (Reddie, 2009). Respondent 18, Paul, considered societal problems in this instance to emanate from negative media:

> I think consumerism is getting us. Everyone's pursuing the urge to spend...there's like a cult of celebrity going on; everyone wants to be famous or live like they're famous. Yeah...I think the media is destroying this country...there needs to be something to control or influence what stories come out, you know? Three million people a day read The Sun and the Sun prints shit. You've got to try and influence that.[44]

Does Islam have a contribution to make to British society?

Twenty one (70%) of the sample group expressed certainty regarding Islam as a positive driving force among British society. Only three (10%) of the group disagreed, responding in the negative about Islam providing a possible constructive contribution within society, due to respective perceptions regarding the religion's incompatibility with societal norms and values. Six respondents (27%) were uncertain as to whether Islam could make a positive societal contribution in view of the prevalent negative portrayal of the religion and its adherents. Reference need only be made therefore to observations of the predominant sample mentioned above:

Respondent 18, Paul:
Absolutely...it's like anything, any other religion in society, or any other belief that's a minority...people live and breathe it and do

things in a certain way. So we need to contribute...the fact that we live in a democracy means that people have the free will to do what they want, whether they want to go and choose to become a Muslim...take on the structure and discipline and live a decent life...so is there stuff this society could learn? Absolutely. Should it be implemented in some...government strategy? Probably not.[45]

Respondent 26, Abdul Halim:
Definitely. There's a lot which society can learn from Islam, such as morals, most importantly.[46]

Respondent 27, Ishaq Thompson:
Yes, I think that Islam has a great contribution to make towards British society. You know, Islam propagates peace, good manners, a good structure for the home, good structure for society; if you just really listen to the teachings of Islam for a minute and stop ridiculing it and stop saying it's a savage culture.[47]

Respondent 29, Rahim McDonald:
Definitely. The fact that I, for one, was somebody that was involved in criminal activity before I accepted Islam, and Islam has come into my life now, and it's made me an honest person...I'm accountable for my own actions...that in itself has benefited the wider community...I'm a responsible member of society, but I have become responsible through my religion. And you'll find many, many Muslims who were in prison, people who've done some serious crimes...they accept Islam in prison, they come out on the street and they're honest individuals now. They don't go back to crime. And better than that: they become responsible members of society...and this is something which obviously benefits everybody.[48]

The positive response from a majority of the sample group regarding Islam's possible impact upon society as a whole points to the research question in that it identifies possible grassroots roles for young British converts who have the type of urban and cross-cultural/religious credibility that extends across the host/majority society and Muslim communities. Roald also raised the question of new Muslims acting as mediators between Muslim communities and Scandinavian society, in view of them having 'one foot in each culture'. She proceeded to highlight her findings of converts as 'bridge-builders' and the ambition of realising this role within a British context (Roald, 2004: 289, 291–2). Roald expresses her surprise that: 'In Britain representatives from Muslim organisations in most interfaith dialogues were mainly first- or second-generation male immigrants' (2004: 291–2). This contrasted with her experience within a Scandinavian context, 'where new Muslims have a key official role to play in interfaith dialogues as well as in dialogues with majority society' (2004: 291–2).

Roald's observations in this regard could not be more pertinent to the suggestion of a greater degree of involvement from convert Muslims, especially those at grassroots, to address prevalent misunderstandings/misconceptions regarding Islam as a religion among the wider society on the one hand, and on the other imbuing Muslim communities with a greater appreciation for societal shared values and participation beyond restrictive cultural parameters. Zebiri accedes to findings which suggest that converts figure less prominently among wider society; however, she maintains that their active contribution to Islamic orientated programmes and events, etc. remains disproportionately large despite their constituting a relatively small part of the British Muslim population, She describes her interviewees' beliefs that they and converts in general can contribute as 'bridge-builders' in a similar way to that described by Roald above (Zebiri, 2008: 82–4).In fact, one of them noted:

> There's a certain type of person we call a cultural deviant, where they stand between two cultures and are able to act as a bridge between them. That's what I think converts in this country can do, is really explain Islam to non-Muslims and explain Britishness to Muslims.
> (Zebiri, 2008: 84)

In view of existing academic discourses which support the intimations of the above findings, a strong case can be mounted for converts to act as conduits/bridge-builders between the non-Muslim majority society and Muslim communities in Britain. This can be seen to be particularly pertinent in light of the existing climate and increasing polarisation between the two entities.

Convert perceptions of violent extremism/terrorism

The author found that a significant number of respondents were either uncomfortable or lacked sufficient knowledge in answering questions specifically relating to extremism. Chapter 5 discussed some of the limitations experienced with the sample group, particularly CGA and their suspicion of academic research emanating from governmental sources, etc. This resulted in over a third (36.6%) pleading ignorance in matters relating to extremist groups/entities. A few simply refused to answer questions on the topic, highlighting the sensitivities and mistrust, even among members of the same communities with similar backgrounds. In any event, the data garnered from the remaining respondents are rich in detail and provide interesting insights of convert perceptions around the violent extremist phenomena.

Questions relating to the success of Al Qaeda/extremist propaganda elicited varying responses (see Table 7.8 and Chart 7.8). Approximately 16.6% of the sample group attributed extremist propagandists' success, in part, to news coverage by western media. Media reporting of extremist

Table 7.8   Why does Al Qaeda attract support?

Reasons for Al Qaeda support	Number/percentage of respondents
Because of negative Media reporting/portrayal of Muslims and their grievances etc.	5 (16.6%)
Muslim lack of religious knowledge/ignorance	5 (16.6%)
Al Qaeda's ability to tap into emotional psyche of Muslim communities	6 (20%)
Other, e.g. unfair treatment of Muslims, Al Qaeda's are trying to make a difference, they don't attract support	3 (10%)
No knowledge of Al Qaeda/refusal to answer questions related to this subject	11 (36.6%)

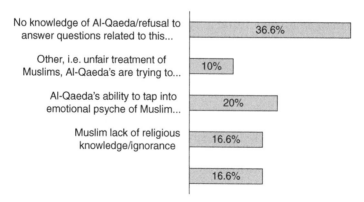

Chart 7.8   Why does Al-Qaeda attract support?

propaganda, the prevailing wars and atrocities committed in predominantly Muslim occupied lands, not to mention the negative portrayals of Muslims, all served to strengthen support for Al Qaeda and its counterparts among grassroots Muslims, according to these respondents. Michael opined that:

> The youth, obviously, they're watching the media, stuff like this, they see that they're getting attacked left, right and centre, the Muslim lands are getting attacked. The non-Muslims are in Muslim lands, they want them to get them out. Then the people go to the youth and they hype them up, in a way that's like, with the media, videos and so forth.[49]

Abdul Halim shared a similar view that Al Qaeda's success was:

> Primarily because of the way the media and news portrays the events that are happening in Muslim countries, i.e. the use of language to manipulate people into believing that Muslims, when they do an act or they commit a crime, that it's murder and killing, whereas when it's a crime done against Muslims, it's ... words which convey different meanings.[50]

Thomas, on the other hand refused to accept that Al Qaeda even existed, holding, as a significant section of Muslims do, that:

> This whole Al Qaeda thing is just gassed up by the media, they ain't got support like they say they have ... I've not met no-one that says they support Al Qaeda, they wanna join Al Qaeda. Does Al Qaeda even exist? It's just a gassed up thing the media has just put out there.[51]

An equal percentage among the sample group (16.6%) attributed the success of violent extremists' ability in attracting support to the lack of religious knowledge and understanding prevalent among Muslim communities today. These particular respondents were also emphatic in their replies to questions regarding this issue. Paul articulated his opinion that there are Muslims:

> out there who are lost ... they are pissed off as well. They see what's going in Palestine – wherever else around the world – in Iraq and they can be easily influenced ... They [(Al Qaeda] are tapping into a group of people ... who are looking for some way to channel their belief or

what they've got on their chest and there's no vehicle to do that in the UK or wherever they're from, so they choose to do it through Al Qaeda.[52]

Uthman believed there to be a few reasons behind the success of Al Qaeda/extremist protagonists, ignorance among the Muslims being one of them:

Ignorance amongst the Muslim community, especially with a lot of the youth...They don't really know what's going on and it's easy to manipulate them if they don't understand the religion. A couple of friends of mine who went to my school...they later became quite extreme and I felt it was down to the fact that they didn't know enough about Islam; and when they wanted to (they were Pakistanis) start practising, they didn't know the direction to go to, who to talk to, didn't have any religious scholars or authority.[53]

Carl also cited a lack of religious knowledge as being among the reasons for the success of Al Qaeda related extremism:

collectively, Muslims as a whole don't practice the religion of Islam properly, and don't have the correct knowledge...Secondly, the amount of scholars who propagate the correct knowledge has diminished; so many people don't understand Islam.[54]

A slightly larger percentage of the sample group (20%) attributed Al Qaeda's success to their ability to tap into the Muslim communities' emotional psyche and evoke various reactions. Gilbert's response to this question, although basic and concise, conveys the sentiment among many Muslims today: 'They're angry innit...a lot of brothers, Muslims are angry at the way they've been treated innit.'[55] Ishaq Thompson's observations are more forceful in illustration when responding to this question:

Because they seem like they're doing something instead of sitting there and doing nothing at all. Somebody slaps you, you want to slap them back...whether you're strong enough or not. People don't want to take things just lying down and this is why they follow Al Qaeda, or this ideology.[56]

Dawud George expressed a similar opinion, emphasising that Al Qaeda:

> play on the emotions of the people, so once something has been highlighted – once an oppression against the Muslims has been highlighted, they can use that to propagate their call, which is to strike back.[57]

Do violent extremist groups fill a void?

Respondents differed as to whether Al Qaeda was filling a void in the Muslim world (see Table 7.9 and Chart 7.9). Abdul Halim believed that a common perception among some Muslims was that Al Qaeda filled a superficial void:

> Apparently, yes. Not that that's the case, but it would seem that way to new Muslims, to people who don't have a full understanding of Islam, perhaps... it would appear that they're filling a void but in reality they're not filling any void. What they are doing is actually creating a problem.[58]

Dawud George, on the other hand, was of the opinion that a void was definitely being filled:

> Yes, they're filling a gap, definitely, yes. They're filling a gap where people have remained quiet for so long, haven't been as vocal as they should be regarding these people. And also there's a gap in terms of the way the daw'ah [propagation] is given... the daw'ah should be given in a way that even current affairs... are discussed, and they're [the Muslims] told about how they should be dealing with these situations. So when someone's not talking about the way we should be dealing with these current situations, then it gives a platform to the people who are prepared to take it, and it's been Al Qaeda for a little while.[59]

Table 7.9   Is Al Qaeda filling a void?

Is Al Qaeda filling a void?	Number/percentage of respondents
Yes	5 (16.6%)
No	8 (26.6%)
Don't know	9 (30%)
No response	8 (26.6%)

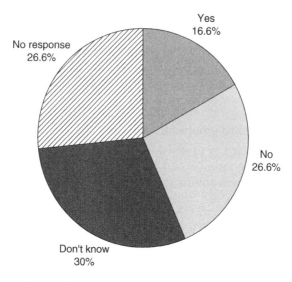

Chart 7.9   Is Al-Qaeda filling a void?

Carl also affirmed that a void was being filled as a result of an unprecedented interest in Islam among western societies:

> I believe Muslims, people in general, want to know about Islam. From all walks of life they want to know about Islam. And if there aren't enough people who are propagating Islam in the correct way, and in the way that people can understand it properly, then Al Qaeda will step in and gather those people who want to learn about Islam but can't find it from the right sources. They will attract those people.[60]

In contrast to the above opinions, Abdul Basit rejected the notion of Al Qaeda filling a void for the simple reason that he did not believe there was one to be filled:

> I don't think they are filling a void, because I don't think there's a void to be filled. I feel that the people who are practising the religion correctly have dealt with how a Muslim should respond to certain events.[61]

Personal exposure and/or attraction to extremist propaganda and reasons for eventually rejecting it

Final questions focused on respondents' exposure to violent extremist propaganda. They were asked:

- whether they had ever been exposed or attracted to violent extremist propaganda, and
- what caused them to reject it.

Only 26.6% (just over a quarter) were prepared to address these questions in detail and the author surmised that the majority of the sample group's reluctance to provide sufficient detailed responses was due either to ignorance or concern surrounding the intent of the research conducted. Nevertheless, the data obtained provides an apt conclusion for the ambit of this particular chapter. Although Uthman was not attracted to such propaganda, he became aware of groups like Hizb ut-Tahrir during his time at university:

> University at the moment is thriving with different groups. Hizb ut-Tahrir were on my campus... different/other groups were all trying to get support and get students and things. One of the first people who told me about Islam was actually a follower of an extremist in England: Abu Hamza. So I came across some of his followers. When it became apparent to me what they were upon, I left them ... It seemed to me that these people were just trying to find an excuse for criminality. It just seemed really like a con. It didn't appeal to me as being much more than that. I just saw people who were into petty crime before and they were clearly attracted to another type of 'gang' ... they felt like it was giving them some kind of status.[62]

Uthman's observations of Abu Hamza's followers resonates strongly with Richard Reid's pre- and post-conversion experiences as well as Sean O'Reilly's account of his friends' progression from petty criminality, prior to conversion, and during their subsequent gravitation towards religiously motivated terrorist activity afterwards (see Chapter 7, case studies 2 and 4 respectively). Evidence continues to emerge, indicating a possible propensity among converts to maintain pre-conversion gun, knife and gang criminality coupling this with violent extremism under the guise of this being legitimate in *darul harb* (an abode of war). Having said this, more vigorous research around this subject is required if sufficient empirical evidence is to be yielded and substantive correlations between such criminality and extremism are to be established. Rahim McDonald acknowledged that he was first attracted to violent extremist rhetoric during the Balkans conflict in the early to mid-1990s. He recalls:

> That was a conflict which was solely... probably one of the most unjust experiences that I have ever experienced as a Muslim, aside from what's happening in Palestine. But Bosnia was intense in its brutality... at that time, many Muslims were going over there to join the Mujahideen. Muslims were sending money to help the relief effort, to pay for food, and also to pay for arms so the Muslims could defend themselves. And this is the right... this is enshrined within the Geneva Convention, that people have the right to resist if they are being oppressed. Yet you will find that the people were being oppressed and slaughtered, and the Geneva Convention... it wasn't being implemented. So what are we to do as Muslims, when we see that our people or these people are not being defended according to the laws of that have been made by the United Nations?[63]

When asked to elaborate further and confirm whether in fact assistance for Bosnian Muslims constituted extremism, Rahim replied:

> I would say, no matter what it is, there are elements of extremism. You have some people that were fighting – yes – justifiably; they were fighting to protect the people... But when you're talking about suicide missions, and blowing things up and killing innocent people, then that's where you draw the line. So that is extremism but unfortunately these things fuel extremism.[64]

He went on to describe the propaganda that was distributed during that period and the fact that the propagatory sources included extremists as well as mainstream Muslim entities.[65] However, most tellingly he recounted the more covert nature of the extremist propaganda which was to:

> lead you away from the path of justice and more towards extremism and following their agenda, which is basically to bring war to your own environment – to bring war to a people who are not directly involved in the war; they've got nothing to do with the war but

because of the fact that they are not Muslims, they automatically become our enemies.[66]

Rahim's final account accords to the author's experience during his tenure as chairman at the time of the Balkans Conflict when some enthusiastic Muslim youth returned to the UK confused at advice they had received while in Bosnia; namely, to return to the UK and maintain a low profile until the opportune moment arrived to wage war on mainland Britain. Dawud George first became aware of extremist propaganda immediately after the 9/11 attacks in the US. He examined Al Qaeda's perspective and compared it to the Salafists' position. Once deciding to look at the circumstances of these attacks from a knowledge-based, as opposed to an emotional, perspective, he was able to discern the erroneous nature of Al Qaeda's propaganda.[67] Perhaps Ishaq Thompson's response encapsulates the latent view of many among Muslim communities, not to mention the respondents in this study who expressed reluctance to answer these somewhat sensitive questions:

I think we all have [extremism] in some respect, whether it's Al Qaeda, or whether it's within our own selves. And it's what reaction we've taken or what stance we've taken – we know what we're about to do is wrong. Somebody slaps me, I want to go and kick his head off, break his arms, break his ribs, and put him in hospital... Really, is that necessary? Do we have to go beyond bounds? So, I think individually, we've all been faced with that, but how do we deal with it? We deal with it by, first of all, knowing what the Prophet would have done. And if we don't know that, and if we don't have a strong belief, then we're going to go the other way.[68]

Conclusions

This chapter has provided empirical evidence from a sample group not too dissimilar from the case studies in the preceding chapter. Parallels have been drawn from the experiences between the respective group and case studies to determine whether any common socio-religious and economic factors existed that could possibly explain why and/or how converts are attracted to, and subsequently embark upon, violent extremist activity. Evidence emanating from the sample group has pointed to the lack of religious knowledge and the effectiveness of extremist protagonists' ability to tap into the emotional psyche of members of Muslim communities, particularly the youth because of their relatively new and either 'founding' or 'youthful' phases of development. The author has asserted throughout the case studies that, with the exception of el-Faisal, young British convert Muslims are most susceptible at the above-mentioned phases of their religious development. The factors highlighted among the sample group arguably support this observation. In fact, the author would further suggest that, due to the nature of answers received from the sample group, a significant number of them have reached the 'youthful' phase of religious development with a few having progressed to the 'adult' and even 'mature' phase. That said, without being in a position to question or examine the group in more detail, it is difficult to accurately identify the stage of religious development for each respondent. Additionally, when addressing the first part of the research question related to converts' susceptibility to violent extremism or, as the case may be, their effectiveness in countering it, certain factors need to be taken into consideration. First, a significant percentage from the sample group (36.6%) expressed reluctance to provide answers or simply pleaded ignorance on questions related to Al Qaeda or violent extremist entities. While an explanation was proffered in the first instance, the author acknowledges that no definitive response can be given, completely negating this section of the group's susceptibility to violent extremism. By extension, neither can affirmation be provided regarding their effectiveness in countering extremism. In fact, an assertion could be made in the absence of empirical evidence from this section of the group that their reluctance to engage and/or their ignorance regarding this essential aspect of research, is indicative of their susceptibility towards violent extremism. However, in any event it would be unwise to discard the rest of the data already extrapolated from this section of the group in view of it corresponding, by and large, with evidence obtained from the remainder of the sample group. Indeed, such data is supported by Sean O'Reilly's case study account of the stagnation in learning he initially experienced followed by his gravitation from the violent extremist narrative towards Salafism. It is therefore prudent to assume that the respondents from the sample group who expressed reluctance in engaging on the subject of extremist entities are progressing in a similar manner to the rest of their cohort.

The question surrounding the group's effectiveness in countering violent extremism extends, according to the evidence provided here, to the more established and older Muslims who were interviewed.

This can be surmised from the detail and lucidity provided during their interviews which clearly indicate their progression beyond the 'founding' and 'youthful' phases of religious development. Accounts from respondents such as Rahim McDonald, Ishaq Thompson and Carl clearly illustrate a more 'mature' phase of development, particularly in view of their ages, periods of conversion, and ability to recount earlier experiences and events during the 1990s. The author's observation in this regard accords with Roald's findings when discussing her interviewees' more reflective stages of development as they progress as Muslims (Roald, 2004: 160). Slightly more youthful but mature insights gained from respondents such as Uthman, Abdul Halim and Abdul Basit support their older cohorts' experiences surrounding pre- and post-conversion issues of identity, etc., particularly in view of the fact that two of them received private school education in predominantly white populated schools where they had to address issues regarding their ethnicity. Despite their respective ages constituting an average of 25 years, (the three older members of the group mentioned above constituted a median age of 42 years), the author would also place them at the 'adult' phase of development. In any event, the relevance of the older respondents' data in relation to the case study of Zacarias Moussaoui cannot be ignored. First and foremost, at least two of the three respondents are likely to have attended Brixton Mosque at the same time as Moussaoui. Secondly, their accounts and experiences, so far as identity issues throughout the 1970s and 80s are concerned, almost echo those of Moussaoui's during his upbringing in France. Rahim McDonald's experiences of racism were vividly recounted earlier in this chapter. The subsequent anger and frustration which developed as a result of such racism undoubtedly caused indelible psychological scars for some of the older respondents much in the same way as it affected Moussaoui (Moussaoui, 2002). However, the demarcation between these individuals' post-conversion religious development is significant. The respondents' varying degrees of focus, understanding and embeddedness of established ideological tenets of Islam contrasted with Moussaoui's eventual concentration on political delineations which were used to present alternative ideological and methodological interpretations of these same foundational principles (e.g. the introduction of a fourth ideological classification of Tawheed – *Tawheed al-Haakimiyah* – which conflicted with existing and accepted categories of which *haakimiyyah* is already a part). Moussaoui's departure from these established principles was arguably the starting point for his journey towards violent extremism.

Other members of the sample group shared experiences similar to that of Reid; in particular his pre-conversion experiences that resulted in his imprisonment and subsequent conversion during incarceration. Similarly to Reid, members of the sample group, upon leaving prison were exposed to Salafism or Salafist communities; however, most of the group remained among such communities while Reid gravitated across to the extreme 'Jihadi' constituency according to the Combating Terrorism Center's theoretical framework (see Figure 1.1). This section of the group's raison d'être for remaining among Salafist communities is similar to that of their older counterparts referred to above. Reid's religious development proceeded in similar vein to Moussaoui. In fact, Moussaoui's case study has highlighted that they even became associates during the time spent at either Brixton or Finsbury Park Mosque together during the mid- to late 1990s.

Finally, it is relatively easy to discern the similar experiences of the majority of the sample group with Sean O'Reilly's case study, especially considering the fact that many of them are from the same generation, converted in similar circumstances and continue to progress along the same routes of learning as O'Reilly. Cultural and religious differences appear minimal among the younger cohort as do any negative or racial encounters with the wider, more culturally-orientated Muslim communities. An explanation for this was shown above when citing Zebiri's observations regarding converts suffering less disillusionment owing to the existence of support networks that were unavailable when older converts embraced Islam (Zebiri, 2008: 62).

To be or not to be susceptible to violent extremism

The question of susceptibility to extremist propaganda, judging by what has transpired during the case studies and interviews depends on multiple factors related to socio-economic, socio-political, socio-religious and psychological drivers that serve to affect or influence the psyche of Muslim converts at both pre- and post-conversion stages of their lives. Unsurprisingly, the scope of this study is limited in part to identifying specific ideological and methodological drivers that may precipitate violent extremist tendencies in a young Muslim convert. The interviews yielded some unexpected results so far as the propensity for violence and extremism are concerned. For instance, Ishaq Thompson and Carl were among the older cohort of the sample group and the author expected their responses regarding the subject of violent extremism to be unequivocal in its condemnation of all Al Qaeda related extremism.

Although they both emphatically eschew all forms of violent extremism and terrorism, nonetheless they continue to display a degree of empathy as to why Muslims are attracted to extremist propaganda, providing eventual tacit approval for extremist acts:

> It's stemming...basically [from] the first oppressors, you know what I mean? Like, you step on my foot – it's as simple as this – someone's going to react, they have to react. And maybe if the rest of the Muslim world isn't doing anything at all, and this ideology is saying 'Ok, we've got to do this, we've got to go and do that' [i.e. terrorism]...The young men are reactives. They react to certain actions against them, you know...the elders wouldn't, the younger ones will. Because they're young, they're naive, they're uneducated and they're just acting on impulse. Some of the things which the ideology of Al Qaeda give as well, is when you come into the religion, you have hang-ups which you don't want to let go...and it's like a green light for you to do these things against the non-Muslims.[69]

Carl noted:

> Al Qaeda...what they stand for, in some Islamic terms, can look romantic. It looks like the smaller individual standing up against the bigger individual. Everybody likes that David and Goliath. So it looks like a small band of people standing up against the worlds' superpower and actually doing something...so romantically that affects people.[70]

A few younger respondents, such as Dawud George also intimated his empathy for Al Qaeda's ability to attract support when asked whether they were filling a void. It should be noted that such empathy or, as the case appears in each instance, understanding of extremist entities' rationale for violence/terrorism should not be misunderstood. In fact, as will be discussed in Chapter 8, it is increasingly acknowledged among statutory bodies and security services that those most effective in countering violent extremism are grassroots communities that understand the psychology and ideology of extremist groups and have experience/expertise in tackling them. Nevertheless, the question of susceptibility to extremism remains and it is the author's summation that so long as new converts, regardless of their respective ages of conversion, are engaged with from an ideological and methodological standpoint during the 'founding' and 'youthful' phases of development where they are most susceptible, the risk of and exposure to violent radicalisation/extremism can be effectively reduced. This would, of course, have to take place among other related socio-economic and possibly psychological interventions depending on the psyche of each convert. Evidence extrapolated from case study 4, alongside the interviews and documentary analyses, point to new converts' susceptibility or vulnerability to violent extremism diminishing as they proceed towards the more 'adult' and 'mature' phases of religious development.

8
Countering Terrorism in the UK: A Community Perspective

This chapter highlights the findings of preceding research chapters drawing on earlier discussions that identified historical and ideological delineations relating to violent extremism. Discourse follows regarding community development of counter-radicalisation/ intervention initiatives that have been developed to address and effectively tackle the issue of violent extremism at a grassroots level. In bringing these threads together the author intends to address the primary research question as well as highlight the implications and subsequent effects of the government's Preventing Violent Extremism agenda (PVE) on Muslim communities.[1] The PVE Pathfinder Fund was launched by the Department for Communities and Local Government (DCLG) in October 2006 and introduced publicly in February 2007.[2] Initial funding of £5 million was allocated to 'support priority local authorities, or groups of local authorities, to take forward a programme of activities to tackle violent extremism at a local level'.[3] Its more specific remit was to develop a community whereby Muslims were empowered to:

- Identify themselves as a welcome part of a wider British society and are accepted as such by the wider community
- Reject violent extremist ideology and actively condemn violent extremism
- Isolate violent extremist activity, and support and co-operate with the police and security services
- Develop their own capacity to deal with problems where they arise and support diversionary activity for those at risk.[4]

Contrary to earlier criticisms regarding Muslim communities' reluctance to tackle extremism among its ranks, acknowledgement has been given to the fact that a small minority have been engaged in countering violent extremist propaganda since the early 1990s – well before any significant government strategy was introduced (Lambert, 2009). In fact, counter-radicalisation initiatives, such as 'Strategy To Reach Empower & Educate Teenagers' (STREET) were conceptualised before the PVE agenda was introduced (Baker, 2006). The 2006 Demos report provided a case study of the organisation. This is when DCLG first became aware of STREET (Briggs et al., 2006: 75–6). It is, therefore, interesting to note certain government departments' cautious approach to such organisations because of their Salafist delineations on the one hand and their championing the same entities as models of good practice on the other.[5] Nevertheless, the PVE agenda continues to court controversy, due to general perceptions of it being either a mechanism for stigmatising Muslim communities and encouraging its members to spy, providing intelligence to statutory agencies on one hand (Kundnani, 2009) and on the other, being criticised for failing to differentiate between funding 'Islamist'/extremist and moderate groups (Maher and Frampton, 2009). In the event, this chapter and indeed, part of the research conducted, are concerned with descriptors which more accurately define extremism irrespective of it being at the 'liberal' or 'fanatical' end of the spectrum (Table 1.1 – see p. 16).

The need for a local counter radicalisation 'bottom-up' approach

With the exception of Finsbury Park Mosque, no empirical evidence exists of any other registered mosques ever being taken over or administered by violent extremists. Finsbury Park Mosque, after its infiltration and subsequent take-over by Abu Hamza and his followers, became a haven for takfeeri orientated adherents (Lambert, 2009). A significant minority of Muslims convicted under anti-terrorist legislation attended the mosque during Abu Hamza's tenure (Cole and Cole, 2009: 4). Suffice it to say that it only remained under his control up until its reclamation on 5 February 2005 as a result of a collaborative effort between local community representatives and the Metropolitan police (Lambert, 2009). Prior to this widely publicised event, Brixton Mosque had also come under scrutiny from the intelligence services, due to Moussaoui and Reid's former association. The mosque was initially labelled a violent extremist institution; however, extensive media coverage served to provide a platform whereby these negative allegations could be effectively countered (Gibson, 2002). The mosque management was also able to confirm the extent of its opposition to violent extremism during the 1990s. Chapter 2 provided a historical synopsis of the mosque's encounters with violent extremist propagandists and their takfeeri ideology. It must be conceded that, while engaged at a community level, the management was unable to extend its remit and authority beyond the mosque premises in Gresham Road. It could not therefore prevent or restrict the expansive activities of extremist protagonists like el-Faisal within the local area. In fact, it proved difficult averting mosque attendees from his activities and events. This was compounded further by the management's inability to determine the extent to which violent radicalisation was occurring at such events. The creation of a vacuum between such individuals and the mosque was inevitable in the absence of comprehensive intervention or diversionary mechanisms. This left susceptible young individuals to choose their preferred path of learning and influence. The subsequent process of an individual's gradation from wider, more established communities towards violent extremism was depicted in the funnel model of Figures 1.6 and 1.7 (see p. 19).

In support of the 'Funnel' model theory are Moskalenko and McCauley's observation regarding the 'conveyor-belt metaphor' – that is, the stage-by-stage process whereby: 'terrorists seek to manipulate grievances in order to radicalize others by pulling them further and further into illegal activities' (Moskalenko and McCauley, 2009: 240). This metaphor belongs to part of a larger 'pyramid model of radicalization' with each ascending level towards the peak or 'apex' representing the degree of an individual's political commitment. The final stage of this upward gradation is, they suggest, illegal and political violence (Moskalenko and McCauley, 2009). This theory concurs with the frameworks illustrated in Figures 1.6 and 1.7 in that both reflect the gradation and increasing susceptibility towards extremism.

After taking into account Finsbury Park Mosque's temporary tenure as one of the few, if not only, extremist mosques, it is easy to discern that the vast majority of UK mosques have never been platforms for violent extremist ideologies or teachings. A reasonable question may then be proffered: 'Where then do young Muslims go to receive violent extremist instruction/teachings?' The author suggests that such a question is the subject of further research. That said, however, this study can illustrate the counter-measures introduced in an attempt to address the problem of susceptible Muslim youth being attracted away from more conventional institutions of religious learning and worship towards the more surreptitious venues where violent extremist propaganda proliferates.

Establishing a strategy to reach, empower and educate

> Because terrorist recruitment in the UK is a 'bottom-up' process of radicalised individuals seeking to join the jihad, facilitators who can make the connections between would-be jihadis and established jihadi and terrorist groups play a key role.... These individuals do not appear to compromise a connected and coherent recruitment operation, but rather act as individuals, each with their own contacts in the UK and overseas.
>
> (Cole and Cole, 2009: 203)

The establishment of a credible grassroots initiative to engage young Muslims who had become divorced from mosques and mainstream avenues of religious/social interaction was considered an essential step by the author. The proliferation of the gun and gang culture alongside various avenues of criminality among some of the youth provided a potentially lethal cocktail of violence. The propensity for this increased once a religious legitimacy was identified through violent extremist teachings. Drs J. and B. Cole support this view, observing in the first instance: 'In order for someone to kill another human being, a change in the psychological state of that individual is necessary' (2009: 234). Secondly, they note:

> Religious figures also played a significant role in motivating the dataset and providing the 'religious' justification for their actions... Evidence... indicates quite clearly that increased belief in the religious justification for violence, through adherence to an Islamist ideology, was a feature along the path to the violent radicalisation of virtually all of these [the dataset's] individuals.
>
> (2009: 245)

Primarily, STREET was set up to provide alternative and safe environments for young Muslims to interact and comfortably express themselves among peers sharing ideas, aspirations and concerns. The opportunity for them to engage with experienced counsellors and mentors from similar social backgrounds was integral to the effectiveness of the work delivered at grassroots. This familiarity enabled youth to develop confidence in articulating their religious belief/understanding to someone they could trust. When appropriate, any erroneous religious/civic beliefs or concepts could be challenged or redressed. Effective deconstruction of extremist understandings/ideology, referencing authentic mainstream texts and legislature, therefore remains at the forefront of STREET's work. The Deconstruct Programme underpins many aspects of the organisation's work as it enables a critical analysis and evaluation of extremist propaganda, particularly audio-visual footage posted via the Internet. An exposition is then provided highlighting both media and religious misrepresentations propounded therein. A synopsis of a deconstruct template for one Al Qaeda's 'as-Sahab' videos featuring Shehzad Tanwir is cited to emphasise the rationale behind the programme:

> The deconstruction attempts to isolate the various media components that have been utilised to construct the media text in question...This report will identify the various messages being encoded within the text and the subtleties at play that are deliberately put together for effect and impact upon the viewer.[6]

The theological thread compromises:

> a counter-narrative from an Islamic perspective, using authentic sources to repel justifications offered by the producers of the named video. [The counter-narrative is] aimed at devaluing the arguments put forth by highlighting the weaknesses...in light of the Qur'an and Sunnah.[7]

Hussain, in his MA examination of the same 'as-Sahab' video, concluded:

> This discussion has demonstrated that in the existing discipline of media studies there is a framework that can be developed to expose the manipulative encodings employed by Al-Qaeda. Such an approach would better equip the most vulnerable in society with the necessary tools to at least decode a different reading to the one preferred by Al-Qaeda as well as potentially reject it.
>
> (2009: 44)

He also expressed optimism that:

> The Media Deconstruction approach presented...becomes the foundation of further extensive deconstructions of material like the text analysed above. The fact that the approach is widely used in schools and colleges teaching Media Studies, supports the notion that it can be made easily accessible for the susceptible young Muslims that Al-Qaeda's propaganda clearly targets.
>
> (2009: 45)

Although an essential aspect of STREET's remit, deconstruct counselling constitutes part of a wider strategy of engagement with often 'hard to reach' youth. The organisation is divided into four interlinked Work Streams (WS), illustrated in Figure 8.1. Conventional activities conducted in Work Stream (WS) 1 attract the largest number of participants and enables interactivity and engagement for target audiences in the familiar territory of sports/outreach projects. Engagement at this level yields varying results – from individuals seeking advice regarding social and/or legal issues to others highlighting their misunderstandings or misconceptions concerning religious interpretations etc. They are referred to Work Streams 2 and/or 3 depending on the nature of the issues raised and counselled accordingly. Work Stream 3 also incorporates referrals from local statutory bodies such as the Youth Offending Services and London Probation with whom Service Level Agreements (SLAs) exist. Regular meetings take place between these parties in order to highlight issues relating to each referral case. The appropriate course of action is then devised to facilitate individual requirements. Work Stream 4 provides a mainstream, theological and religious framework which underpins the other work streams.

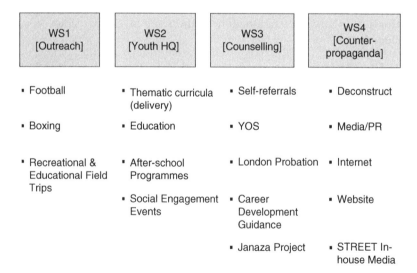

WS1 [Outreach]	WS2 [Youth HQ]	WS3 [Counselling]	WS4 [Counter-propaganda]
• Football	• Thematic curricula (delivery)	• Self-referrals	• Deconstruct
• Boxing	• Education	• YOS	• Media/PR
• Recreational & Educational Field Trips	• After-school Programmes	• London Probation	• Internet
	• Social Engagement Events	• Career Development Guidance	• Website
		• Janaza Project	• STREET In-house Media

Figure 8.1   STREET organisational and operational structure, 2009

Grassroots partnerships: An innovative and daring approach?

Unsurprisingly, many British black converts, not to mention a minority of white ones also, continue to view statutory authorities and governmental agencies with mistrust. Negative pre-conversion experiences have, in many cases, left indelible impressions on the racial psyche of such individuals. The murder of Stephen Lawrence in 1993 and the ensuing ineptitude that followed in the wake of a public enquiry is a case in point as it revealed the extent of institutionalised racism within the police and government (Hall, 2009: 195). Among the 70 recommendations provided by the subsequent Macpherson Report was one advocating 'that a Ministerial Priority...be established for all Police Services "To increase trust and confidence in policing amongst ethnic minority communities"' (Hall, 2009 citing Macpherson, 1999).

Unfortunately, post-conversion experiences have only served to exacerbate any pre-existing mistrust and suspicions, especially in view of the government's and its associated bodies' response to the 9/11 and 7/7 attacks:

> In 2001, the UK joined the US in invading Afghanistan...Two years later, they joined the US again to invade Iraq and overthrow the regime of Saddam Hussein. Both invasions were successful in achieving their immediate objectives, but the political fallout from these conflicts would be felt on the streets of UK cities in the following years. Since 2003, there has been a dramatic increase in terrorist activity in the UK by individuals and groups based within the Muslim population.
>
> (Cole and Cole, 2009: 111)

Within this context, any development of symbiotic relationships between grassroots Muslim communities and statutory agencies or government would be viewed with suspicion from many angles. Those from the Muslim communities, averse to establishing any type of relationship of this nature, would consider their colleagues to have betrayed their religion. At worst, Muslim individuals or organisations embarking upon such relationships would be considered to have apostastised from the pale of Islam. On the opposite end of this spectrum, negative statutory and governmental agency perceptions of symbiotic 'partnerships' continue to be stoked by entities warning that support is being afforded to extremists considered at the embryonic stage of violent extremism:

> The problem is that PVE – however well intentioned – isn't work-ing. Not only is it failing to achieve its stated objectives, in many places it is actually making the situation worse: a new generation is being radicalised, sometimes with the very funds that are sup-posed to be countering radicalization ... The central theoretical flaw in PVE is that it accepts the premise that non-violent extremists can be made to act as bulwarks against violent extremists. Some within government and the police service believe that only non-violent radicals – otherwise known as 'political Islamists' – possess the necessary 'street cred' to control angry young Muslims. Genuine Muslim moderates are regularly dismissed by key authority figures as 'spoken for', and thus marginalised. Non-violent extremists have consequently become well dug in as partners of national and local government and the police. Some of the government's chosen col-laborators in 'addressing grievances' of angry young Muslims are themselves at the forefront of stoking those grievances against British foreign policy; western social values; and alleged state-sanctioned 'Islamophobia'. PVE is thus underwriting the very Islamist ideol-ogy which spawns an illiberal, intolerant and anti-western world view.
>
> (Maher and Frampton, 2009: 5)

Against this backdrop, the Brixton Mosque management deemed it imperative to engage, on equal terms, with local statutory and govern-mental bodies with whom it had infrequent contact. Contrary to media and existing perceptions of a top-down, coercive relationship, typified by an informant/police arrangement, both the author [as chairman] and mosque management had seldom liaised or corresponded with statutory bodies. Exceptions to this occurred during the few occasional and peri-odic community liaison meetings where discussions ensued around the subject of the growth of the Muslim population in Lambeth. On such occasions distinctions were made between the practice and ideologies of the various groups that had begun to emerge in the local area, such as the Nation of Islam, the Ahmadi movement (Qadianyis), etc. Clear distinctions were also provided to differentiate the mosque's activities from el-Faisal's local extemporaneous events. In fact, the manage-ment felt almost compelled to embark upon engagement at a statutory level, albeit on terms conducive to both the local Muslim and wider non-Muslim communities, due to existing perceptions prevalent at the time; namely, that Brixton Mosque was a venue for recruiting extremists. Terms of any engagement with statutory agencies, it must be reiterated, would have to be mutually agreed. The issue of providing intelligence on the Muslim community, e.g. informing or spying on its members, therefore was an unviable proposition from the outset. This was not to be confused however with the continued commitment of civic respon-sibility to report identified potential terrorists or terrorist actions. Spalek et al. highlighted the partnership approach of the Metropolitan Police's Muslim Contact Unit established in the aftermath of 9/11:

> The Muslim Contact Unit [MCU]... developed a close working part-nership with black convert community groups... and many others of a similar nature. The essence of this work is to empower and facil-itate local Muslim Community groups and their efforts to educate and support convert Muslims and, where they have been released from prison, to re-integrate them into a devoutly practising faith community.
>
> (Spalek et al., 2009: 176)

Empowerment and facilitation were key components that distinguished the initial partnership between the mosque management and statu-tory agencies. This arrangement was in stark contrast to the somewhat archaic top-down coercive approaches which were always rejected by the mosque, hence the level of disengagement and non-cooperation that initially punctuated any communication between the two entities. In fact, previous relations with the local police were, for a number of years, tenuous to say the least and on a few notable occasions stand-offs and physical confrontations occurred. Nonetheless, STREET emerged as a result of the facilitatory nature of some of these partnerships and was able, to some extent, to deflect 'opposition from powerful commenta-tors who regularly conflate Salafism (and Islamism) with extremism and terrorism' (Spalek et al., 2009: 177). Spalek et al. further suggest that in the absence of this facilitation, 'These groups would have otherwise been excluded from engagement processes as a result of their perceived links with terrorism, or because of their real or perceived opposition to established secular values' (Spalek et al., 2009).

It is important to reproduce comments made by the US Counter Terrorism Center in its report on militant ideologies in order to empha-sise the minimal extent of collaboration required between effective grassroots organisations – Salafist entities in this instance – and statutory and/or government agencies in their collective fight against violent extremism. Whilst not entirely accurate in its summation of Salafism so far as secularism, gender equality, etc. is concerned, the authors' message as it relates to the effectiveness of the Salafi counter-radicalisation approach is unequivocal:

> Finally, a word about 'moderate' Muslims. The measure of moderation depends on what type of standard you use. If by 'moderate' one means the renouncement of violence in the achievement of political goals, then the majority of Salafis are moderate. But if by 'moderate' one means an acceptance of secularism, capitalism, democracy, gender equality, and a commitment to religious pluralism, then Salafis would be extremists on all counts. Then again, there are not many Muslim religious leaders in the Middle East that would qualify as moderates according to the second definition. Until there are, the international community should focus on alienating Jihadis from the broader Salafi Movement. While it may be distasteful to work with non-violent Salafi leaders, they are best positioned to delegitimize Jihadi violence.
>
> (McCants et al., 2006: 11)

Shared values

In order to address the inaccuracies contained in the CTC's above summation, it is necessary to confront allegations and concerns regarding Salafism's socially conservative approach within today's society. Accusations of insularity and isolation may, particularly in the not too distant past, have been accurate. Explanations surrounding the initial reasons for this somewhat reclusive nature were offered in Chapter 2 when discussing converts' establishment of new identity constructs and the application/misapplication of *al-uzlah* (seclusion). Considering that Salafism, in its present UK context, emerged relatively recently – during the early 1990s – the inexperience and indeed immaturity of its adherents in those formative years are akin to the 'founding' and 'youthful' phases of development depicted in Figure 1.2. The author not only suggests that many Salafis have progressed beyond these somewhat idealistic phases, he also asserts that a significant number, particularly after 9/11 and 7/7, re-evaluated their understanding and subsequently progressed along routes similar to those described by Patel, arriving at conclusions resembling a form of religious pluralism within a western societal context:

> On one side of the faith line are religious totalitarians. Their conviction is that only one interpretation of one religion is a legitimate way of being, believing, and belonging on earth. Everyone else needs to be cowed, or converted, or condemned, or killed. On the other side of the faith line are the religious pluralists, who hold that people believing in different creeds and belonging to different communities need to learn to live together. Religious pluralism is neither mere coexistence nor forced consensus. It is a form of proactive cooperation that affirms the identity of the constituent communities while emphasizing that the well being of each and all depends on the health of the whole.
>
> (Reddie, 2009: 229 citing Patel, 2007)

Evidence of STREET's success in reintegrating many of its target audience into the local community is well documented via a robust reporting system. More importantly, this success is acknowledged by statutory partners who continue to refer 'hard to reach' cases to the organisation. If an isolationist approach had been detected by these agencies, existing agreements would have undoubtedly ceased. While saying this however, acknowledgement must be given to the reality of Salafi adherents, or any other religious delineation for that matter, being at different stages of understanding so far as societal participation is concerned. With this in mind, it is necessary to revisit the adaptation of Hudson's model once more to establish whether it is comprehensive as a theoretical framework to encapsulate the varying religious *and* social spheres of development. In Chapter 6 limitations were observed concerning the applicability of this framework (Figure 1.2) to el-Faisal's case study. In view of his religious education and sojourn in Riyadh it was difficult to determine whether he had progressed beyond the 'youthful' and even 'adult' phases of religious development. His qualifications and successive appointment/s as an imam in the UK would certainly suggest that an 'adult' or 'mature' stage of development had been reached. The adaptation of an additional theoretical model is necessary if el-Faisal's position is to be more accurately determined. This new model could also possibly be applied more comprehensively to the remaining case studies and the sample group, alongside Hudson's adapted framework.

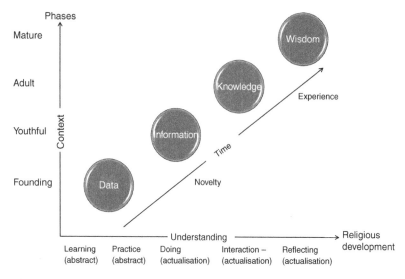

Figure 8.2　Adaption of 'The Continuum of Understanding' model
Source: (Cleveland, 1982: 34–9)

An explanation of the original model, from which Figure 8.2 has been adapted, provides interesting definitions regarding the terminologies used. These could also be adapted to fit within the context of religious understanding, development and practice:

- **Data** comes about through research, creation, gathering, and discovery.
- **Information** has context. Data is turned into information by organizing it so that we can easily draw conclusions. Data is also turned into information by 'presenting' it, such as making it visual or auditory.
- **Knowledge** has the complexity of experience, which comes about by seeing it from different perspectives. This is why training and education is difficult – one cannot count on one person's knowledge transferring to another. Knowledge is built from scratch by the learner through experience. Information is static, but knowledge is dynamic as it lives within us.
- **Wisdom** is the ultimate level of understanding. As with knowledge, wisdom operates within us. We can share our experiences that create the building blocks for wisdom; however, it needs to be communicated with even more understanding of the personal contexts of our audience than with knowledge sharing.

Data and information deal with the past. They are based on the gathering of facts and adding context. Knowledge deals with the present. It becomes a part of us and enables to perform. However, when we gain wisdom, we start dealing with the future as we are now able to vision and design for what will be, rather than for what is or was.

(Cleveland, 1982; Clark, 2004)

The above framework and definitions provided therein place el-Faisal at the 'founding' phase so far as his understanding of religious tenets, etc. are concerned. The *'data'* phase of development reflects formative learning stages connected to the acquisition of information through research, etc. This phase of development lacks the prerequisite understanding of contexts within which to *actualise* or practise what has been learned. El-Faisal's misrepresentation and indeed distortion of religious texts throughout his lectures are indicative of this primary learning phase. The author suggests that this additional model, incorporating Hudson's adapted framework, provides an effective tool against which to chart stages of converts' development and understanding as they progress in their new faith.

The author has endeavoured to introduce, as well as adapt, relevant and existing theoretical models to the research conducted throughout this study. Further examination of these models could possibly yield additional, more robust frameworks against which emerging studies could also be applied. In any event, additional testing of the frameworks introduced in this study is necessary in order to determine the validity of the theories propounded.

STREET's positioning – between violent radicalism and secular liberalism

The need to understand the array of drivers affecting the process of violent radicalisation/extremism continues to be of utmost priority for policy makers, academics and practitioners alike. The introduction of a final theoretical framework, therefore, attempts to incorporate the earlier, more general model depicted in Table 1.1, the bipolar spectrum of religious extremism among the Muslim community in Britain. Figure 8.3 perhaps illustrates the positioning of known personalities and groups within the British Muslim context today. However, it does not encapsulate all religious entities. As can be seen from the source and date of referencing, the framework was advocated prior to the emergence of organisations like the Quilliam Foundation when other entities such as the Muslim Council of Britain (MCB) were more closely aligned with government than at present (Dodd, 2009). Nonetheless, the author has taken the liberty of inserting the Quilliam Foundation into this already illustrative model because of the organisation's emerging personification of a liberal extreme that continues to turn many sections of the Muslim (and increasingly non-Muslim) communities against them:

> The Guardian revealed that Ed Husain, co-director of the government-funded thinktank the Quilliam Foundation (QF), believes that spying on British Muslims who are 'not committing terrorist offences' is 'good and right'. He has expressed some pretty extreme views in the past, but this is beyond anything that anyone who believes in liberal democracy could extol... The importance of this episode is that it highlights something that has become increasingly clear: that QF has become part of the problem rather than the solution.
>
> (Murray, 2009)

While the proposed model provides a subjective gauge against which the positive/negative influences and secular/political extremes of organisations etc. are measured, it should not be ignored, especially when considering the experience and former position of its author (Lambert, 2005). Furthermore, in the absence of frameworks that either challenge or reject the assertions made therein, due consideration is necessary to understand the political and ideological landscape of Muslim activity in Britain.

Figure 8.3 provides a more detailed illustration so far as identifying movements, groups and their perceived effectiveness in relation to the bipolar perspective of extremism highlighted earlier in Table 1.1. Lambert elaborated upon the distinctive features of the groups and movements referred to in this particular model (with exception of Quilliam Foundation) and made the following observations:

1. **Al Qaeda:** At that particular stage, i.e. up until 2005 (when this workshop was convened), the movement's interest in the political climate in Britain was heightened to an extent that infiltration into opposition parties and groups, etc., was considered a significant strategy to cause further disruption among which subsequent terrorist attacks could be launched
2. At the other end of the continuum, *secularised* (and what has increasingly become liberal) input was considered negative or, unhelpful during that period
3. **Muslim Council of Britain (MCB):** This organisation was not considered by the Muslim communities to be close enough to the actual

problem of home-grown terrorism and violent extremism. However, the government chose to promote its positive relations with MCB prior to invasion of Iraq. These became tenuous following MCB's subsequent criticism of the government's foreign policy in reference to Iraq, Palestine and the US-led 'war on terror.'

4. **Muslim Association of Britain (MAB):** Lambert's observations were that this group was among the few to have effectively tackled Al Qaeda. It was an organisation that had gained significant credibility owing to its stance regarding the Palestinian issue

5. **Islamic Human Rights Commission (IHRC):** Again, considered to be a very effective and credible organisation in the field of countering violent extremism

6. **Salafis:** In Lambert's estimation, the Salafis remain among the most influential and effective groups that have experience and expertise in effectively countering violent extremist propaganda and its protagonists. He acknowledges that, while apparent similarities exist between Salafis and violent extremists, the Police have increasingly been able to distinguish between the two movements and ideologies.

(Lambert, 2005)

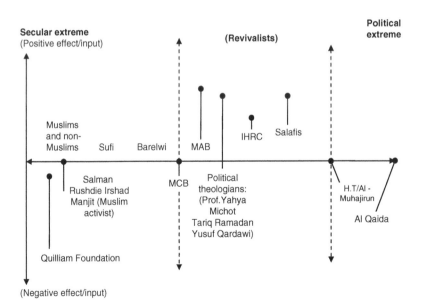

Figure 8.3 Theoretical positioning and effectiveness of some Muslim movements/individuals in Britain today
Source: (Lambert, 2005)

This final observation is significant inasmuch as part of the ambit of this research was to examine whether Salafism comprises an ideology and practice in which violent extremism proliferates, or whether it is in contrast an effective antidote to the extremist phenomenon. The framework depicted in Figure 8.3, the author suggests, is complementary to Table 1.1, with the earlier model providing more detailed ideological and political definitions.

Susceptibility vs. effectiveness

Some academic research continues to assert the incorrect notion of Salafism comprising three branches that encapsulate these separate and disparate movements. This study has endeavoured, in part, to highlight such distinctions by providing empirical and documentary evidence through triangulation of the various sources of primary and secondary data used. Indeed, the author suggests that some muted success has been achieved insofar as appreciating the negative effects of the Salafi-purist, Salafi-politico and Salafi-jihadi typology upon the true adherents to Salafism. The case studies have, to a certain degree, also reflected the subtle yet distinct gravitation of three of the subjects across ideological 'constituencies' depicted in the Combating Terrorism Center's Muslim constituency model (Figure 1.1, see p. 9) towards violent extremism. Each constituency possesses separate ideological characteristics which demarcate the difference between the movements. While saying this, however, acknowledgement must be given to possible overlaps between the constituencies. In light of this model, the author submits that the respective 'Islamist', 'Salafi' and 'Jihadi' constituencies confirm the assertion regarding the three movements being ideologically and methodologically distinct from each other.

Documentary evidence has been provided to highlight behavioural extremist similarities between over-zealous Muslims irrespective of religious delineation. The ascetic practice of *al-uzlah* (isolation/seclusion) from wider society was provided as an example of a behavioural characteristic which, if performed without understanding of context and/or environment in which it may be practicable, could lead to an extreme interpretation. The author suggests that not all extremist tendencies, in isolation, cause violent extremism to take root but that collectively they can, and occasionally do, propel an individual towards violent extremism if certain social or psychological factors/drivers are in place. Behavioural extremism in its entirety cannot therefore be cited as an accurate indicator of an individual's gravitation towards violent extremism: it has to be preceded by an ideological extremism. Upon identifying the ideological root, the degree of behavioural extremism can then possibly be determined.

Chapter 7 examined the sample groups' understanding of Al Qaeda inspired violent extremism and whether they were susceptible to the propaganda that ensued from these extremist entitities. With the exception of the respondents who refrained from answering questions of this nature, the remaining group was emphatic in its rejection of violent extremism. The interviews further determined that the likely reason for such an outright rejection was due to the extent and *nature* of religious instruction received at the most formative years of the converts' lives. The data extrapolated highlighted the importance of imparting the fundamentals of the religion, i.e., Tawheed, etc. at the 'founding' phase of converts' religious development. This provided a firm ideological grounding. Political studies and discourses were avoided as they could arguably be considered a potentially disastrous element of instruction at such an early stage of a convert's development owing to his/her heightened level of susceptibility. Moskalenko and McCauley's research observations in this instance are poignant while expounding upon converts' susceptibility at this stage:

> An inert sympathizer can be moved directly from the base of the pyramid to the apex [political violence] by experiencing personal loss or affront, by identification with a new vivid example of loss or affront to the cause, or simply by a loved one who is already radicalized.
>
> (Moskalenko and McCauley, 2009: 241)

Beyond the founding phase, further development could encapsulate historical perspectives of the religion in order to provide a classical context in which to understand how the religion was previously actualised. Examples of how extremism emerged and was tackled during these periods are essential at this particular stage of development provided the convert is conversant with the fundamental tenets acquired during the 'founding' phase. Ideological deviations such as Tawheed al-haakimiyyah as a fourth category could, thereafter, be introduced in view of the grounding received. The 'adult' and 'mature' phases enable actualisation of the above fundamental tenets while being cognisant of historical contexts and circumstances, etc. This process is necessary as it increases the individual's capacity to contextualise the practice of Islam within his/her own environment. It also increases resilience to political mobilisation as described above. Figure 8.2 and its associated definitions incorporate the processes described above.

Failure to adequately ground converts during the first two formative phases renders them susceptible to the type of politicisation witnessed among Islamist constituencies depicted in Figure 1.1. Although the doctrines of these particular groups cannot, in their entirety, be directly attributable to violent extremism, the effect of any 'adverse' politicisation can be considered dangerous for a new convert/revert. This was witnessed during the radicalisation process of Moussaoui (case study 1) during the time he spent mixing with foreign students in Montpellier University. Salafism, in its most basic form, is intrinsically apolitical and the strong attraction to its ideology and methodology is due to an emphasis on the acquisition of authentic knowledge-based foundations, coupled with socially conservative practices (Inge, 2008). Indeed, the Salafist position is considered antithetical to the takfeeri understanding of Jihad. The latter's emphasis on both political and apparently knowledge-based principles of Islam, although misrepresented by them, appeal to susceptible young Muslims who are disgruntled by a perceived over-emphasis on politics from the Islamist/Ikhwani constituencies on the one hand. On the other, the youth, while attracted to the ideological and knowledge-based focus of Salafism, are disillusioned by the movement's apparent political disengagement. Violent extremists are thus successful in attracting youth due to their ability to amalgamate Islamist politicisation with Salafist ideological underpinnings. These two powerful components provide the impetus behind the attraction for violent extremist propaganda.

The research interviews provided evidence confirming the majority of the sample group received little or no religious instruction around political affairs. Instead, the vast majority of them were educated on foundational tenets of Islam, e.g., tawheed and prayer. They also learned about historical accounts relating to the Prophet, his life and companions (*Sahaba*). This perhaps explains the reason for their structured progression towards both 'youthful' and 'adult' phases of development. Indeed, provided those respondents who continue to remain at the 'founding' phase develop according to the methodology illustrated in Figures 1.2 and 8.2, they could gradually progress in a manner which actually renders them *unsusceptible* to violent extremist propaganda. This process of religious maturation is significant to their resilience against violent extremism. In fact, it could provide them with a premise upon which to effectively refute or counter violent extremist rhetoric.

The theoretical frameworks introduced throughout this research, although independent, are complementary in their potential to explain the varying positions and stages of development among some Muslim communities in Britain today. They provide a premise upon which to test or further research Salafi converts using theories developed from a primary, empirical insider perspective. To date, research of this nature remains scant because of the inaccessibility of Salafi converts and/or their communities. It is therefore hoped that further insider perspectives emerge as a result of this research.

Finally, when considering Salafi converts' possible position as conduits within society, the theoretical frameworks provided in Figures 1.6 and 1.7 indicate an influential role at grassroots level. This has already been intimated during case study 4 when examining Sean O'Reilly's maturation and gravitation from violent extremist propaganda. STREET's success among it's predominantly convert target audience is another example to consider in this vein. Coincidentally, the opportunity to develop existing bridge-building roles between grassroots community leaders and statutory agencies/government should not be ignored in light of the success garnered from partnership arrangements. If the government continues to be serious about its strategy to address extremism from a grassroots bottom-up perspective it would do well to choose its advisers carefully and ensure that, not only are they credible, but that their objectives are none other than to identify effective grassroots partners to progress the PVE agenda among Muslim communities that are most in need of support. Recent trends among some government departments continue to suggest their preference to seek advice from purported think-tanks and advisers intent on marginalising community groups and organisations that have established track records in countering radicalisation. The government should evaluate this advice as it risks becoming prey to entities already positioned strategically among its ranks whose sole intention appears none other than to advance their own religious preferences and persuasions. If the government accedes to the advice and warnings proffered by these groups it could unwittingly contribute towards supporting existing religious factionalism and tensions already prevalent among Muslim communities. Impartiality could no longer be a defining feature of government in view of it having fallen prone to developing policies which risk being inherently biased, and therefore flawed, owing to the nature of advice received. In view of continuing concerns and criticism from various sections of the British public over the PVE agenda (Kundnani, 2009), the government should endeavour to avoid allowing entities' carte blanche narratives which subsequently prove to be counter-productive among Muslim communities. Perhaps particular caution should be exercised regarding entities that have:

> come to represent the toxic juncture at which intense personal ambition and government propaganda meet...using public money to advocate increasingly totalitarian attitudes towards the general public...judging Muslims by their own early standards.
>
> (Murray, 2009)

Continuing governmental support for such groups and/or personalities has already served to alienate Muslim communities even further. Such support, in the author's estimation, risks exacerbating the 'pendulum swing' effect among Muslim youth from a more mainstream understanding of Islam towards a politicised and violent extremist interpretation. Additionally, an unwitting or indeed deliberate bias to support such narratives may lead to increased conflation of socially conservative but mainstream revivalist groups with extremism. This would compound the status quo and detract from existing evidence that continues to identify these very groups as the most effective antidote to tackling violent extremism at the heart of where it currently proliferates – the grassroots.

Glossary

Almaniyya	Almaniyya: 'The word for secularism in Arabic...is new in Arab political literature. It is derived from the word for "world" ("alam") and not from the word for "science" ("ilm") – that is, [it refers] to the world we live in', cited in interview with Shaker, A.N., 'Secularism will Triumph in the Arab World; Terrorism's Crimes are the Death Struggle of Fundamentalism', The Middle East Media Research Institute (MEMRI) December 11 2008, no.2148, http://www.memri.org
Ahl ul-Sunnah wa al-Jamaah	The People of the Sunnah and Congregation: This refers to Muslim adherents to the Prophetic ideology, methodology and practice. Its general usage incorporates all Sunni groups whereas its specific usage refers to more orthodox groups among Sunni adherents.
Ayah (plural: ayat)	Verse/s of the Qur'an
Bay'ah	Oaths of allegiance
Dar al-Harb	Abode of War
Dar al-Islam	Abode of Islam
Dar al-Kufr	Abode of Disbelief
Dawah	Propagatory work: call to Islam
Deen	Religion/way of life
Fatwa (pl. Fatawaa)	Judicial verdict
Fiqh	Islamic jurisprudence
Ghulu	Extremism
Haakimiyyah	In reference to this research, the phrase refers to the Shariah concept that Allah alone has the right to prescribe all laws, irrespective of jurisdiction, e.g., societal, governmental, etc.
Hadith (pl. ahadeeth)	Narration, action or tacit approval of Prophet Muhammad
Halal	Permissible
Haram	Impermissible
Hijrah	Emigration/migration
Ijtihad	Personal reasoning to derive the correct import/understanding of the Shariah. This is usually applied by established scholars in the religion
Jahiliyah	Jahiliyya can be translated into English only through approximations and paraphrases. As it is used in 'Signposts', it is one of the axes of Syed Qutb's view of the world. Derived from the Arabic root meaning to be

'ignorant', this word is used by Muslims to designate the pre-Islamic society of the Arabian Peninsula. This society 'was ignorant' of God until Muhammad's mission. As the orientalist Goldziher has remarked, the concept of *jahiliyya* plays a part in Islamic tradition much akin to that of 'barbarism' in the Western tradition. 'Islamism or barbarism' would thus be the alternative posited by Qutb. Kepel, G: *The Roots of Radical Islam* SAQI, 2005, footnote, p.43

Jihad	Linguistically, it means 'to exert oneself, strive or struggle'. This is encapsulated within the Shariah meaning which points more emphatically to fighting against disbelievers in order to promote Islam. This particular meaning has prerequisites to such Jihad being established
Kaafir (pl. Kuffar)	Disbeliever
Madhab (pl. Madhaahib)	Jurisprudential school of thought
Raafidah	A synonymous name for the Shia faith, founded years after Prophet Muhammad's death; they claim Ali ibn Taalib should have been the first caliph instead of Abu Bakr
Saheeh/Sahih	Authentic or verified Prophetic narration [hadeeth]
Shahada	Linguistic meaning: witness. The Shariah meaning is more comprehensive and relates to the testimony of faith which constitutes part of the first foundational pillar of faith. It is to declare that none deserves to be worshipped except Allah and that He is alone with associates/partners
Surah	Chapter of the Qur'an
Takfeer	Excommunication, or the act of declaring another Muslim a disbeliever
Tawheed	Unification of Allah's worship – monotheism (singling out Allah alone for worship). It is the antithesis to polytheism
Ummah	Nation of people. In this research it refers specifically to the universal Muslim nation

Notes

1 Introduction

1. The Quilliam Foundation is one such organisation. Both founding directors claim to have been extremists, i.e. Islamists that have now recanted such beliefs for a more liberal understanding of Islam. Refer to www. Quilliamfoundation.org
2. Hamed, S., 'The Attraction of "Authentic" Islam: Salafism and British Muslim Youth', in Meijer, R. (ed.), *Global Salafism: Islam's new Religious Movement*. London: Hurst, 2009.
3. See Naqshbandi, M., 'Problems and Practical Solutions to Tackle Extremism; and Muslim Youth Community Issues,' Shrivenham Papers: Defence Academy of the United Kingdom, 2006.
4. Barnett, A., Doward, J. and Townsend, M. 'Terror suspect numbers soar', *The Observer*, Sunday 14 May, 2006.
5. The 1991 Gulf War, the Balkans Conflict of 1992–95, Chechnya and Kosovo, to name but a few: Naqshbandi, 'Problems and Practical Solutions to Tackle Extremism; and Muslim Youth Community Issues,' pps. 11, 12 and Zebiri, K. 'British Muslim Converts: Choosing Alternative Lives'. One World, Oxford, 2008, pps. 23 and 29.
6. CDLR was first established in the UK by the Saudi Dissident, Muhammad al-Mas'ari who was forced into exile in London: Teitelbaum, J. 'Holier Than Thou: Saudi Arabia's Islamic Opposition'; Washington Institute for Near East Policy, 2000.
7. Dissension arose among the ranks of Saudi Arabia's clerics after the issuance of a fatwa from the Mufti, Shaykh Abdul Azeez bin Baz, permitting the arrival of non-Muslim troops into the Kingdom during Operations Desert Shield and Desert Storm: Teitelbaum, 'Holier Than Thou: Saudi Arabia's Islamic Opposition'.
8. See www.salafimanhaj.com, e-book, 'The Barbarism of Aboo Qatadah', 2007, p.10.
9. See www.salafimanhaj.com, e-book, 'The Devil's Deception of Abdullah El Faysal (Sheikh Faisal), 2007, for examples of rhetoric against the Arab/Muslim world.
10. See the demeaning terminology of scholars being government stooges, scholars for dollars and 'dodgy' (Ibid., pp. 15–17), transcript (dated 26 June 2006) of Abu Hamza al-Misri's lecture, 'Learning from Experience'; Lambert, R.; PhD Candidate, University of Exeter, 2005–8, and the dissent of Safar Hawali and Salman Awdah following the Gulf War; Teitelbaum, Holier Than Thou: Saudi Arabia's Islamic Opposition'; and Bakier, A.H., 'Terrorism Monitor', Volume 4, Issue 20, 19, 2006.
11. See www.salafimanhaj.com, e-book 'The Devil's Deception of Abdullah El Faysal (Sheikh Faisal).

12. http://uk.youtube.com/watch?v=xig_1odh4pw&feature=related: Muhammad al-Mas'ari, on a panel alongside Omar Bakri and Abu Hamza and http://uk.youtube.com/watch?v=KSBl0fi_uyE: Omar Bakri and Abu Hamza.
13. See Macpherson, Lord, 1999, 'The Stephen Lawrence Inquiry: Report, Cm.4262-1 which highlighted a long established fact among the black community, namely, that institutional racism existed among the Metropolitan Police and, most likely, other statutory bodies.
14. This is a slight adaptation of the model cited in Elworthy and Rifkind 'Making Terrorism History' DEMOS, Rider 2006.
15. Wilton Park Conference, in association with DEMOS: 'Towards a Community Based Approach to Counter-Terrorism', Report WPS06/5, Conference held 20–22 March 2006, paragraph 32, p.8
16. 'From the manifestations of the Khaarijee (singular of Khawaarij) ideology in recent times is: Many of them resort to using caution and carefulness in secretiveness, since their beliefs and ideologies conflict with what the people of knowledge and the rest of the Muslims are upon', Al-Fowzan, S. and Al-Khumayyis, A.R., 'The Characteristics of the Extremist Khawaarij', al-ebaanah book, 2005, p.16.
17. Dodd, V., 'Anti-terror code "would alienate most Muslims",' *The Guardian*, 17 February 2007, http://www.guardian.co.uk/politics/2009/feb/17/counterterrorism-strategy-muslims
18. Ibid.

2   Brixton Mosque's Early Encounters with Extremism

1. The arrest and subsequent charges levelled against Zacarias Moussaoui relating to the twin towers attack, and arrest of Richard Reid, aka the Shoe Bomber, who attempted to bring down a transatlantic flight in December 2001.
2. Iqra Independent School's (a community school established by the mosque in September 1994) Ethnicity Profile (12 October 1998) showed the composition of its students to be: 17.9% Arab, 14.9% African, 16.4% Asian, 44.7% Afro-Caribbean from convert parents, and 5.9% Other.
3. See present leadership's application: Connecting Communities Plus Community Application Grant 2006, Point 15, page 6.
4. Out of 290 mosques in London an estimated 254 are Barelvi and Deobandi: Naqshabandi, M: 'Muslims in Britain', http://www.muslimsinbritain.org/index.html
5. Ash Shahada Housing Cooperative, which eventually developed into an Association: http://www.ash-shahada.org/html/aboutus.html
6. 'The purists emphasize a focus on non violent methods of propagation, purification, and education', Wictorowicz, Q. 'Anatomy of the Salafi Movement' 2006, p. 208.
7. After the Prophet Muhammad's death, the most senior of his companions gathered and decided upon his successor who would become the first Caliph of the Muslims. Abu Bakr As-Siddique was subsequently nominated and appointed. See Mukhtasar Seerah Ar-Rasool (Abridged Biography of the

Prophet Muhammad), M. Ibn Abdul Wahhab At-Tamimi, Darussalam, 2003, pps. 316–22.

8. Interview with Shaykh Kamaludin 8 January 2008 cited in Lambert, R., 'The London Partnerships: An Insider's Analysis of Legitimacy and Effectiveness', University of Exeter, Draft PhD, September 2009, p.148.

9. Letter from Raja and Partners, Solicitors, 28 March 1998, confirming completion of the acquisition of 1 Gresham Road, Brixton Mosque's premises.

10. Brixton Mosque and Islamic Cultural Centre Charitable Trust Deed, 19 October 1997.

11. Other initiatives were introduced such as Community Dinners and excursions/activities for the community – see Brixton Mosque's Fundraising Prospectus on the mosque website: http://www.masjidit.co.uk/

12. An Introductory Community Profile of Brixton Islamic Cultural Centre, Past, Present & Future, 19 August 2001, p.9.

13. See correspondence between Lambeth Council and Brixton Mosque, dated 19 June, 2 and 28 July 2001 respectively.

14. The then Leader to the Council, Jim Dickson, stated in his letter of 18 April 2001: 'You are involved in an impressive range of community activity. I believe it is very much to the council's disadvantage that we have not worked closely with you on key projects up to now. I hope very much that we can start to get some joint projects up and running soon and I will do my best to facilitate that.'

15. *An Introductory Community Profile of Brixton Islamic Cultural Centre, Past, Present & Future*, 19 August 2001, p.16.

16. Ibid., p.151.

17. Suleaman, N., 'Restless Convert in Quest for Jihad', http://news.bbc.co.uk/1/hi/uk/4942924.stm

18. Shaykh Ali Hasan during his lecture in Luton entitled 'The Evils of Takfeer' (August/September 1997) invited extremists and followers of Abu Hamza in the local vicinity to sit and discuss ideological points of disagreement; however, none of the leaders turned up, with the exception of a few followers.

19. This was remedied once the mosque was purchased in March 1998 and confirmed by official documentation, edition date: 14 April 1998 – see Official Copy of Register Entries, Title Number TGL145425. Holding trustees now held sole responsibility for the premises. They could then expel/prevent whomever they considered a threat, and failure to comply effectively meant that the offending individual was contravening the law by trespassing/unlawful entry.

20. According to media reports, Abu Hamza arrived there in 1997: http://news.bbc.co.uk/1/hi/uk/4644960.stm

21. See Amnesty International: 'The backlash – human rights at risk throughout the world', AI Index, ACT 30/027/2001, 4 October 2001, p.1 and in Los Angeles, the LA County Commission on Human Relations recorded a 700% increase in reported anti-Middle Eastern hate crime between September and December 2001 compared with the previous year. Conference research presented at annual meeting of American Sociological Association 16–20 August 2002.

22. 'Anonymous Mosque is the hotbed of extremism', *Evening Standard*, 22 July 2005, p. 6.

3   British Muslims and Identity

1. Singer Billy Bragg told the BBC it was right to have a national debate about what it means to be British: 'I do think we need to talk about the issue of identity, about who we are', Story from BBC NEWS:http://news.bbc.co.uk/go/pr/fr/-/1/hi/uk_politics/4611682.stm, Published: 2006/01/14 15:09:35 GMT and Alibhai-Brown, 2000, pp. 26–30.
2. Current estimates place British converts to Islam at 14 200, slightly under 1% of the British Muslim population: Ehsan Masood, *British Muslims*, Media Guide, British Council, p.6, while Tariq Modood places the number at 5–10 000: Modood et al., p. 70.
3. Multicultural Britain: Leading Article, 21 January 2005; Guardian Unlimited © Guardian Newspapers Limited.
4. *Daily Telegraph*, 13 October 2000.
5. *Observer*, 'A monster in our own making', 21 August 2005 and *Financial Times*, 'When multiculturalism is a nonsense', 31 August 2005.
6. See Bhui, H.S., 'Muslim Communities and Criminal Justice: A stigmatised faith identity post 9/11', *Race and Criminal Justice*, Sage Publications, 2009.
7. See Scarman, Lord Justice (1981), 'The Brixton Disorders, 10–12 April 1981', paragraphs 2.22 and 4.63: Cmnd 8247 London: Home Office. The Scarman Report (as it is commonly known) raised issues pertaining to factors adversely affecting the Afro-Caribbean community that precipitated the Brixton and Toxteth riots in 1981.
8. Gordon Brown's speech promoting patriotism: Story from BBC NEWS: http://news.bbc.co.uk/go/pr/fr/-/1/hi/uk_politics/4611682.stm. Published: 2006/01/14 15:09:35 GMT
9. By the nineteenth century a Moroccan merchant community was already established as were Somali and Yemeni communities in Cardiff and South Shields: see N. Matar, *Islam in Britain 1558–1685*; Cambridge, 1998; F. Halliday, *Arabs in Exile: Yemeni Migrants in Urban Britain*, London 1992; R.I. Lawless, *From Tai'zz to Tyneside, an Arab Community in the North-East of England during the Early Twentieth Century*, Exeter, 1995.
10. 4797 Church of England schools, 2138 Roman Catholic, 28 Methodist, 23, Jewish, 238 'others' were present in 1998 compared to 0 Muslim schools: Source – State Funded Schools in England in 1996; DFEE Statistical Branch.
11. The actions, sayings and tacit approvals of Prophet Muhammad.
12. Literal translation is striving, seeking inferences of the divine rules pertaining to specific circumstances that arise and lack of an explicit dictate from the more general and express principles of Islam based upon authentic sources of Islamic legislature, or to formulate a specific legal opinion in the absence of specific texts of reference.
13. Reference should be made to the Combating Terrorism Center's Executive Report (November 2006), 'Militant Ideology Atlas', which 'identifies the most influential thinkers in the Jihadi movement and delineates the movement's key ideological vulnerabilities', p. 5.

14. *Daily Mail*, 12 October 2000.
15. David Green, Director of Civitas, a rightist independent think-tank: *Daily Mail*, 11 October 2000.
16. European Monitoring Centre on Racism and Xenophobia: 'The Impact of 7 July 2005 London Bomb Attacks on Muslim communities in the EU', Report, November 2005, pp. 10–11.
17. 'i. the environment produces stimuli, ii. which in turn produces emotions (bodily reactions), iii. which the [individual] perceives and rationalizes into feelings, iv. which affects his autobiographical self, v. which is experienced through the delicately shaped machinery of their imagination [identity], vi. which is affected by feelings induced by the emotions.' G. Marranci, *Jihad Beyond Islam*, Berg, 2006a, and G. Marranci, Muslim Inside: Islamic religiosity & identity in Scottish Prisons, University of Aberdeen, 2006b, p.6.
18. Beckford et al., 2005, p. 186.

4 British Muslims and Religious Conversion

1. Research presented at Muslim network meeting, Selly Oaks, University of Birmingham: 'An Introduction to Muslims in the 2001 Census, 7 September 2004.
2. National Prison Statistics of England and Wales, 30 June 2002 http://www.official_documents.co.uk/documents/cm59/5996/5996pdf
3. 'The Brixton Mosque and Islamic Cultural Centre is located in the Coldharbour ward of [the London Borough of] Lambeth, which has the largest population in the borough. It rose from 13,272 in 1991 to 14,376, an increase of 8.3%. This is 5.4% of the borough population. White British people make up only 33% of the population of the ward, compared to 49% of the [entire] Borough population', Lambeth Community Grant Application by the Muslim Youth Concern (youth initiative of Brixton Mosque), 2006, p.6.
4. Rambo refers to the following typology: 'i. Apostasy or defection from a faith, ii. Intensification/revitalization of commitment to a faith iii. Affiliationn to a movement, iv. Institutional Transition from one group or community to another and v.Traditional Transition from one religion to another', Rambo, 1993, pp. 12–14.
5. Al-Uthaimeen, M.S., *Islamic Verdicts on Pillars of Islam*, Vol.1: Creed and Prayer, Darussalam, Riyadh 2003, pp. 72–9.
6. Note: Upon utterance of this testimony, an individual becomes a Muslim. Also, it is important to note that the term 'slave' denotes a devout servant of God and should not be understood according to the human relationship between slave and master.
7. This terminology refers to the Muslim Brotherhood movement and its distinctive ideology that has a political interpretation and impetus at its foundation.
8. Examples of these are many: i) Shias' rejection of traditional hadeeth collections from the Sunni branch and ii) their belief in the infallibility of their imams. These are only two examples of significant ideological differences between Sunni and Shia Islam. Further elaboration on these ideological differences would prove exhaustive for the remit of this particular study. See,

however, Al-Afghanee, A. *The Mirage in Iran*, Tawheed Publications, 1987, translated by A.A.B. Philips.
9. Shaykh Taqi al-Din al-Nabhani (d.1977), see Roald, 2004, p.142.

5   Methodology

1. The STREET programme (of which the author is the founding and Managing Director) will be discussed in more detail towards the conclusion of this research.
2. Further reference can be made to Boehm, V.R. in Hakel, M.D., Sorcher, M., Beek, M. and Moses, J.L. 'Making it Happen: designing research with implementation in mind.' NewburyPark and London: Sage. 1982, pp. 451, 454, 455 and Robson, 1993, pp. 451–2.
3. After receiving assurances of anonymity, the entire target group felt comfortable in participating in the interviews that were conducted.
4. Strategy To Reach Empower & Educate Teenagers (Muslim Youth initiative launched in 2007).
5. 'Revert' is a term used synonymously with conversion and denotes a 'return' to Islam as Muslims believe that mankind was born upon a natural disposition, see Roald, 2004.
6. See the transcript of the interview conducted by Anne Chapman, Assistant Federal Public Defender for the Eastern District of Virginia on 11 October 2005 in London.
7. The Supreme Court of Judicature, Court of Appeal (Criminal Division), R v. El-Faisal, 17 April 2004, Case No: 2003-01860.

6   Case Studies

1. The Al-Sahwa Islamiyyah (Islamic Awakening) movement with Safar Hawali and Salman Awdah at its helm during the nineties is yet another example of religious internal political tensions affecting an increasingly globalised Muslim community or Ummah.
2. Zacarias Moussaoui and Abdullah el-Faisal.
3. United States v. Zacarias Moussaoui, Criminal No. 01-455-A; Defense Trial Exhibits: http://vaed.uscourts.gov/notablecases/moussaoui/exhibits/defense
4. United States of America v. Zacarias Moussaoui aka Shaqil aka Abu Khalid al Sahrawi, Case Number: 01-cr-00455 June 13th 2002.
5. Linder, D.O.: 'The Trial of Zacarias Moussaoui: An Account' 2006 http://www.law.umkc.edu/faculty/projects/FTRIALS/moussaoui/zmaccount.html
6. Ibid.
7. Ibid.
8. 'El-Wafi' is the surname cited in more recent articles, such as the CNN article: 'London Radicals made my son terrorist' CNN.com 4 May 2006, http://edition.cnn.com/2006/WORLD/europe/05/04/moussaoui.radicalized and the *Guardian Unlimited* article: 'Moussaoui turned to extremism in the UK' also, 4 May 2006; http://www.guardian.co.uk/uklatest/story/0..-5797981.00.html. It is not mentioned in Abd Samad Moussaoui's book.

9. Burckhard, M.J. (Social Worker): Moussaoui Family History, United States v. Zacarias Moussaoui, Criminal No. 01-455-A; Defense Trial Exhibits: http://vaed.uscourts.gov/notablecases/moussaoui/exhibits/defense/ JV002. 17T, Mulhouse, 25 August 1972.

10. Ibid.

11. Ibid.

12. Ibid.

13. Ibid.

14. Ibid.

15. Ibid.

16. The Attorney General for the Republic at the District Court of Bayonne: Trial documents for Omar Moussaoui for light violence against Aicha; United States v. Zacarias Moussaoui, Criminal No. 01-455-A; Defense Trial Exhibits: 20 January 1970, http://vaed.uscourts.gov/notablecases/ moussaoui/exhibits/defense/ JV002.3T

17. Doctor A. Chevalier; Medical Certificate on observations made of Ms. Aicha Moussaoui's injuries, United States v. Zacarias Moussaoui, Criminal No. 01-455-A; Defense Trial Exhibits: Paris Faculty of Medicine, Bayonne, France, 9 December 1970 http://vaed.uscourts.gov/notablecases/ moussaoui/exhibits/defense/ JV002.9T

18. Alquie, P (Solicitor): Spouses' Non-Reconciliation authorisation no. 71. 00074, 19 May 1971: United States v. Zacarias Moussaoui, Criminal No. 01-455-A; Defense Trial Exhibits: http://vaed.uscourts.gov/notablecases/ moussaoui/exhibits/defense/ JV002.10T

19. Public Hearing of the Tribunal De Grande Instance De Bayonne, Department of Pyrenees Atlantiques Ruling: Divorce Judgement, June 28 1971: United States v. Zacarias Moussaoui, Criminal No. 01-455-A; Defense Trial Exhibits: http://vaed.uscourts.gov/notablecases/moussaoui/exhibits/ defense/ JV002.12T

20. Burckhard, M.J. (Social Worker): Moussaoui Family History, United States V. Zacarias Moussaoui, Criminal No. 01–455-A;Defense Trial Exhibits: Mulhouse, August 25, 1972, p.4 http://vaed.uscourts.gov/notablecases/ moussaoui/exhibits/defense/ JV002.17T

21. Ibid., p.5

22. Court of Appeal, Childrens' Court, Periguex: Temporary Placement Order; United States v. Zacarias Moussaoui, Criminal No. 01-455-A; Defense Trial Exhibits: http://vaed.uscourts.gov/notablecases/moussaoui/exhibits/ defense/ JV002.13T

23. United States v. Zacarias Moussaoui, Criminal No. 01-455-A; Defense Trial Exhibits: http://vaed.uscourts.gov/notablecases/moussaoui/exhibits/ defense/ JV002.1T Also refer to JV002.5T, JV002.15T, JV002.18T, p.5 of Trial Exhibits.

24. Office for Departmental Solidarity, Department of Pyrenees Atlantiques: Decree for Admission to Childhood Welfare Services, 24 June 1968. United States v. Zacarias Moussaoui, Criminal No. 01-455-A; Defense Trial Exhibits: http://vaed.uscourts.gov/notablecases/moussaoui/exhibits/ defense/ JV002.1T

25. Court of Appeals of Pau, Childrens' Court of Bayonne: Order to cease placement, references Docket nr: 46/1969, dated 8 February 1972,

United States v. Zacarias Moussaoui, Criminal No. 01-455-A; Defense Trial Exhibits: http://vaed.uscourts.gov/notablecases/moussaoui/exhibits/defense/ JV002.1T6T

26. Burckhard, M.J. (Social Worker): Moussaoui Family History, United States v. Zacarias Moussaoui, Criminal No. 01-455-A; Defense Trial Exhibits: Mulhouse, 25 August, 1972, p. 6 http://vaed.uscourts.gov/notablecases/moussaoui/exhibits/defense/ JV002.17T

27. The author was enrolled on an MBA [Education] course, whereas Zacarias was studying a Masters Degree in International Business Studies.

28. Academic Year Reports, 1974–79, Montesquieu School: United States v. Zacarias Moussaoui, Criminal No. 01-455-A; Defense Trial Exhibits: http://vaed.uscourts.gov/notablecases/moussaoui/exhibits/defense/ JV002.31T. Also refer to JV002.32T of Trial Exhibits.

29. Ibid., http://vaed.uscourts.gov/notablecases/moussaoui/exhibits/defense/ JV002.35T

30. Academic Year Reports; First Trimester, Jules-Ferry School, 1981–82: United States v. Zacarias Moussaoui, Criminal No. 01-455-A; Defense Trial Exhibits: http://vaed.uscourts.gov/notablecases/moussaoui/exhibits/defense/ JV002.41T

31. Second Semester Trimester, 1982–83 and First Trimester, 1983–84; Jules-FerrySchool: http://vaed.uscourts.gov/notablecases/moussaoui/exhibits/defense/ JV002.43T and JV002.44.

32. Cite Technique, certification that Zacarias Moussaoui is pursuing his studies as a day boarder in the 'seconde' class, 10 November 1984: United States v. Zacarias Moussaoui, Criminal No. 01-455-A; Defense Trial Exhibits: http://vaed.uscourts.gov/notablecases/moussaoui/exhibits/defense/ JV002.47T

33. Cite Technique, Academic Report, First, Second and Third terms; 1984–85: United States v. Zacarias Moussaoui, Criminal No. 01-455-A; Defense Trial Exhibits: http://vaed.uscourts.gov/notablecases/moussaoui/exhibits/defense/ JV002.48T. Also JV002.49T and JV002.50T.

34. Montesquieu College School, Narbonne; 1980–81, Second Trimester, Physical Education: United States v. Zacarias Moussaoui, Criminal No. 01-455-A; Defense Trial Exhibits: http://vaed.uscourts.gov/notablecases/moussaoui/exhibits/defense/ JV002.38T

35. Jules-FerrySchool, Narbonne; 1983–1984 2nd Trimester, Physical Education & Sports: United States v. Zacarias Moussaoui, Criminal No. 01-455-A; Defense Trial Exhibits: http://vaed.uscourts.gov/notablecases/moussaoui/exhibits/defense/ JV002.42T

36. Cite Technique, Academic Report, Physical Education, First Term; 1984–85: United States v. Zacarias Moussaoui, Criminal No. 01-455-A; Defense Trial Exhibits: http://vaed.uscourts.gov/notablecases/moussaoui/exhibits/defense/ JV002.48T

37. Technical-Commercial License from Acemie de Montpelier for Session 1990 (Lycee Arago): United States v. Zacarias Moussaoui, Criminal No. 01-455-A; Defense Trial Exhibits: http://vaed.uscourts.gov/notablecases/moussaoui/exhibits/defense/ JV002.56T

38. Transcript of videotaped interview of Abdul Haqq Baker; Brixton Mosque, London, England – 11 October 2005 p.6, conducted by Anne Chapman,

Assistant Federal Public Defender for the Eastern District of Virginia. Filmed and recorded by Simon Rutson, European Video. Also, United States v. Zacarias Moussaoui, Criminal No. 01-455-A; Defense Trial Exhibits: http:// vaed.uscourts.gov/notablecases/moussaoui/exhibits/defense/ JV002.V2

39. Ibid.
40. *The Sunday Times*: British Library quest of 9/11 plotter; 6 August 2006, p.7
41. Transcript of videotaped interview of Abdul Haqq Baker; Brixton Mosque, London, England – 11 October 2005, p.6, conducted by Anne Chapman, Assistant Federal Public Defender for the Eastern District of Virginia. Filmed and recorded by Simon Rutson, European Video. Also, United States v. Zacarias Moussaoui, Criminal No. 01-455-A; Defense Trial Exhibits: http:// vaed.uscourts.gov/notablecases/moussaoui/exhibits/defense/ JV002.V2
42. Ibid., p.7.
43. Ibid., p.9.
44. Ibid., pp.10–11.
45. Ibid., p.12.
46. Ibid., p.7–8.
47. Kokaz.com was a site that provided up to date information on the fighting in Chechyna.
48. Transcript of videotaped interview of Abdul Haqq Baker, p.14.
49. Ibid.
50. *The Sunday Times*; British Library quest of 9/11 plotter, Gadher, Dipesh, 6 August 2006, p.7.
51. The Zacarias Moussaoui (September 11) Trial: A Chronology: http://www. law.umkc.edu/faculty/projects/ftrials/moussaoui/zmchronology.html p.3.
52. United States District Court for the Eastern District of Virginia, Alexandria Division: 'December 2001 Term Indictment'.
53. Ibid.: 'Transcript of Jury Trial before the Honourable Leonie M. Brinkema, United States District Judge'.
54. Alexandria Court Schedule, updated: Monday July 31, 2006, 9:30am ET: United States v. Zacarias Moussaoui, Criminal No. 01-455-A: http://vaed. uscourts.gov/notablecases/moussaoui/index.html
55. Substitution for the Testimony of Khalid Shaykh Mohammed: United States v. Zacarias Moussaoui, Criminal No. 01-455-A: Defendant's Exhibit 941, p.1.
56. Ibid.
57. Ross, B and Esposito, R: 'CIA's Harsh Interrogation Techniques Described,' ABC News, 18 November 2005: http://abcnews.go.com/Blotter/ Investigation/story?id=1322866
58. Substitution for the Testimony of Khalid Shaykh Mohammed: United States v. Zacarias Moussaoui, Criminal No. 01-455-A: Defendant's Exhibit 941, pp.1–2.
59. Ibid., pp.3, 44–8.
60. Alexandria Court Schedule, updated: Monday July 31, 2006, 9:30am ET: United States v. Zacarias Moussaoui, Criminal No. 01-455-A: http://vaed. uscourts.gov/notablecases/moussaoui/index.html
61. Defendant's Notice Of Expert Evidence Of Mental Condition: United States v. Zacarias Moussaoui, Criminal No. 01-455-A; Government Exhibit: P200348, filed 30 November 2005, p.437.

62. Orientation and Educational Action Department: 'Intervention – Conclusions and Recommendations re: Jamila Moussaoui, 16 May 1978, Judicial File No. I.A.M. 175/75, SOAE File No. 92/76. United States v. Zacarias Moussaoui, Criminal No. 01-455-A; Defense Trial Exhibits: http://vaed. uscourts.gov/notablecases/moussaoui/exhibits/defense/ JV002.25T

63. Specialized Hospital Center examination of Mr Omar Moussaoui on 7 December 1973, conducted by Dr R. Franc, Psychiatrist and expert. United States v. Zacarias Moussaoui, Criminal No. 01-455-A; Defense Trial Exhibits: http://vaed.uscourts.gov/notablecases/moussaoui/exhibits/ defense/ JV002.67T

64. Suleaman, N., Transcript of radio interview, *Today Programme* interview of Abdul Haqq Baker 20 April 2006, Radio 4 (7.40a.m.). Story from BBC NEWS: http://news.bbc.co.uk/go/pr/fr/-/1/hi/world/americas/4874352.stm Published: 2006/04/03 22:33:56 GMT.

65. Ibid., pp.2–3.

66. Ibid.

67. Ibid.

68. Suleaman, N., 'Restless Convert in quest for Jihad', BBC News, Wednesday, 3 May 2006, 20:37 GMT 21:37 UK.

69. Thomas Tallis School website: http://www.school-portal.co.uk/GroupHome page.asp?GroupID=50463

70. Department of Justice Bulletin: 'British National Indicted for Conspiring with 'Shoe Bomber' Richard Reid, Monday, 4 October 2004 CRM (202) 514-2008, TDD (202) 514-1888: http://www.usdoj.gov/opa/pr/2004/October/ 04_crm_673.htm

71. Womack, D.E., Official Court Reporter: 'Transcript of Reid Sentencing,' United States of America vs. Richard C. Reid: http://www3.whdh.com/ news/articles/extra/A8458/ Criminal No. 3 02-10013-WGY 30 January 2003.

72. Government's Sentencing Memorandum: United States of America vs. Richard Colvin Reid, a/k/a Abdul-Rahim, a/k/a Abdul Rahim, Abu Ibrahim, Criminal No. 02-10013-WGY: http://news.lp.findlaw.com/hdocs/docs/ reid/usreid11703gsentm.pdf pp.6–8.

73. Ibid. p.6.

74. Ibid.

75. Ibid. pp.6–8.

76. Ibid., pp.6–7.

77. Ibid., p.14.

78. Ibid., p.7.

79. Ibid.

80. Ibid., p.11.

81. Ibid., p.11.

82. Ibid., p.19.

83. 'Exchange between Reid and Judge follows life sentence,' CNN, 6 December 2003, http://www.cnn.com/2003/LAW/01/31/reid.transcript/

84. Womack, D.E. Official Court Reporter: 'Transcript of Reid Sentencing,' United States of America vs. Richard C. Reid: http://www3.whdh.com/ news/articles/extra/A8458/, Criminal No. 3 02-10013-WGY 30 January 2003, pp.1–2.

85. Attorney General Transcript regarding Richard Reid: Wednesday, January 16, 2002, DOJ Conference Center, http://www.fas.org/irp/news/2002/01/ag011602.html

86. http://www.cnn.com/2003/LAW/01/31/reid.transcript/

87. El-Faisal admitted during interview that he personally knew Lindsay and had advised him, 'to pursue a life of quiet study'. Sandford, D., 'Hate preacher knew 7/7 bomber', BBC News, http://news.bbc.co.uk/go/pr/fr/-/2/hi/uk_news/7465201.stm Published: 2008/06/20 15:55:50 GMT.

88. BBC News: 'Profile: Sheikh Abdullah al-Faisal', Published 25 May 2007, http://news.bbc.co.uk/go/pr/fr/-/2/hi/uk_news/6692243.stm

89. BBC News: 'Profile: Sheikh Abdullah al-Faisal', Published 25 May 2007, http://news.bbc.co.uk/go/pr/fr/-/2/hi/uk_news/6692243.stm

90. 'Shaikh Abdullah al Faisal': http://www.pureislam.co.za/index.php?option=com_content&task=category&sectionid=13&id=91&Itemid=46

91. Supreme Court of Judicature Court of Appeal (Criminal Division) on Appeal from the Central Criminal Court (H.H.J. Beaumont QC) in the Royal Courts of Justice, Strand, London WC2A 2LL: R v. El-Faisal, Case no: 2003-01860-C2, 4 March 2004, p.2.

92. 'Muslim cleric guilty of soliciting murder', *The Guardian*, 24 February 2003, http://www.guardian.co.uk/uk/2003/feb/24/race.world/

93. Supreme Court of Judicature Court of Appeal (Criminal Division) on Appeal from the Central Criminal Court (H.H.J. Beaumont QC) in the Royal Courts of Justice, Strand, London WC2A 2LL: R v. El-Faisal, Case no: 2003-01860-C2, 4 March 2004, Clause 33, p.9.

94. Ibid., Clause 34, p.9.

95. Ibid., transcript of 'Jihad' 24, 73(21:24)–74, p.6.

96. Ibid., Clause 36, p.10.

97. Ibid., Clauses 48 and 49, pp.14–15.

98. 'Race hate cleric Faisal deported', BBC News, 25 May 2007; http://news.bbc.co.uk/go/pr/fr/-/2/hi/uk_news/6691701.stm

99. The name has been changed to maintain confidentiality.

100. Interview transcript of Sean O'Reilly, 22 October 2008, pp.1–3.

101. Ibid., p.3.

102. Ibid.

103. Ibid.

104. Ibid., p.2.

105. Ibid., p.3

106. Ibid.

107. Ibid., pp.3–4.

108. Ibid., p.4.

109. Ibid.

110. Ibid.

111. Ibid.

112. Ibid.

113. Ibid., pp.8–9.

114. Ibid.

115. Ibid.

116. Ibid., p.10.

117. Ibid., p.10.

118. Ibid.
119. Ibid.
120. Ibid.
121. Ibid., p.4
122. Ibid., pp.4–5
123. Ibid., p.5.
124. Ibid.
125. Ibid., p.11.
126. Ibid.
127. Ibid.
128. Ibid., p.6
129. Ibid., p.12.
130. Ibid.
131. Ibid, p.6.
132. Ibid., p.1.
133. Ibid., citing Zubeck, P. 'Cadets' guest speaker will focus on Christianity', Colorado Springs Gazette.
134. Interview transcript of Sean O'Reilly, 22 October 2008, p.7.
135. Ibid., p.6.
136. Ibid.
137. Ibid., p.8.
138. Ibid., p.8.
139. Ibid.
140. Ibid., p.7.
141. Ibid., p.5.
142. Ibid.
143. Ibid., p.11.
144. Ibid., p.12.
145. Ibid., p.10.
146. Ibid., p.15.
147. Ibid.
148. Department of Communities and Local Government: 'The next generation of community leaders', 7 October 2008, http://www.communities.gov.uk/news/corporate/987399
149. Interview transcript of Sean O'Reilly, 22 October 2008, p.18.
150. Zebiri, 2008: p. 40.

7   Research Analysis of Interviews

1. Transcript of interview 30 with Dawud George, 2008, p.1.
2. Transcript of interview 11 with Abdullah Smith, 2007, p.2.
3. Transcript of interview 29 with Rahim McDonald, 2009, pp.1–2.
4. Transcript of interview 27 with Ishaq Thompson, 2009, p.1.
5. Transcript of interview 23 with Hussain, 2007, p.1.
6. Transcript of interview 31 with Abdul Basit, 2008, pp.2–3.
7. Transcript of interview 22 with Thomas, 2007, pp.1–2.
8. Transcript of interview 26 with Abdul Halim, 2008, p.2.
9. Transcript of interview 4 with Michael, 2007, p.1.

10. Transcript of interview 4 with Yusuf, 2007, pp.1–2.
11. Transcript of interview 11 with Abdullah Smith, 2007, p.1
12. Respondent 23, Hussain, considered himself to be non-Muslim prior to converting to Sunni Islam, hence the author has referred to the former's self-categorisation in Table 7.2.
13. Ibid., table 3.2b, p.70.
14. Transcript of interview 26 with Abdul Halim, 2008, p.5.
15. Transcript of interview 29 with Rahim McDonald, 2009, p.10.
16. Transcript of interview 31 with Abdul Basit, 2008, p.2.
17. The MPS Gang Survey conducted by S. Mahomed between October 2006 and August 2007 highlighted the existence of 40 established gangs in Lambeth alone.
18. Transcript of interview 22 with Thomas, 2008, p.2.
19. Transcript of interview 23 with Hussain, 2008, p.1.
20. Transcript of interview 26 with Abdul Halim, 2008, p.2.
21. Transcript of interview 27 with Ishaq Thompson, 2009, p.3.
22. Transcript of interview 28 with Uthman, 2008, p.2.
23. Transcript of interview 1 with Yusuf, 2007, pp.1–2.
24. Transcript of interview 2 with Ahmad, 2007, p.3.
25. Transcript of interview 8 with Rashad, 2007, p.2.
26. Transcript of interview 12 with Hakim, 2007, p.2.
27. Transcript of interview 27 with Ishaq Thompson, 2009, p.5.
28. Transcript of interview 30 with Dawud George, 2008, p.4.
29. Transcript of interview 28 with Uthman, 2008, p.5.
30. Transcript of interview 30 with Dawud George, 2008, p.6.
31. Transcript of interview 26 with Abdul Halim, 2008.
32. Transcript of interview 18 with Paul, 2007, p.7.
33. Transcript of interview 31 with Abdul Basit, 2008, p.4.
34. Transcript of interview 29 with Rahim McDonald, 2009, p.9.
35. Transcript of interview 26 with Abdul Halim, 2008, p.4.
36. Transcript of interview 27 with Ishaq Thompson, 2009, p.6.
37. Ibid.
38. Ibid.
39. Ibid. p.7.
40. Transcript of interview 1 with Yusuf, 2007, p.3.
41. Transcript of interview 30 with Dawud George, 2008, p.6
42. Transcript of interview 17 with Andre, 2007, p.4.
43. Transcript of interview 28 with Uthman, 2008, p.5.
44. Transcript of interview 18 with Paul, 2007, p.3.
45. Ibid.
46. Transcript of interview 26 with Abdul Halim, 2008, p.5.
47. Transcript of interview 27 with Ishaq Thompson, 2009, p.8.
48. Transcript of interview 29 with Rahim McDonald, 2009, pp.10–11.
49. Transcript of interview 4 with Michael, 2007, p.7.
50. Transcript of interview 26 with Abdul Halim, 2008, p.6.
51. Transcript of interview 22 with Thomas, 2007, p.4.
52. Transcript of interview 18 with Paul, 2007, p.4.
53. Transcript of interview 28 with Uthman, 2008, pp.5–6.
54. Transcript of interview 32 with Carl, 2009, p.10.

55. Transcript of interview 7 with Gilbert, 2007, p.3.
56. Transcript of interview 27 with Ishaq Thompson, 2009, p.8.
57. Transcript of interview 30 with Dawud George, 2008, p.8.
58. Transcript of interview 26 with Abdul Halim, 2008, p.6.
59. Transcript of interview 30 with Dawud George, 2008, p.8.
60. Transcript of interview 32 with Carl, 2009, p.11.
61. Transcript of interview 31 with Abdul Basit, 2008, p.6.
62. Transcript of interview 28 with Uthman, 2008, p.6.
63. Transcript of interview 29 with Rahim McDonald, 2009, pp.12–13.
64. Ibid.
65. Ibid., p.13.
66. Ibid.
67. Transcript of interview 30 with Dawud George, 2008, p.8.
68. Transcript of interview 27 with Ishaq Thompson, 2009, p.9.
69. Transcript of interview 27 with Ishaq Thompson, 2009, p.9.
70. Transcript of interview 32 with Carl, 2009, pp.10–11.

8 Countering Terrorism in the UK: A Community Perspective

1. Department for Communities and Local Government: 'Preventing Violent Extremism Pathfinder Fund 2007/8 Case Studies', April 2007, p.4, http://www.communities.gov.uk/archived/publications/communities/preventingviolent pathfinderfundg.
2. Department for Communities and Local Government: 'Preventing Violent Extremism Pathfinder Fund, Guidance Note for Government Offices and Local Authorities in England, 7 February 2007, p.2.
3. Ibid., p.3.
4. Ibid.
5. Ibid., p.9.
6. Media deconstruction and counter-narrative of 'as-Shahab Video 1' STREET UK Ltd Deconstruction Team, August 2008, p.2.
7. Ibid., p.21.

Bibliography

Books, journals and reports

Abbas, T., *British South Asian Muslims: before and after September 11th*, Muslim Britain, Zed Books, 2005.

Abdullah, M., 'al-Itijaahaat al-Taasabiyyah,' in Al-Mutairi, *Religious Extremism in the Lives of Contemporary Muslims*, p.26.

Addae, P., 'The Devil's Deception of Abdullah Faysal (Shaykh Faisal): A Critical Study of his Statements, Errors and Extremism in Takfeer', http://Salafimanhaj.com, 2007.

Adelman, C., 'The Tins' in Ford Teaching Project, University of East Anglia, Centre for Applied Research in Education 1974' and 'On First Hearing' Adelman, C., 'Uttering Muttering', London, Grant McIntyre, 1981.

Ahmad, W. and Husband, C., 'Religious identity, citizenship and welfare: The case of Muslims in Britain', *American Journal of Islamic Social Sciences*, Vol. CII, No. II, 1996.

Akbar, Y.H., *Global Antitrust: Trade and Competition Linkages*, Ashgate Publishing Ltd., 2003.

Al-Mutairi, Dr. A.R.M.L., *Religious Extremism in the Lives of Contemporary Muslims*, translated by Zarabozo, J.M.M., Basheer Company for Publications and Translations, 2001.

Al-Albani, M.N., *The Prophet's Prayer described*, Al-Haneef Publications, 1993.

Al-Fawzan, S., 'Are the Terrorists of Today the Khawaarij?' http://www.fatwa1.com/anti-erhab/Irhabion.html, audio clip no. 20.

Al-Fowzan, S. and Al-Khumayyis, A.R., 'The Characteristics of the Extremist Khawaarij', al-ebaanah book, 2005, p.16.

Alibhai-Brown, Y., 'Muddled Leaders and the Future of British National Identity', in *Political Quarterly*, Blackwell Publishers, 2000, pp. 26–30.

Ali-Shaikh, S., 'The Fitnah of the Khawaarij', www.answering-extremism.com

Ali-Shaykh, S.A.A., 'A Warning Against Extremism', UK, Jamiah Media, 2008.

Al-Majd, A.K., 'Hawaar la Muwaajahah', cited in Al-Mutairi, *'Religious Extremism in the Lives of Contemporary Muslims*, 2001, p.100.

Al-Meedani, A.R., 'Basaair li-l-Muslim al Musaair', cited in Al-Mutairi, *Religious Extremism in the Lives of Contemporary Muslims*, 2001, p.150.

Al-Samuraa'ee, N., 'al-Takfeer: Judhooruhu, Asbaabuhu wa Mabruraatuhu', cited in Al-Mutairi, *Religious Extremism in the Lives of Contemporary Muslims*, 2001, p.8.

Al-Uthaimeen, M.S., *Islamic Verdicts on Pillars of Islam*, Vol.1: Creed and Prayer, Darussalam, Riyadh 2003.

Al-Zawahiri, A., 'Knights under the Prophet's Banner', December 2001, cited in Keppel, G., *The War for Muslim Minds: Islam and the West'*, Belknap Press, 2004.

Amnesty International, 'The backlash – human rights at risk throughout the world', AI Index; ACT 30/027/2001, 4 October 2001, p.1.

An Introductory Community Profile of Brixton Islamic Cultural Centre, Past, Present & Future, 19 August 2001.

Ansari, H. (citing the then Conservative Home Affairs Minister, John Patten), *The Infidel Within: Muslims In Britain since 1800*; Hurst & Company, London, 2004.

Asad, T., 'Multiculturalism and British Identity in the wake of the Rushdie affair', *Politics and Society*, 18, 4, 1990, 455–80.

At-Tuwayjiri, H.A. 'Iqamatul Burhan: (The Establishment of Proof)' The Society for Adherence to the Sunnah Publishers, 1992.

Bagguley, P. and Hussain, Y., *Flying the Flag for England? Citizenship, Religion and Cultural Identity among British Pakistani Muslims,* Muslim Britain, Communities Under Pressure, Zed Books, 2005.

Baker, A.H., 'Proposal for youth initiative', 1ˢᵗ Draft: 'An Introduction to the STREET; Strategy To Reach Empower & Educate Teenagers,' 18 June 2006.

Baker, A., 'The Significance of State Funding for Muslim Education in Britain': SouthBankUniversity, London, 1998.

Baker, A., 'The future is for Islam and the need to be balanced' transcript of Friday sermon, 29 September 2001.

Baker, A: A Historical Account of Tackling Violent Extremist Propaganda in Brixton Mosque, unpublished.

Bakier, A.H., 'Terrorism Monitor', Volume 4, Issue 20, October 19, 2006.

Bakri, M., 'Al Hijrah', cited in Al-Mutairi, *Religious Extremism in the Lives of Contemporary Muslims*, 2001, p.585.

Bauman, Z., *Identity: Conversations with Benedetto Vecchi*, Cambridge: Polity Press, 2004.

Beckford, J.A., Joly, D., Khosrokhavar, F. *Muslims in Prison: Challenge and Change in Britain and France*, Palgrave Macmillan, 2005.

Berger, P. and Luckmann, T., *The Social Construction of Reality*, Allen Lane and the Penguin Press, London, 1967.

Bevir, M. and Rhodes, R.A.W. 'Interpretive Theory' in Marsh, D. and Stoker, G. (eds), *Theory and Methods in Political Science*, Palgrave Macmillan, 2002.

Bhui, H.S., 'Muslim Communities and Criminal Justice: A stigmatised faith identity post 9/11', *Race and Criminal Justice*, Sage Publications, 2009.

Biddle, S., 'War Aims and War Termination', in Colonel John R. Martin (ed.), *Defeating Terrorism: Strategic Issue Analyses*, Strategic Studies Insititute, US Army War College, January 2002, pp.7–8, cited in Hassan M.H.B., 'Key Considerations in Counterideological Work against Terrorist Ideology' *Studies in Conflict & Terrorism*, 29: 531–58, 2006.

Birt, Y, 'Islamic Citizenship in Britain after 7/7: Tackling Extremism and Preserving Freedoms', in A.A. Malik (ed.), *The State We Are in; Identity, Terror and the Law of Jihad*, Amal Press, 2006.

Birt, Y. 'Sufis and Salafis in the West: Discord and the hope of unity', 26 August 2007, www.yahyabirt.com

Birt, Y., 'Lies, Damn Lies, Statistics and Conversion!', Q-News, no. 343–4, May–June 2002, http://www.yahyabirt.com

Bjorgo, T. and Horgan, J., *Leaving Terrorism Behind: Individual and collective disengagement*, Routledge, Taylor & Francis Group, 2009.

Boehm, V.R., in Hakel, M.D., Sorcher, M., Beek, M. and Moses, J.L. *Making it Happen: Designing research with implementation in mind'*, Sage, 1982.

Bonney, R., *Jihad: From Qur'an to bin Laden*, Palgrave Macmillan, 2004, p.55.

Bouerk, C., 'Saudi Arabia's "Soft" Counterterrorism Strategy: Prevention, Rehabilitation and Aftercare', Carnegie Papers, Carnegie Endowment for International Peace, Middle East Program, no.97, September 2008.

Bradley, L., *Bass Culture: When Reggae was King*, Penguin Books, 2001.

Briggs, R., Fieschi, C., Lownsbrough, H., 'Bringing it Home: Community-based approaches to counter-terrorism', DEMOS, 2006.

Brixton Mosque & Islamic Cultural Centre Charitable Trust Deed, 19 October 1997.

Brough, G., 'Shoe bomber brands Obama "no better than Bush" ', *The Mirror*, 22 June 2009: http://www.mirror.co.uk/news/top-stories/2009/06/22/the-shoe-bomber

Bukhari: 'Sahih Al Buhkari' Hadeeth nos. 3610, 6163 and 6933 & Muslim: 'Sahih Muslim' Hadeeth no. 1064.

Burke, J., *Al-Qaeda: The True Story of Radical Islam*, Penguin, 2004.

Cantle Report (2001), Community Cohesion: A Report of the Independent Review Team, London: Home Office pp. 210–12, 239; Clarke, T. (2002), Report of the Burnley Task Force, http://www.burnleytaskforce.org.uk; Denham, J. (2002), Building Cohesive Communities: A Report of the Ministerial Group on Public Order and Community Cohesion, London: Home Office; Ritchie, D. Oldham Independent Review, Oldham, (2001).

Castells, M., *The Information Age: Economy, Society and Culture*, Volume II: *The Power of Identity* Blackwells, 1997. Second Edition, Blackwell Publishing, 2004.

Cesari, J., 'Muslims in Europe and the Risk of Radicalism,' cited from Coolsaet, R. (ed.) *Jihadi Terrorism and the Radicalisation Challenge in Europe*', Chapter 8, p.100, Ashgate Publishing Company, 2008.

Change Institute: 'Studies into violent radicalization: The beliefs ideologies and narratives', A study carried out for the European Commission – Directorate General Justice, Freedom and Security, 2008, Appendix E., Interviewees, pp.181–2.

Church of England Schools, State Funded Schools in England in 1996, DFEE Statistical Branch.

Clark D., dikw2 (2004) http://www.nwlink.com/~donclark/performance/understanding.html

Cleveland, H. 'Information as Resource', *The Futurist*, December 1982 p. 34–9.

Cole, J. and Cole, B., *Martyrdom: Radicalisation and Terrorist Violence Among British Muslims*, Pennant Books, 2009.

Colley, L., *Britons: Forging the Nation 1707–1837*, Yale University Press, 1996.

Cowan, J.M., *The Hans Weir Dictionary of Modern Arabic*, Spoken Language Services Inc., New York 3rd Edition, 1976.

Department for Communities and Local Government: 'Preventing Violent Extremism Pathfinder Fund 2007/8 Case Studies', April 2007, p.4 http://www.communities.gov.uk/archived/publications/communities/preventingviolentpathfinderfundg

Department for Communities and Local Government: 'Preventing Violent Extremism Pathfinder Fund, Guidance Note for Government Offices and Local Authorities in England, 7 February 2007.

Department of Communities and Local Government: 'The next generation of community leaders', 7 October 2008.

Department of Justice Bulletin: 'British National Indicted for Conspiring with "Shoe Bomber" Richard Reid, Monday, 4 October 2004, CRM (202) 514-2008, TDD (202) 514-1888: http://www.usdoj.gov/opa/pr/2004/October/04_crm_673.htm

Eleftheriadou, M., 'Muslim Brotherhood vs Salafi–Jihadi Islam: Confronting the "Black Sheep" of Political Islam', Center for Mediterranean & Middle Eastern Studies, January 2008; Issue 9.

Elworthy, S. and Rifkind, G: *Making Terrorism History,* DEMOS, Rider 2006.

Eriksen, T.H. 'Kulturella Veikryss Cultural Crossroads', Oslo, Universitetsforlaget, 1994.

Esposito, J., cited in 'Islam and Congress', Al-Mujtama, no. 919, p.44.

European Monitoring Centre on Racism and Xenophobia, 'The Impact of 7 July 2005 London Bomb Attacks on Muslim communities in the EU', Report, November 2005, pp. 10–11.

Evans, Ellis D. (ed.), *Adolescents Readings in Behaviour and Development,* Dryden Press, 1970.

Evans, E.D. and Potter, T.H., 'Identity Crisis: A Brief Perspective'.

Faisal, A., *Natural Instincts: Islamic Psychology* Darul Islam Publishers, London, 1997.

Fawzan, S., *A Summary of Islamic Jurisprudence,* Al-Maiman Publishing House, Riyadh, 2005 pp.475–76.

Festinger, L. Riecken, H.W. and Schachter, S. 'When Prophecy Fails.' New York: Harper and Row (1956) 196

Feyerabend, P., *Science in a Free Societ,* London, N.L.B. 1978.

Flinn, F.K., 'Conversion: The Pentecostal and Charismatic Experience', in Lamb, C. and Bryant, D. (eds),*Religious Conversion: Contemporary Practices and Controversies,* London: Cassell, 1999, pp. 51–72.

Fortier, A.M., 'Pride Politics and Multiculturalist Citizenship', *Ethnic and Racial Studies,* Vol.28 no.3, May 2005.

Freud, S., *The Future of an Illusion,* translated by Scott, W., London: Hogarth, 1978/1928.

Furedi, F., *Culture of Fear: Risk-taking and the Morality of Low Expectation',* Cassell, 1997.

Gailani, F. *The Mosques of London,* Elm Grove Books, 2000.

Gardner, K. and Shakur, A. 'I'm Bengali, I'm Asian and I'm Living Here: The Changing Identity of British Bengalis', in Ballard, R. (ed.), *Desh Pardesh: The South Asian Presence in Britain,* Hurst, 1994.

Garfinkel, R., 'Personal Transformations: Moving From Violence To Peace', United States Institute of Peace Special Report, 186, April, 2007.

Gerholm, T., 'Three European Intellectuals as Converts to Islam: Cultural Mediators or Social Critics?' in Gerholm T. and Lithman Y.G. (eds), *New Islamic Presence in Western Europe,* Mansell, 1988.

Greaves, R., 'Negotiating British Citizenship and Muslim Identity', in Abbas, T. (ed.) *Muslim Britain,* Zed Books, 2005

Haadee, M.R. *The Reality of Sufism in light of the Qur'aan & Sunnah,* Al-Hidaayah Publishing, 1995.

Hajar, I., 'Tahdheeb at-Tahdheeb', Hydrabad, 1325–7, vol.10, p.225.

Halliday, F., *Arabs in Exile: Yemeni Migrants in Urban Britain,* I.B. Taurus, 1992.

Hall, N., 'Policing Racist Hate Crime in London: Policy, Practice and Experience after the Stephen Lawrence Inquiry', Research report for the Metropolitan Police Service.

Halstead, J.M. 'The case for Voluntary Aided Schools', Cambridge, Islamic Academy, 1986.

Hamed, S., 'The Attraction of "Authentic" Islam: Salafism and British Muslim Youth', in Meijer, R. (ed.), *Global Salafism: Islam's new Religious Movement.* London: Hurst, 2009.

Hameed, A.H., 'As-Salafiyyatu, limaadhaa? Ma'aadhan wa Malaadhan: Abhaathun wa Maqalaatun wa Haqaa'iq wa Bayyinaat wa Radd 'ala Shubuhaat – [Why Salafiyyah as a Refuge and Safe-Haven? A response to the doubts]' Abridged and translated version: Amman, Jordan: Daar ul-Athariyyah, 2008.

Hamm, M.S. *In Bad Company: America's Terrorist Underground,* Northeastern University Press, 2001.

Hanbal, A. (2/188 and 210) and others with an authentic [saheeh] chain of narration, cited in Abdul-Hameed's, A.H., *Forty Hadeeth on: The Call to Islam and the Caller,* Al-Hidaayah Publishing and Distribution, 1994, p. 39.

Hassan, M.H.B., 'Key Considerations in Counterideological Work against Terrorist Ideology', *Studies in Conflict & Terrorism,* 2006, 29: 531–58.

Hayley, A., *The Autobiography of Malcolm X,* Penguin, 1968.

Haynes, J., 'Religion, Secularization, and Politics: A Postmodern Conspectus', *Third World Quarterly,* 18(4), 1997.

Heirich, M. 'Change of Heart: A Test of Some Widely Held Theories About Religious Conversion', *American Journal of Sociology,* 1977, 83, 653–80.

Hermansen, M. 'Two-Way Acculturation: Muslim Women in America Between Individual Choice (Liminality) and Community Affiliation (Communitas)', in Haddad, Y.Y. (ed.), *The Muslims of America,* Oxford University Presss, 1991, 188–201.

Home Office–Foreign and Commonwealth Office: 'Young Muslims and Extremism', Home Office–FCO Paper, 10 May 2004, p.9, http://www.timesonline.co. uk/article/0,,22989-1688872,00.html.

Hopkins, N. and Kahani-Hopkins, V., 'The antecedents of identification: A rhetorical analysis of British Muslim activists' constructions of community and identity', *British Journal of Psychology,* Department of Psychology, Dundee University, Scotland, UK, 2004, 43, 41–57, p.44.

Hopkins, N. and Kahani-Hopkins, V: 'British Muslim Identities' p.42, 2004.

Horgan, J., *The Psychology of Terrorism,* Routledge, 2005.

Hudson, M., 'Managing Without Profit: The Art of Third-Sector Organizations', Penguin Books, 1995.

Husain, E., *The Islamist,* Penguin Books, 2007.

Hussain, T., 'As-Sahab: A semiotic analysis of The Wills of the Knights of the London raid', BirkbeckCollege: University of London MA Islamic Studies, Final Dissertation, August 2009.

Hutnick, N., 'Aspects of Identity in Multi-Ethnic Society', *New York Community,* 1985, 12, 2: 298.

Inge, A., 'Salafism in Britain: The New Generation's Rebellion,' unpublished MA dissertation, School of Oriental and African Studies, University of London, 2008.

Ingold, T. 'Culture and the Perception of the Environment' in Croll, E. and Parkin, D. (eds), *Bush Base, Forest Farm: Culture, Environment and Development*, Routledge.

International Crisis Group (ICG), Middle East Report [21ˢᵗ September 2004] Chapter 1 – 'Wahhabism'.

Iqra Independent School Ethnicity Profile [12th October 1998].

Jacobson, J., *Islam in Transition: Religion and Identity Among British Pakistani Youth*, Routledge, 1998.

James, O., *Britain on the Couch*, Century, 1997.

Janis, I., *'Victims of Groupthink* (2nd edition), Houghton-Mifflin, 1982.

Johnstone, P., 'July 7 preacher el-Faisal deported', *The Telegraph*, 25 May 2007; http://www.telegraph.co.uk/news/uknews/1552580/July-7-preacher-Abdullah-El-Faisal-deported.html

Joly, D., *Britannia's Crescent: Making a Place for Muslims in British Society*, Avebury, 1995.

Kepel, G: 'The Roots Of Radical Islam' SAQI, 2005.

Kirby, S. and McKenna, K., *Experience, Research, Social Change: Methods from the Margins'*, Garamound. 1989.

Kohlberg, L., *The Psychology of Moral Development*, Harper & Row, London, 1984.

Kose, A. *Conversion to Islam: A Study of Native British Converts*, Kegan Paul International, 1996.

Kundnani, A: 'Spooked! How not to prevent violent extremism', Institute of Race Relations, October 2009, http://www.irr.org.uk/pdf2/spooked.pdf

Lambert, R., 'The Threat from Salafi-Jihadist Groups', NATO Advanced Research Workshop: Developing Currents within Political and Radical Islam: How to construct a differentiated Western response, AmmanJordan, 10–11 October 2005.

Lambert, R., 'Ignoring Lessons of the past', *Criminal Justice Matters*, Issue 73, September 2008: 23.

Lambert, R. 'Salafi and Islamist Londoners: Stigmatised minority faith communities countering al-Qaida' Crime Law Soc. Change, 2008, 50: 73–89.

Lambert, R., 'The London Partnerships: an Insider's Analysis of Legitimacy and Effectiveness', Draft PhD, Department of Politics, University of Exeter September 2009.

Lane, E., *Arabic-English Lexicon*, Islamic Texts Society, Cambridge, 1984, vol.2, p.2287.

Lawless, R.I., *From Tai'zz to Tyneside, an Arab Community in the North-East of England during the Early Twentieth Century*, Exeter University Press, 1995.

Levtzion, N., 'Towards a Comparative Study of Islamisation', in Levtzion, N. (ed.), *Conversion to Islam*, Holmes and Meier, 1979.

Linder, D.O., 'The Trial of Zacarias Moussaoui: An Account' 2006 http://www.law.umkc.edu/faculty/projects/FTRIALS/moussaoui/zmaccount.html

Lofland, J. and Skonovd, N., 'Conversion Motifs', *Journal for the Scientific Study of Religion*, 20: 373–85, 1981.

Lofland, J. and Stark, R., 'Becoming a World-Saver: A Theory of Conversion to a Deviant Perspective,' *American Sociological Review*, 1965, 30: 862–75.

Lonergan, B., *Method in Theology*, Darton, Longman & Todd, 1972.

Macpherson W., 'The Report of the Stephen Lawrence Inquiry', 1999, The Stationery Office.

Macpherson, Lord, 1999, 'The Stephen Lawrence Inquiry: Report, Cm.4262-1

Maher, S. and Frampton, M., 'Choosing Our Friends Wisely: Criteria for engagement with Muslim groups', Policy Exchange, 2009, www.policyexchange.org.uk

Mahmood, E. 'British Muslims', Media Guide, 2005; p.6.

Malik, A.A; *The State We Are In; Identity, Terror and the Law of Jihad,* Amal Press, 2006.

Malik, S., 'The Making of a Terrorist: My brother, the bomber,' *Prospect Magazine,* Issue 135: June 2007 www.prospect-magazine.co.uk

Marr, A. *The Day Britain Died: The Subject of a Major BBC TV Series,* Profile Books, 2000.

Marranci, G., *Jihad Beyond Islam,* Berg: Oxford and New York, 2006a.

Marranci, G., 'Muslim Inside: Islamic religiosity and identity in Scottish Prisons', University of Aberdeen, 2006b.

Matar, N., *Islam in Britain 1558–1685;* Cambridge University Press, 1998.

Maudoodi, A., 'Tadween al-Dustoor', from 'Majmooah Nadhariyyah al-Islaam wa Hadyihi', p.251.

McBeth, J., 'No way would he have got there on his own. He doesn't have the capacity to think it through.' *Living Scotsman,* 27 December 2001, p.2: http://living.scotsman.com/features/No-way-would-he-have.2289424.jp

McCants W., Brachman, J. and Felter, J., 'Militant Ideology Atlas' Executive Report, November 2006, Combating Terrorism Center, US Military Academy.

Media Deconstruction and Counter-narrative of 'as-Shahab Video 1', STREET UK Ltd Deconstruction Team, August 2008, p.2.

Miles, M.B. and Huberman, A.M., *Qualitative Data Analysis: A sourcebook of new methods,* London: Sage, 1984.

Milton, K. and Svasek, M. (eds), *Mixed Emotions: Anthropological Studies of Feelings,* Berg, 2005.

Modood, T., *Not easy being British. Colour, culture and citizenship,* Runnymede Trust and Trentham Books, 1992.

Modood, T., 'Remaking multiculturalism after 7/7' openDemocracy Ltd. 29 September 2005, www.openDemocracy.net

Modood, T., Beishon S., and Virdee S., *Changing Ethnic Identities,* PSI, 1994.

Mol, H. *Identity and The Sacred: A Sketch for a New Social-Scientific Theory of Religion,* Basil Blackwell, 1976.

Moskalenko, S. and McCauley, C., 'Measuring Political Mobilization: The Distinction Between Activism and Radicalism,' *Terrorism and Political Violence,* 21: 239–60, 2009, p. 240.

Moussaoui, A.S., *Zacarias Moussaoui: The Making of a Terrorist,* Serpent's Tail, 2003.

Mukhtasar Seerah Ar-Rasool (Abridged Biography of the Prophet Muhammad), M. Ibn Abdul Wahhab At-Tamimi, Darussalam, 2003, pp. 316–22.

Mustafa, S., 'Al-Khilaafah', vol.5 p.13 cited in Al-Mutairi, *Religious Extremism in the Lives of Contemporary Muslims',* 2001, p.585.

Naqshbandi, M., 'Problems and Practical Solutions to Tackle Extremism; and Muslim Youth Community Issues', Shrivenham Papers: Defence Academy of the United Kingdom, 2006.

National Prison Statistics of England and Wales, 30th June 2002 http://www.official_documents.co.uk/documents/cm59/5996/5996pdf

Neuman, P., 'Perspecives on Radicalisation and Political Violence' The International Centre for the Study of Radicalisation and Political Violence; Papers from the First International Conference' (ICSR), London 17–18 January 2008, p.3.

New York Police Department Intelligence Division: 'Radicalization in the West: The Homegrown Threat', May 2007.

Nielsen, J., *Muslims in Western Europe*, Edinburgh University Press, 1992, 3rd edition 2004.

Nielsen, J., 'Muslims in Europe: history revisited as a way forward?' Islam and Christian Muslim Relations (8) 2: 135–287, 1997.

Niyazi, B. *The Development of Secularism in Turkey*, McGill Press, 1964.

Office For Standards in Education: http://www.ofsted.gov.uk/Ofsted

O'Neill, S. and McGrory, D., *The Suicide Factory: Abu Hamza and the FinsburyPark Mosque*, Harper Collins, 2006.

Oliveti, V., *Terror's Source: The Ideology of Wahhabi-Salafism and its Consequences*, Amadeus Books, 2001.

openDemocracy.net, 'Europe's answer to Londonistan', 24 August 2005.

Pargeter, A., *The New Frontiers of Jihad: Radical Islam in Europe*, I.B. Taurus, 2008.

Patel, E., *Acts of Faith: The Story of an American Muslim, The Struggle for the Soul of a Generation*, Beacon Press, 2007.

Paxman, J. *The English: Portrait of a People*, Penguin, 1999.

Peach, C., *Britain's Muslim Population: Muslims in Britain*, Zed Books, 2005.

Philips, A.A.B., *The Evolution of Fiqh (Islamic Law & The Madh-habs)*, Tawheed Publications, 1988.

Philips, A.A.B., *The Fundamentals of Tawheed (Islamic Monotheism)*, International Islamic Publishing House, 1997, p.12.

Pipes, D. 'Radicalized Muslim Converts Critical to Terrorist Operations' Human EventsOnline Copyright © 2006 HUMAN EVENTS, 7 December 2005.

Poston, L., *Islamic Da'wah in the West: Muslim Missionary Activity and the Dynamics of Conversion in Islam*, Oxford University Press, 1992.

Powney, J. and Watts, M., *Interviewing in Educational Research*, Routledge and Kegan Paul, 1987.

Qutb, S., *Ma'alim fi'l-Tariq (Signposts)*, Dar al-Shourouk, Cairo, 1980; edition of the World Islamic Union of Students, p.10.

Qutb, S., 'Muqawwimaat al-Tasawur' p.177 and 'Muallim fi al-Tareeq' p.118 in Al-Mutairi, *Religious Extremism in the Lives of Contemporary Muslims*, 2001, p.107.

Qwidi, al-, 'Understanding the Stages of Conversion to Islam: The Voices of British Converts', PhD, University of Leeds, 2002, p.155.

Rai, M., *7/7: the London Bombings, Islam and the Iraq War*, Pluto Press, 2006.

Raja and Partners Solicitors, 28th March 1998: Letter confirming completion of sale of Brixton Mosque.

Ramadan, T. *Western Muslims and The Future Of Islam*, Oxford University Press, 2004.

Ramadan, T., *To be a European Muslim*, The Islamic Foundation, 1999.

Rambo, L.W. *Understanding Religious Conversion*, Yale University Press, 1993.

Reddie, R.S., *Black Muslims in Britain: Why are a growing number of young Black people converting to Islam?*, Lion Hudson plc, 2009.

Renani, S.R.A., 'The Impact of Globalization on British Muslims Identity', Royal Holloway, University of London, PhD, 2001.

Roald A.S., *New Muslims in the European Context: The Experience of Scandinavian Converts*, Brill 2004.

Robson, C., *Real World Research: A Resource for Social Scientists and Practitioner-Authors*, Blackwell, 1993.

Runnymede Trust, *The Future of Multi-Ethnic Britain* (also known as the Parekh Report) 2000, p.36.

Ruthven, M., *Fundamentalism: A Very Short Introduction*, Oxford University Press, 2007.

Saggar, S., 'The One Per Cent World: Managing the Myth of Muslim Religious Extremism,' University of Sussex, Lecture Transcript, 16 March 2006.

Salafimanhaj.com, 'The Devil's Deception Of Abdullah Faysal Al Kharijee ('Shiekh Faisal'), 2007.

Sander, A., 'The Status of Muslim Communities in Sweden', in Nonneman, G., Niblock, T. and Szajkowski, B. (eds), *Muslim Communities in New Europe*, Ithaca, 1992, pp. 269–303.

Scarman, Lord Justice (1981), 'The Brixton Disorders, 10–12 April 1981', paragraphs 2.22 and 4.63: Cmnd 8247, Home Office.

Schacht, J., *The Origins of Muhammadan Jurisprudence*, Oxford, 1950.

Scott, J., *A Matter of Record*, Polity Press, 1990.

Shaykh Taqi al-Din al-Nabhani (d.1977): see Roald, A.S., *New Muslims in the European Context*, 2004, p.142.

Shepard, W.E. 'Islam and Ideology: Towards a Typology', *Middle East Studies*, no. 19, 1987: 307–36.

Smith, C., *Islam and Modern History*, New American Library, Mentor, 1957.

Smith, H.W., *Strategies of Social Research: The methodological imagination*, Prentice-Hall, 1975.

Sommer, R. and Wicker, A.W., 'Gas Station Psychology: The case for specialization in ecological psychology. Environment and Behaviour,' 1991, pp. 23, 131–49, cited in Robson, C., 1993, p. 446.

Spalek, B., Lambert, R. and Baker, A.H., 'Minority Muslim Communities and Criminal Justice: Stigmatized UK Faith Identities Post 9/11 and 7/7', cited from Bhui, H.S., *Race and Criminal Justice*, Sage, 2009.

Stemmann, J.J.E., 'Middle East Salafism's Influence and the Radicalization of Muslim Communities in Europe', The GLORIA Center, Interdisciplinary Center, Herzliya, vol. 10, no. 3, Article 1/10, September 2006.

Sunan Abu Daud, 'Kitab al-Sunna' hadeeth collection no. 17718.

Taimiyyah, I., 'Al-Fataawa' vol.7.

Taji-Farouki, S., *A Fundamental Quest: Hizbut al –Tahrir and the Search for the Islamic Caliphate*', Longmans, 1996, pps. 57–63.

Teitelbaum, J., *Holier Than Thou: Saudi Arabia's Islamic Opposition*, Washington Institute for Near East Policy, 2000.

Tesch, R. *Qualitative Research: Analysis types and software tools*, Falmer, 1990.

Thomas Tallis School website: http://www.school-portal.co.uk/GroupHomepage.asp?GroupID=50463

Thouless, R.H., *An Introduction to the Psychology of Religion*, Cambridge University Press, 1979.

Tippett, A. 'Conversion as a Dynamic Process in Christian Mission', *Missiology*, 1977, 2: 203–21.

University of Birmingham: 'An Introduction to Muslims in the 2001 Census, 7 September 2004.

Wehr, H., *A Dictionary of Modern Written Arabic*, MacDonald & Evans Ltd, 1974.

Whitehead, A.J. and McNiff, J. *Action Research: Living Theory*, Sage Publishers, 2009.

Whyte, W.F. *Learning from the Field: A guide from experience*, Sage, 1984, pp. 147, 197, 240, 439.

Whyte, W.F. *Street Corner Society: The social structure of an Italian slum*, 3rd edn, University of Chicago Press, 1981, pp,147, 197.

Wiktorowicz, Q., *Radical Islam Rising: Muslim Extremism in the West*, Rowman & Littlefield Publishers, 2005.

Wiktorowicz, Q., 'Anatomy of the Salafi Movement: Studies in Conflict and Terrorism' Routledge, Taylor and Francis Group 29: p.218, 2006a.

Wiktorowicz, Q., 'The New Global Threat: Transnational Salafis and the Global Threat', Rhodes College 2006b.

Wilson, M., Robinson, E.J., and Ellis, A., 'Studying Communication between Community Pharmacists and their Customers', *Counselling Psychology Quarterly*, 1982, 2, 367–80.

Wilton Park Conference, in association with DEMOS: 'Towards A Community Based Approach To Counter-Terrorism,' Report WPS06/5 Conference held 20–22 March 2006, paragraph 32.

Winter, R., *Action-Research and the Nature of Social Enquiry*, Gower, 1987, p.34, cited in Robson, C., 1993, p.448.

Winter, T. 'Conversation as Nostalgia: Some Experiences of Islam', in Percy, M.(ed) *Previous Convictions: An Anatomy of Religious Conversion*, SPCK Publishing, 2000.

www.muslimer.com/shia.htm

www.salafimanhaj.com e-book entitled 'The Devil's Deception of Abdullah El Faysal (Shaykh Faisal) 2007.

Yin, R.K., *Case Study Research, Design and Methods*, Applied Social Research Methods Series, Volume 5, SAGE, 2009.

Zarabozo, J.M., 'Commentary on The Forty Hadith of Al-Nawawi', 'Hadith no. 2: The Hadith of Angel Jibreel', Al-Basheer Company for Publications and Translations, 1999.

Zebiri, K., *British Muslim Converts: Choosing Alternative Lives*, One World, 2008.

Media articles and broadcasts

'Al Salafiya Jihadia al-Maghrebia takrouj min taht al-anqath' (The Moroccan Salafiyah Jihadia emerges from under the rubble), Al-Ansar magazine, 19 August 2003, cited in Pargeter, A., 'The New Frontiers of Jihad: Radical Islam in Europe,' I.B. Taurus, 2008 pp.119.

'Anonymous Mosque is the hotbed of extremism', *Evening Standard*, 22 July 2005.

'Exchange between Reid and Judge follows life sentence,' CNN, 6 December 2003, http://www.cnn.com/2003/LAW/01/31/reid.transcript/

'Malaf al-harakat al-Islamiya fil Magreb' (A file on the Islamic Movements in Morocco), Nuctasa Kheina (Hot Topic), 25 September 2003. Available in Arabic at http://www.aljazeera.net/NR/exeres/20589211-8460-40E7-9A5A-68BC9F2F002A.htm cited in Pargeter, A., 'The New Frontiers of Jihad: Radical Islam in Europe,' I.B. Taurus, 2008.

'Muslim cleric guilty of soliciting murder', *The Guardian*, 24 February 2003, http://www.guardian.co.uk/uk/2003/feb/24/race.world/

'Race hate cleric Faisal deported', BBC News, 25 May 2007; http://news.bbc.co.uk/go/pr/fr/-/2/hi/uk_news/6691701.stm

'Shaikh Abdullah al Faisal': http://www.pureislam.co.za/index.php?option=com_content&task=category&sectionid=13&id=91&Itemid=46

'The Home Office case against Abu Qatadah', *Daily Telegraph*, 27 February 2007, http://www.telegraph.co.uk/news/uknews/1543944/The-Home-Office-case-against-Abu-Qatada.html

Alleyne, R., 'How a streetwise tearaway became a jihad fanatic', *The Telegraph*, 5 October 2002: http://www.rickross.com/reference/alqaeda/alqaeda48.html

Barnett, A., Doward, J. and Townsend, M., 'Terror suspect numbers soar', *The Observer*, Sunday 14 May 2006.

BBC News: 'Profile: Sheikh Abdullah al-Faisal', Published 25 May 2007, http://news.bbc.co.uk/go/pr/fr/-/2/hi/uk_news/6692243.stm

BBC News: Abu Hamza arrived in 1997, http://news.bbc.co.uk/1/hi/uk/4644960.stm

Boulden, J., 'London mosque leader recalls bomb suspect', CNN.com/WORLD, 26 December 2001, http://archives.cnn.com/2001/WORLD/europe/UK/12/26/bake.cnna/index.html

Daily Mail, 12 October 2000.

Dodd, V., 'Anti-terror code "would alienate most Muslims"' *The Guardian*, 17 February 2007, http://www.guardian.co.uk/politics/2009/feb/17/counterterrorism-strategy-muslims

Dodd, V., 'Government suspends links with Muslim Council of Britain over Gaza', *The Guardian*, 23 March 2009, http://www.guardian.co.uk/politics/2009/mar/23/muslim-council-britain-gaza

Elliott, M., The Shoe Bomber's World,' Time Magazine in Partnership with CNN, 16 February, 2002.

Gardiner, B., 'Mosque leader says he warned police,' Associated Press, 27 December 2001, http://multimedia.belointeractive.com/attack/investigation/1227reid.html p.1

Gibson, H., 'Looking for Trouble', Time Magazine, 14 January 2002, http://www.time.com/time/world/article/0,8599,193661,00.html

Gordon Brown's speech promoting patriotism: Story from BBC News, http://news.bbc.co.uk/go/pr/fr/-/1/hi/uk_politics/4611682.stm Published: 2006/01/14 15:09:35 GMT

Green, D., Director of Civitas, a rightist independent think-tank: Daily Mail; 11th October 2000

Hattersley, G., 'Turning from Britain's youth culture to Islam's certainties', *Sunday Times News Review*, 10 July 2005.

Herbert, P., 'I knew exactly what I was doing', *The Guardian*, 24 August 2006, http://www.guardian.co.uk/print/0,,329560226–111026,00.html

http://uk.youtube.com/watch?v=xig_1odh4pw&feature=related: Muhammad al-Mas'ari, on a panel alongside Omar Bakri and Abu Hamza and http://uk.youtube.com/watch?v=KSBl0fi_uyE: Omar Bakri and Abu Hamza

Iqra Independent School Ethnicity Profile [12th October 1998].

Jacobsen, M., 'The bombers who weren't', *Washington Post*, 23 March 2008.

King Abdul Aziz al Saud's address to pilgrims, November 1946; 'Al-Mus-haf wa's-Sayf' pp.135–6 cited in Suhaymee, A.S., 'Be a Serious Salafi!' (forthcoming), p. 6.

Knight, S., 'Inside the mind of the shoebomber,' *Times Online*, 2 August 2005, http://www.timesonline.co.uk/tol/news/world/us_and_americas/article 550799.ece

Lister, S., 'Blood curdling brand of hatred taken on tour of Britain', *The Times*, 25 February 2003, http://www.timesonline.co.uk/tol/news/uk/article1 112524.ece

Lister, S., 'Profile: El-Faisal, the sheikh of race hate', *Times Online*, 24 February 2003, http://www.timesonline.co.uk/tol/tools_and_services/specials/article111 2221.ece & 'Profile of Shaikh Faisal'; http://www.pureislam.co.za/index.php? option=com_content&task=category&sectionid=13&id=91&Itemid=46

Multicultural Britain: Leading Article, 21 January 2005; Guardian Unlimited © Guardian Newspapers Limited

Murray, D., 'Quilliam's toxic take on liberty', *The Guardian*, 23 October 2009, http://www.guardian.co.uk/commentisfree/2009/oct/23/quilliam-islamic-fundamentalists-terrorism/print

Naqshabandi, M., 'Muslims in Britain', http://www.muslimsinbritain.org/index.html

Nzerem, K., 'At School with the Shoe Bomber', *The Guardian*, 28 February 2002, http://www.guardian.co.uk/world/2002/feb/28/september11.race

Oldham, J., 'Teenage thug to suicide bomber', *Scotsman*, 31 January 2003, http://news.scotsman.com/shoebomber/Teenage-thug-to-suicide-bomber.2398104.jp

Pipes, D., 'Time to begin watching Islamic converts to see which are radicalized', *Jewish World Review*, 6 December 2005: http://www.JewishWorldReview.com

Plunkett, N., ' "Terrorist" preacher was a quiet boy – mother', *Jamaica Gleaner Online*, th August 2008, http://www.jamaica-gleaner.com/gleaner/20060827/news/news7.html

Ramadan, T., *The Guardian*, 21 January 2005: Guardian Unlimited © Guardian Newspapers Limited.

Ross, B and Esposito, R., 'CIA's Harsh Interrogation Techniques Described,' ABC News, 18 November 2005: http://abcnews.go.com/Blotter/Investigation/story? id=1322866

Ryan, M., 'Cleric preached racist views', *BBC News Online*, 23 February 2003. http://news.bbc.co.uk/go/pr/fr/-/2/hi/uk_news/2784591.stm

Sandford, D., 'Hate preacher knew 7/7 bomber', BBC News, http://news.bbc.co.uk/go/pr/fr/-/2/hi/uk_news/7465201.stm Published: 2008/06/20 15:55:50 GMT

Seaton, M., 'My son the fanatic', *The Guardian*, 2 January 2002, http://www.guardian.co.uk/world/2002/han/02/september11.uk

Suleaman, N., Transcript of radio interview; *Today Programme* interview of Abdul Haqq Baker, 20 April 2006 Radio 4 (7.40am). Story from BBC News.

Suleaman, N; 'Restless Convert in quest for Jihad' BBC News, 3 May 2006, 20:37 GMT 21:37 UK, http://news.bbc.co.uk/1/hi/uk/4942924.stm

Syal, R., 'I wouldn't work in a tall building, says wife of jailed extremist', *The Telegraph*, 23 July 2003.

The Daily Telegraph, 13 October 2000.

Financial Times, 'When multiculturalism is a nonsense', 31 August 2005.

The Guardian.co.uk; 'Muslim cleric guilty of soliciting murder', 24 February 2003, http://guardian.co.uk/uk/2003/feb/24/race.world

The Jamaica Gleaner: http://www.jamaica-gleaner.com/gleaner/20060827/news/news7.html

The Observer: 'The making of a human timebomb,' War on Terrorism: Observer Special, Observer, 30 December 2001, http://observer.guardian.co.uk/waronterrorism/story/0,,625868,00.html

The Observer: 'A monster in our own making', 21 August 2005.

The Sunday Times: 'British Library quest of 9/11 plotter', 6 August 2006, p.7.

The Sunday Times: 'British Library quest of 9/11 plotter, Gadher, Dipesh, 6 August 2006.

Zubeck, P. 'Cadets' guest speaker will focus on Christianity', *Colorado Springs Gazette*.

Interview Transcripts

Interview with Shaykh Kamaludin (community interviewee CZA) 8.1.08 cited from Lambert, R., 'The London Partnerships: An Insider's Analysis of Legitimacy and Effectiveness', University of Exeter, Draft PhD, September 2009, p.148.

Transcript of interview 1 with Yusuf, 2007

Transcript of interview 2 with Ahmad, 2007

Transcript of interview 4 with Michael, 2007

Transcript of interview 7 with Gilbert, 2007

Transcript of interview 8 with Rashad, 2007

Transcript of interview 11 with Abdullah Smith, 2007

Transcript of interview 12 with Hakim, 2007

Transcript of interview 17 with Andre, 2007

Transcript of interview 18 with Paul, 2007

Transcript of interview 22 with Thomas, 2007

Transcript of interview with Sean O'Reilly, 22 October 2008

Transcript of interview 23 with Hussain, 2008

Transcript of interview 26 with Abdul Halim, 2008

Transcript of interview 27 with Ishaq Thompson, 2009

Transcript of interview 28 with Uthman, 2008

Transcript of interview 29 with Rahim McDonald, 2009

Transcript of interview 30 with Dawud George, 2008

Transcript of interview 31 with Abdul Basit, 2008

Transcript of interview 32 with Carl, 2009

Court transcripts

2nd Semester Trimester, 1982–1983 and 1st Trimester, 1983–1984; Jules-FerrySchool: http://vaed.uscourts.gov/notablecases/moussaoui/exhibits/defense/ JV002.43T and JV002.44

Academic Year Reports; 1974–1979 Montesquieu School: United States V. Zacarias Moussaoui, Criminal No. 01-455-A; Defense Trial Exhibits: http://vaed. uscourts.gov/notablecases/moussaoui/exhibits/defense/ JV002.31T Also see JV002.32T of Trial Exhibits

Academic Year Reports; 1974–1979 Montesquieu School: United States V. Zacarias Moussaoui, Criminal No. 01-455-A; Defense Trial Exhibits: http://vaed. uscourts.gov/notablecases/moussaoui/exhibits/defense/ JV002.31T Also see JV002.32T of Trial Exhibits

Academic Year Reports;1ˢᵗ Trimester, Jules-Ferry School, 1981–1982: United States V. Zacarias Moussaoui, Criminal No. 01-455-A; Defense Trial Exhibits: http:// vaed.uscourts.gov/notablecases/moussaoui/exhibits/defense/ JV002.41T

Alexandria Court Schedule, updated: Monday July 31, 2006, 9:30am ET: United States V. Zacarias Moussaoui, Criminal No. 01-455-A: http://vaed.uscourts.gov/ notablecases/moussaoui/index.html

Alquie, P (Solicitor): Spouses' Non-Reconciliation authorization no. 71.00074, 19 May 1971: United States V. Zacarias Moussaoui, Criminal No. 01-455-A; Defense Trial Exhibits: http://vaed.uscourts.gov/notablecases/moussaoui/ exhibits/defense/ JV002.10T

Attorney General Transcript regarding Richard Reid: Wednesday, 16 January 2002, DOJ Conference Center, http://www.fas.org/irp/news/2002/01/ ag011602.html

Burckhard, M.J. (Social Worker): Moussaoui Family History, United States V. Zacarias Moussaoui, Criminal No. 01-455-A; Defense Trial Exhibits: http://vaed.uscourts.gov/notablecases/moussaoui/exhibits/defense/ JV002.17T Mulhouse, 25 August 1972

Burckhard, M.J. (Social Worker): Moussaoui Family History, United States V. Zacarias Moussaoui, Criminal No. 01-455-A; Defense Trial Exhibits: http://vaed.uscourts.gov/notablecases/moussaoui/exhibits/defense/ JV002.17T Mulhouse, 25 August 1972

Chevalier A., Medical Certificate on observations made of Ms. Aicha Moussaoui's injuries, United States V. Zacarias Moussaoui, Criminal No. 01-455-A; Defense Trial Exhibits: Paris Faculty of Medicine, Bayonne, France, 9 December 1970 http://vaed.uscourts.gov/notablecases/moussaoui/exhibits/defense/ JV002.9T

Cite Technique, Academic Report, 1ˢᵗ, 2ⁿᵈ and 3ʳᵈ Terms; 1984 -1985: United States V. Zacarias Moussaoui, Criminal No. 01-455-A; Defense Trial Exhibits: http://vaed.uscourts.gov/notablecases/moussaoui/exhibits/defense/ JV002.48T. Also: JV002.49T and JV002.50T

Cite Technique, Academic Report, Physical Education, 1ˢᵗ Term; 1984 –1985: United States V. Zacarias Moussaoui, Criminal No. 01-455-A; Defense Trial Exhibits: http://vaed.uscourts.gov/notablecases/moussaoui/exhibits/defense/ JV002.48T

Cite Technique, certification that Zacarias Moussaoui is pursuing his studies as a day boarder in the 'seconde' class, 10 November 1984: United States V. Zacarias Moussaoui, Criminal No. 01-455-A; Defense Trial Exhibits: http:// vaed.uscourts.gov/notablecases/moussaoui/exhibits/defense/ JV002.47T

Court of Appeal, Childrens' Court, Periguex: Temporary Placement Order; United States V. Zacarias Moussaoui, Criminal No. 01-455-A; Defense Trial Exhibits: http://vaed.uscourts.gov/notablecases/moussaoui/exhibits/defense/ JV002.13T

Court of Appeals of Pau, Childrens' Court of Bayonne: Order to cease placement, references Docket nr: 46/1969, 8 February 1972, United States V. Zacarias Moussaoui, Criminal No. 01-455-A; Defense Trial Exhibits: http://vaed.uscourts.gov/notablecases/moussaoui/exhibits/defense/ JV002.1T6T

Defendant's Notice Of Expert Evidence Of Mental Condition: United States V. Zacarias Moussaoui, Criminal No. 01-455-A; Government Exhibit: P200348, filed 30 November 2005, p.437

Government's Sentencing Memorandum: United States of America vs. Richard Colvin Reid, a/k/a Abdul-Raheem, a/k/a Abdul Raheem, Abu Ibrahim, Criminal No. 02-10013-WGY: http://news.lp.findlaw.com/hdocs/docs/reid/ usreid11703gsentm.pdf p.7

Jules-Ferry School, Narbonne; 1983–1984 2nd Trimester, Physical Education & Sports: United States V. Zacarias Moussaoui, Criminal No. 01-455-A; Defense Trial Exhibits: http://vaed.uscourts.gov/notablecases/moussaoui/ exhibits/defense/ JV002.42T

Montesquieu College School, Narbonne; 1980–1981 2nd Trimester, Physical Education: United States V. Zacarias Moussaoui, Criminal No. 01-455-A; Defense Trial Exhibits: http://vaed.uscourts.gov/notablecases/moussaoui/ exhibits/defense/ JV002.38T

Office for Departmental Solidarity, Department of Pyrenees Atlantiques: Decree for Admission to Childhood Welfare Services, 24 June 1968. United States V. Zacarias Moussaoui, Criminal No. 01-455-A; Defense Trial Exhibits: http://vaed.uscourts.gov/notablecases/moussaoui/exhibits/defense/ JV002.1T

Orientation and Educational Action Department: 'Intervention – Conclusions and Recommendations re: Jamila Moussaoui, 16 May 1978, Judicial File No. I.A.M. 175/75, SOAE File No. 92/76. United States V. Zacarias Moussaoui, Criminal No. 01-455-A; Defense Trial Exhibits: http://vaed.uscourts.gov/ notablecases/moussaoui/exhibits/defense/ JV002.25T

Public Hearing of the Tribunal De Grande Instance De Bayonne, Department of Pyrenees Atlantiques Ruling: Divorce Judgement, 28 June 1971: United States V. Zacarias Moussaoui, Criminal No. 01-455-A; Defense Trial Exhibits: http://vaed.uscourts.gov/notablecases/moussaoui/exhibits/defense/ JV002.12T

Specialized Hospital Center examination of Mr. Omar Moussaoui on 7 December 1973, conducted by Dr. R. Franc, Psychiatrist and expert. United States V. Zacarias Moussaoui, Criminal No. 01-455-A; Defense Trial Exhibits: http://vaed.uscourts.gov/notablecases/moussaoui/exhibits/defense/ JV002.67T

Substitution for the Testimony of Khalid Sheikh Mohammed: United States V. Zacarias Moussaoui, Criminal No. 01-455-A, Defendant's Exhibit 941

Supreme Court of Judicature Court of Appeal (Criminal Division) On Appeal from the Central Criminal Court (HHJ Beaumont QC) in the Royal Courts of Justice, Strand, London WC2A 2LL: R v. El-Faisal, Case no: 2003-01860-C2, 4 March 2004

Technical-Commercial License from Acemie de Montpellier for Session 1990 (Lycee Arago): United States V. Zacarias Moussaoui, Criminal No. 01-455-A; Defense Trial Exhibits: http://vaed.uscourts.gov/notablecases/moussaoui/ exhibits/defense/ JV002.56T

The Attorney General For The Republic at the District Court of Bayonne: Trial documents for Omar Moussaoui for light violence against Aicha; United States V. Zacarias Moussaoui, Criminal No. 01-455-A; Defense Trial Exhibits:

20 January 1970 http://vaed.uscourts.gov/notablecases/moussaoui/exhibits/defense/ JV002.3T

The Supreme Court of Judicature, Court of Appeal (Criminal Division), R v. El-Faisal, 17 April 2004, Case No: 2003-01860

The Zacarias Moussaoui (September 11) Trial: A Chronology: http://www.law.umkc.edu/faculty/projects/ftrials/moussaoui/zmchronology.html p.3

Transcript of videotaped interview of Abdul Haqq Baker, Brixton Mosque, London, England – 11 October 2005, conducted by Anne Chapman, Assistant Federal Public Defender for the Eastern District of Virginia. Filmed and recorded by Simon Rutson, European Video. Also, United States V. Zacarias Moussaoui, Criminal No. 01-455-A; Defense Trial Exhibits: http://vaed.uscourts.gov/notablecases/moussaoui/exhibits/defense/ JV002.V2

United States District Court for the Eastern District of Virginia, Alexandria Division: 'December 2001 Term Indictment'

United States of America v. Zacarias Moussaoui aka Shaqil aka Abu Khalid al Sahrawi, Case Number: 01-cr-00455 13 June 13 2002

United States V. Zacarias Moussaoui, Criminal No. 01-455-A; Defense Trial Exhibits: http://vaed.uscourts.gov/notablecases/moussaoui/exhibits/defense/ JV002.1T Also see JV002.5T, JV002.15T, JV002.18T, p.5 of Trial Exhibits

United States V. Zacarias Moussaoui,Criminal No. 01-455-A; Defense Trial Exhibits: http://vaed.uscourts.gov/notablecases/moussaoui/exhibits/defense

Womack, D.E. Official Court Reporter: 'Transcript of Reid Sentencing,' United States of America vs. Richard C. Reid: http://www3.whdh.com/news/articles/extra/A8458/ Criminal No. 3 02-10013-WGY 30 January 2003, pp.1–2

Womack, D.E. Official Court Reporter: 'Transcript of Reid Sentencing,' United States of America vs. Richard C. Reid: http://www3.whdh.com/news/articles/extra/A8458/ Criminal No. 3 02-10013-WGY 30 January 2003

Quranic references

The Qur'an Surah 2 (Chapter Al Baqarah) verse 256

The Qur'an, Surah (Chapter) al-Nisaa 4 verse 35

The Qur'an, Surah (Chapter) Anbiyya 21, verse 7

The Qur'an, Surah An-Nisaa (Chapter) 4, verse 59

The Qur'an: Surah (Chapter) al Baqarah 2, verse137, Surah Ali Imran 3, verse 110, Surah an-Nisaa 4, verse 115

The Qur'an: Surah (Chapter) Yusuf, 12, verses 54–102

The Qur'an, Surah (Chapter) al-Maidah, 5, verse 8

Index

Page numbers in *italics* denotes a table/diagram